Praise for Jay Parini's

BORGES AND ME

"This is a jewel of a book. Very funny, clever, moving, luminous with love of literature and landscape. Parini's portrait of both Borges and Scotland is exquisite, deeply affectionate, sometimes comically irritable. He uses all a novelist's art, all his smoke and mirrors, to let the great man step shambolically from these pages to trap and beguile us, like a modern Ancient Mariner, with his brilliant, freely associative and heady metaphysics and literary table talk. . . . The young Parini's painful writing ambitions are beautifully wrought; so too is a long-lost time of the draft dodgers who washed up on these shores, of poetry recited at the kitchen table, and hash cookies (Borges loved them) and sudden fierce friendships that go on to last a lifetime. I read it in a greedy gulp. My laughter (at poor Parini's long night in bed with his subject) kept my wife awake. But by the end, I was damp around the eyes; I was sad to let this little cast of characters go.

"It's hard to conceive of how an old and frail blind man could have had such psychological force, such unworldly innocence, such redeeming sway over others, but Jay Parini persuades us fabulously in a high-style Borgesian marriage of fiction and history."

—Ian McEwan

"An important contribution to the biography of a major writer. . . . For readers who already admire Borges, this memoir will be a delicious treat. For those who have yet to read him, Parini provides the perfect entry point to a writer who altered the way many think of literature."   —*The New York Times Book Review*

"A tender bond forms between the eccentric sage and his caretaker. . . . Fans of both Borges and Parini will delight in this touching coming-of-age memoir."
     —*Publishers Weekly* (starred review)

"Many of the book's loveliest passages are pure geography. . . . The pressure to capture Scotland in words for the great Jorge Luis Borges forces Jay to think about language in a new way, to 'up his game' as a poet, and this artistic journey, occurring alongside their physical journey, becomes the book's emotional backbone."
     —*The Wall Street Journal*

"A captivating chronicle and homage." —*Kirkus Reviews*

"*Borges and Me* is a road-trip book like no other. . . . Full of wonderful energy and humor, with underpinnings of sadness and seriousness I can't shake."   —Ann Beattie

"A loving portrait of [a] singular writer. . . . As Parini chronicles their misadventures with the hilarity of hindsight, he palpably re-creates his youthful anxiety and Borges' own sometimes infuriating sanguinity."
     —*BookPage*

JAY PARINI

BORGES AND ME

Jay Parini is a poet, novelist, and biographer who teaches at Middlebury College. He has written eight novels, including *The Damascus Road, Benjamin's Crossing, The Apprentice Lover, The Passages of H.M.*, and *The Last Station*, the last made into an Academy Award–nominated film. His biographical subjects include John Steinbeck, Robert Frost, William Faulkner, and, most recently, Gore Vidal. His nonfiction works include *Jesus: The Human Face of God, Why Poetry Matters*, and *Promised Land: Thirteen Books That Changed America*.

www.jayparini.com

Also by Jay Parini

FICTION

The Damascus Road
The Passages of H.M.
The Apprentice Lover
Benjamin's Crossing
Bay of Arrows
The Last Station
The Patch Boys
The Love Run

POETRY

New and Collected Poems: 1975–2015
The Art of Subtraction: New and Selected Poems
House of Days
Town Life
Anthracite Country
Singing in Time

NONFICTION AND CRITICISM

The Way of Jesus: Living a Spiritual and Ethical Life
Empire of Self: A Life of Gore Vidal
Jesus: The Human Face of God
Promised Land: Thirteen Books That Changed America
Why Poetry Matters
The Art of Teaching
One Matchless Time: A Life of William Faulkner
Robert Frost: A Life
Some Necessary Angels: Essays on Writing and Politics
John Steinbeck: A Biography
An Invitation to Poetry
Theodore Roethke: An American Romantic

BORGES AND ME

BORGES AND ME

An Encounter

JAY PARINI

ANCHOR BOOKS

A Division of Penguin Random House LLC

New York

FIRST ANCHOR BOOKS EDITION, NOVEMBER 2021

Copyright © 2020 by Jay Parini

All rights reserved. Published in the United States by Anchor Books,
a division of Penguin Random House LLC, New York, and distributed
in Canada by Penguin Random House Canada Limited, Toronto.
Originally published in hardcover in the United States by Doubleday,
a division of Penguin Random House LLC, New York, in 2020.

Anchor Books and colophon are registered
trademarks of Penguin Random House LLC.

Grateful acknowledgment is made to The Colchie Agency for
permission to reprint eight lines from the poem "Daedalus"
from *Barefoot: The Collected Poems* by Alastair Reid, edited
by Tom Pow (Cambridge, England: Galileo Publishers,
2018), pp. 175–176. Copyright © 1978 by Alastair Reid
and copyright © 2018 by Leslie Clark. All rights reserved.
Reprinted by permission of The Colchie Agency.

The Library of Congress has cataloged the
Doubleday edition as follows:
Names: Parini, Jay, author.
Title: Borges and me : an encounter / Jay Parini.
Description: First edition. | New York : Doubleday, 2020.
Identifiers: LCCN 2019038775 (print) | LCCN 2019038776 (ebook)
Subjects: LCSH: Parini, Jay. | Borges, Jorge Luis, 1899–1986—
Influence. | Authors, American—20th century—Anecdotes.
Classification: LCC PS3566.A65 Z46 2020 (print) |
LCC PS3566.A65 (ebook) | DDC 813/.54 B—dc23
LC record available at https://lccn.loc.gov/2019038775
LC ebook record available at https://lccn.loc.gov/2019038776

Anchor Books Trade Paperback ISBN: 978-1-9848-9949-1
eBook ISBN: 978-0-385-54583-9

Author photograph © Oliver Parini
Book design by Michael Collica

www.anchorbooks.com

Printed in the United States of America

*For Devon, my companion on the
road for over forty years*

One's real life is often the life
that one does not lead.

—*Oscar Wilde*

BORGES AND ME

I

ONE JUNE MORNING in 1986, at my farmhouse in Vermont, I stepped from bed as the sun had only just lifted an eyebrow over the Green Mountains: always a coveted moment in my day, when I lean into beginnings, thinking about the work ahead of me—in this case, a novel about the last days of Tolstoy that had begun to glimmer at the edges of my conscious mind. My wife and children were still asleep, and I couldn't help but look at them fondly. How could I resist these sweet little boys who drove me nuts at times, as children must do, as it's their job? Or a bright, affectionate wife who didn't seem to mind my occasional flights of idiocy, offering a rueful smile at times, sometimes a deep laugh? This bounty felt undeserved and probably was. With a sense of gratitude, even amazement, I made my way downstairs into the country kitchen, where I brewed a strong cup of Irish Breakfast tea for myself before going into my study at the other end of the house.

As I often did before settling at the stained trestle table that still anchors my study, I turned on the radio to catch the headlines, tuning in to the BBC on a shortwave radio that my old friend and mentor, Alastair Reid, had recently given to me as a gift for my thirty-eighth birthday. When the newscaster read the day's top stories, I was stunned to hear that Jorge Luis Borges, the great Argentine writer "who blended fact and fiction in a peerless sequence of narratives that defied all boundaries and set off the Boom in Latin American literature," had died in Geneva at the age of eighty-six. "He was a man of many stories," the announcer said. "As a writer, he explored the most idiosyncratic spaces in the human experience, a lover of labyrinths and mirrors, a shapeshifting writer who could never be defined."

Memories surfaced now. I had met Borges when I was a graduate student many years before, in Scotland, and traveled with him from St. Andrews to the Highlands and back. Our encounter lasted only a week or so, but it forced a shift in me, a change of perspective, hitting me at just the right time. And all I knew for sure was that my way of being in the world was never quite the same after Borges.

Standing at the window, I looked into the garden below at a bed of Oriental poppies, the blood-bright cheeks of the flowers turning toward me. Did they notice my stinging eyes? I thought so, and stepped away from the window. I'm not someone who cries easily, but I wept that day. Weeping as much for myself as for Borges, remembering the callow, overly serious, shy, and often terrified fellow I was when we met, trying to weigh this against the man I'd become, still wondering what on earth had happened to me in Scotland some fifteen years before.

In 1970, having just graduated from Lafayette College and moved (briefly, I hoped) back in with my parents in Scranton, Pennsylvania, I saw two choices: stay at home, where my mother would chop off my balls, or go to Vietnam, where they'd be blown off by a landmine. A third choice, less apparent at first but finally obvious, was to leave the United States altogether, getting as far away as possible. The place that called to me was a small town on the East Neuk of Fife, in Scotland.

St. Andrews had already provided me with a much-needed escape and given me a feeling of vocation, as I'd studied there for my junior year abroad. During a memorable year, I'd made friends easily, much to my surprise, mixing with Scottish and English students, befriending a handful of Continental students, too. The lectures I attended were often appealing—florid rhetorical performances of a kind unfamiliar to me—and I'd learned a good deal, especially from intense one-on-one tutorials with a range of eccentric but erudite teachers. (One of them held tutorials at his ramshackle flat, where his wife served us tea wearing a face mask as she was "sensitive to germs.")

Most important, in Scotland I'd begun to write, recording my daily life in a journal, which I hoped (mentally cribbing a phrase from Robert Lowell) would shimmer with "the grace of accuracy." No detail seemed too inconsequential to record, and I often filled pages with quotations from things I'd read or recorded snippets of conversation I'd overheard in tea shops or pubs. I also began to write my own poems. They were imitative and unmemorable, as one might expect, but this was a thrilling turn. I'd decided—for reasons based on no demonstrable talent or experience—to make a profession of writing.

I thought I knew quite a bit about literature, though I had a skim of learning, the lightest froth on a cup which was not even an especially big cup. Nonetheless, I'd begun to read with a sense of urgency. I gulped more than read books like *Walden* and *Leaves of Grass*, *The Great Gatsby* and *Look Homeward, Angel*. I scooped up Hesse, Woolf, Kerouac, Lawrence, McCullers, Nabokov, Beckett, and others. In libraries I leafed eagerly through the large, crisp pages of *The New York Review of Books*, drawn to provocative pieces by the likes of Gore Vidal, Joan Didion, Norman Mailer, and Susan Sontag. I attended readings by writers, some of them famous (Allen Ginsberg, James Dickey, Paul Goodman), and felt quite sure that literature would provide access to worlds far beyond Scranton.

I set my sights on graduate study in St. Andrews, though I knew it would be a battle to persuade my parents that this sort of move made sense. I was my mother's first child, and she had been possessive from the first breath I drew. (My sister, Dorrie, was two years behind me, and her being a girl did not make it any easier with my mother, to put it mildly.) I was "backward," my mother frequently said, which meant I was frightened by strangers, put off by everyone and everything. As a baby, I screamed whenever somebody unfamiliar stepped into the room. Only my mother could comfort me, and she encouraged this dependence. It wasn't intentionally smothering, I suspect, but the results were the same. Needless to say, I would have great difficulty separating from her. Adulthood seemed a far, impossible kingdom.

My mother all but had a nervous breakdown when I left for Scotland the first time. "You're going where?" she asked. "Scotland? Are you crazy? Nobody goes to Scotland!" The night before my first departure, in 1968, she hurled herself onto the bed in the hotel in New York in a state of emotional disarray. Her bitter wailing kept me awake in the adjacent room throughout the night, and she looked exhausted when she said goodbye to me at the docks the next morning, hardly uttering a word. I sailed away to Britain on a rickety Italian liner that she told me "was unstable and would probably sink." It's no wonder I wept quietly in my bunk on that low-rent ship on the eight-day journey from New York to Southampton. This was a kind of weaning for me, as I now see. I was shedding my old life as best I could. I could easily imagine my mother crying herself to sleep in Scranton, night after night, but I steeled myself, knowing that I had to go through whatever lay before me, no matter how painful.

My father was a genial worrywart, the son of Italian immigrants who spoke very little English and could offer their five sons few advantages beyond bowls of handmade linguini and homegrown vegetables. (My grandmother shot rabbits from her back porch and turned them into ragu.) Like many of his generation, children of the Great Depression, my father suffered from a pervasive cautiousness. The sidewalks of his mind were strewn with banana peels. He had been forced to leave high school well before graduating, but with a bit of luck and grit he made his way in the insurance business, selling local families policies that (I fear) he never quite understood himself. Every day he wore a suit with a starched white shirt and a colorful silk tie, holding his head high in Scranton. He polished his shoes before leaving the house with an exaggerated fervor. He had "made it." And yet he continued to worry intensely about the future, especially *my* future.

So did I, and I was given a bottle of tranquilizers (old-fashioned barbiturates that would have stunned a horse) by our family doctor "to steady my nerves" before I set off to graduate school. "Don't be so anxious," Dr. Evans said to me. "All this nervousness isn't good for you. If you stay up all night, you won't get enough sleep. Just take the pills and stop worrying."

So what exactly was I worried about? Pretty much everything, I think. The tidal wave of sex, drugs, and rock and roll on which my peers gleefully surfed felt to me more like a sea I might drown in. I was a virgin and afraid I might stay one forever. And more than anything, I was terrified of Vietnam, furious about a war fought over an illusion of freedom or world dominance or—more probably—something I couldn't even imagine.

I had turned against the war during my freshman year in college, marching on Washington in 1967 and again in the spring of 1970. Like most college kids, I knew what I thought I knew: the war in Southeast Asia was immoral, stupid, and cruel. The antiwar writings of Howard Zinn, Noam Chomsky, and others became part of my permanent mental library. Making matters worse, my draft board had recently taken an interest in me, shifting my status after graduation from 2-S (student deferment) to 1-A (fit for active duty), even though I had drawn a reasonably high number in the lottery. I never quite metabolized this lucky draw and feared the worst, as my draft board in Lackawanna County was notorious, a prolific maw that gobbled up young men. Several of my friends from high school had been swept into the army, and one of them would soon end up in some godforsaken camp near the DMZ.

I still have nightmares about that morning at the armory in Scranton when, standing naked in line with dozens of others, I was prodded and poked by army doctors. "You call that a prick?" one sergeant yelled as I tried to hide my shriveled penis, which prompted barking laughter at my expense. One skinny guy I'd known from a tenth-grade physics class was there, and he passed out cold on the floor, foaming at the mouth, drawing his knees into a fetal position. "Send him first," one of the recruiters said. "He'll scare the shit out of them gooks."

My mother was as determined as I was to keep me out of the action. Though I passed the army physical with flying colors, she was convinced I was unfit for service. "Think about your allergies. All night as a young boy you were coughing. That wheeze! You kept your poor sister awake all night. You still cough too much, especially in the spring, with the flowers, and it would keep the other soldiers awake in the barracks. They have enough to deal with in Vietnam without your health problems." She had no end of schemes to keep me out of the military. As she wrote in one letter during my senior year in college, "Your Uncle Julie is well connected, and he knows a doctor who will certify that you can hardly breathe. Think how your chest feels when you exert yourself! And those feet of yours, without the arches. You couldn't walk more than a few miles without sitting. What kind of army wants that? And by the way: Stop being so political. Why did you have to march on Washington, not once but twice? You're not one of those hippies. You don't understand as much about these things as you think you do."

I spent many nights in the summer of 1970 arguing about the war with family and friends, especially Billy Giordano (as I will call him here), who had been a companion for some years, playing on my baseball team in junior high, joining me in pickup football after school in the fall, sometimes camping with me in the Poconos. He wasn't a "smart kid," as they say: not in any academic way. But I liked his freshness, his energy, and the kind of wild, subversive intelligence that doesn't show up on exams. I made a point of seeking him out in the cafeteria at West Scranton High and finding ways to hang around him.

"This is our time," he said only a day or so before he enlisted in the infantry that July, doing this "to avoid the draft"—a move that was perversely illogical and self-defeating. Unless, of course, what you really wanted was to go to Vietnam. "My dad was in the war against Hitler and Tojo," he told me, "and he never regretted it. He thinks I should go."

"Does he think I should go?"

"You should do whatever the fuck you want."

When Billy came over to my house for a final visit before his induction, it was hard to look at him closely: the once innocently smooth face had become craggy, full of worry lines that summer. He had somehow broken a front tooth, which gave his smile a threatening appearance. He'd let his beard grow, unevenly; it showed itself in clumps of bristle on his cheeks and chin. His long and greasy hair brushed against his shoulders, and his neck needed shaving. He smelled of beer and cigarettes, had grown a little heavy, and spoke with a kind of pressured speech, as if History itself leaned over his shoulder and listened. Images of him at various stages in his adolescence floated in my head as I watched him talking. I saw him beside me in a canoe, fishing on some remote pond. Or dancing in the high school gym, making a fool of himself by leaping onto a table and bobbing his head obscenely to the lyrics of "Barbara Ann." I always hoped to pitch on the baseball team in high school, and Billy was a gifted catcher who would let me throw lousy pitch after pitch into the dwindling pink-orange dusk at the sandlot field in Keyser Valley. When dark fell, we would sit together under a canopy of stars on the railroad tracks, talking about the nature and strangeness of life.

"I don't know if there's a God," Billy had said to me once, "but there is pussy in the world. And I want to get as much of it as I can before I die. I do, yes, dear God." I didn't know whether or not to believe him, but I found his stories irresistible. And I loved Billy in part for the fearless way he lived his life. He took risks, and he encouraged me—without much success—to take risks.

"If you don't lay it on the line, Jay," he would say, "what is the fucking point? *Is* there a fucking point?"

My mother, too, kept asking, "Is there any point?" But what she questioned was my plan to return to Scotland, an unimaginable place. And my wish to leave *her*. She thought I should go to law school or just find a job of some kind. To this day I have a recurrent nightmare about opening a law practice in Scranton. I occupy the top floor of a nondescript building near the courthouse on North Washington Avenue. My mother sits at the metal receptionist's desk, bellowing at would-be clients on the telephone or in person. This was a fantasy of hers, too: she wanted to sit at that desk, in control of all communications with her son, a dragon folded in the gate of Jay Parini, Attorney at Law. And woe to all who dared to enter this sacred space without her approval.

But I intended to make a profession of literature, as I announced one morning at breakfast with my father.

"Is literature a profession?" he asked plaintively.

I didn't let on that I was troubled by the same question. Could I really make a go of writing—especially if what I wanted to write was poetry? There was always journalism, I told myself. I could write dogmatic book reviews for newspapers or do lofty interviews with writers or intellectuals, the sort of pieces that fatten the Sunday supplements and sometimes grow into books. Making a living by one's pen wasn't easy, I knew that much. You could write thrillers or detective stories, even tales of horror, but as I almost never read this kind of fiction, the fantasy of success in those genres was simply that, a fantasy.

The one thing I knew for sure was that I would never return to the safe, simple, unquestioning life that my parents had sought and found for themselves in northeastern Pennsylvania in the wake of a war that had killed sixty million people around the world. I had to get away from them and Scranton, away from all the long suffocating meals and nonsensical conversations, the fatal lethargy of "normal" life.

During my final year at Lafayette, I wrote to Professor Alec Falconer, chair of the English Department at St. Andrews, asking to be admitted as a Ph.D. student. I had very little awareness of what exactly my studies would entail, were I lucky enough to be accepted, or how long they might take, as the catalogue descriptions were opaque. The main thing, it seemed, was that "after at least nine terms of residence" one must submit "an original thesis of some length." It would be "conducted under the supervision of the university." That seemed like something I could manage, though I didn't know the specifics.

During my previous stint in Scotland, I had discovered, in a used bookstore in Edinburgh, a volume of poems called *Loaves and Fishes* by George Mackay Brown. His tart, oddly inflected voice—like nothing I'd ever heard before—was a bell that rang in my head as I walked through the streets of that beautiful city. I had memorized half a dozen of his poems, and tried to write like him myself. Soon I discovered *A Time to Keep*, a slim volume of his stories set on Orkney, a remote island off the north coast of Scotland. The lyrical sway of his prose moved me, the way he dug into the emotional lives of ordinary people living in isolation from the rest of the world. The protagonists ranged from Viking raiders to lonely crofters and fishermen: figures so far from anything I had ever known but nonetheless present on the page in crisp, elemental language. I half wondered if one day I might not apply some of the same techniques to my own little world of Scranton.

In my application to Professor Falconer, I proposed a thesis on George Mackay Brown, talking knowledgeably about his unfolding career as a poet and writer of fiction, though I had only a few scraps of information about him and hardly knew the full range of his work. To my satisfaction and surprise, Falconer wrote back within a few weeks in his tiny hand with black India ink on letterhead. "The University has accepted your application for postgraduate study, and I think this is a reasonably good idea for a thesis. In any case, we shall discuss the matter, and I will be glad to admit you into the doctoral program under my supervision. Good luck in your journey from distant parts."

I showed this letter to my parents, and we sat around the kitchen table discussing it. "Are we living in distant parts?" my father wondered with a smirk. My mother was less philosophical. "You can't do this to me," she said. I tried to explain that I was doing nothing "to her." This was something "for me." My father, bless him, suggested that "it could probably do no harm to try my hand at this sort of thing." Upon graduation, I had been given an award by Lafayette that pretty much paid for my first two years of graduate study in St. Andrews, and I knew my father would help me financially as needed. He wasn't sure what "graduate study in literature" meant, but the military option—going to Vietnam—held no mythic pull for him, never having himself served in the army because he had a hernia and flat feet, and he hoped (I think) that if I got out of the way for a few years, the war would pass, and I would return to Scranton and resume "normal" life.

In any case, I insisted that I was going to Scotland, knowing that my parents would not stop me. The alternative was Vietnam, as I noted. "At least you'll be safe in Scotland," my mother said grudgingly, "though Scotch girls have a bad reputation, and the men apparently wear skirts."

And so, with anxiety and fear but also hope, I traveled back to Scotland. I dearly wished, as Thoreau put it in my favorite sentence from *Walden*, "to live deliberately, to front only the essential facts of life, and see if I could not learn what it had to teach, and not, when I came to die, discover that I had not lived." It's embarrassing to admit, but I wrote that too-famous sentence on the front page of the first journal I bought in St. Andrews at a little stationer's shop on the corner of Church and South Street, in late September, when I was twenty-two.

2

WHEN I ARRIVED, in the fall of 1970, for my second period of study, St. Andrews seemed a universe to itself, out of communication with the rest of the world. The effects of the Second World War had not faded completely in Scotland, even after twenty-five years, and a kind of austerity persisted in the scantily heated rooms of residence halls and student flats, in the thin soup served up at lunch and dinner, and in the wizened faces of veterans who walked the streets on crutches or hovered over pints in dark pubs with a vacant look in their eyes. They had seen the worst, in far-flung parts of a world at war, and their wounds, physical and emotional, would never heal. I had one genial tutor, Cedric Collier, who never tired of talking about the Italian campaign, remembering the Eighth Army under Monty and their unhappy assault on German forces in Sicily. "In the rocky foothills of Mount Etna," he would say, "they foiled us. What?"

That startled "What?"—the final beat in any statement of his—always took me aback. It was as if he were still reliving his bafflement and shame at Britain's having been foiled in those remote foothills.

If there was an element of suppressed madness about the place, St. Andrews also inspired me with its beauty. Long beaches defined the town. On one side was the East Sands, an inlet full of fishing boats that had known more bountiful times. These salt-weakened vessels smelled of rotting fishnets and old lines and reeked with the memory of hauls gone by. A few barnacle-encrusted skiffs had been dragged onto the sands and waited for summer, the paint flaking on their hulls. I rarely visited this particularly scraggy bit of shoreline, which had an alien quality. The West Sands was another story. That brilliant wide beach curled westward around the bay toward an inlet of the River Tay. Its sands were glassy where the tide fell away and made an excellent route for runners, who would pick their way through bladderwrack and shells, the white bones of driftwood and the skeletons of fish or crabs. Oystercatchers called *cheep cheep*, wading into the surf with their orange beaks and spindly legs, while gulls swooped from the sky. The air tingled, and the water in the early morning or late afternoon was a shield of gold.

During my first term, I settled into a pattern of life that included an early run along the West Sands. This struck me as the most beautiful beach in the universe, a place where I could connect with a deep spiritual reality. God was there, in the sand and tumbling surf, in the blue-green bay. I followed my run with a long bath (I liked to read in the tub), coffee with fellow students in a nearby café, then a long day in the university library on South Street, where I found a chilly upper room in Parliament Hall where I seemed the only occupant. I settled at a table in one corner and began to write my thesis on Mackay Brown.

Professor Falconer had agreed to supervise this project in our initial correspondence, though he said unnervingly in a subsequent letter that "we should deliberate on the choice of subject when you arrive in St. Andrews. Brown is perhaps unsuitable for research. He is not a well-known writer, and he seems to be still alive." That Falconer had already been prey to second thoughts on my thesis topic actually terrified me, and it only got worse on subsequent meetings, when his reservations became increasingly clear. "I'm not sure this is going to work out," he would say. "Americans come here, but they don't understand." The problem was, I had no fall-back position. If my thesis didn't go forward, what then? I could too easily imagine myself being sucked back, caught in Scranton or Saigon—and sometimes I didn't see much difference between them.

On the other hand, it was a little hard to take Alec Falconer seriously. He was a vaguely senescent fellow in his late sixties, a man who had been an officer in the Royal Navy during the war and had spent much of his subsequent life thinking about the relationship between Shakespeare and the sea. The Bard, Falconer argued, had shown a remarkable familiarity with shipboard protocol, so he must surely have been a naval man during his famous "lost years." He made this improbable case at length in his 1964 "masterwork," *Shakespeare and the Sea.* As Falconer suggested, "A naval officer of the twentieth century can have little difficulty in recognizing, even in its Elizabethan and Jacobean setting, a familiar world of intelligence reports, fleet orders, signals, strategy, maneuvers and royal naval ceremony." He noted, by way of evidence from *Othello*, that when a second ship is sighted on the horizon, an age-old cry invariably went up: "A sail! A sail!"

It was, Professor Falconer told me, most unfortunate that "an American so-called scholar" from a "minor university in the hinterlands" had recently argued that during his lost years Shakespeare would almost certainly have been working in the legal field at the Inns of Court in London; otherwise he could never have written with such ease about these matters, nor would he have relied so heavily on tort law and jurisprudence for metaphors, as in Sonnet 46, where a litigation between the speaker's heart and eye provides the explicit structure and context of the poem, complete with pleadings and a final verdict. Falconer, showing me a copy of this book, referred to his rival as a "mountebank and a fraud."

Once on a wet evening I ran into Falconer on The Scores, a windblown street overlooking the bay near Castle House, home of the School of English. Holding his oversized fedora in place with one hand, he said to me wistfully, his face pinched, "It's a cruel night on the sea, lad. A cruel night." It didn't surprise me to learn that a decade later he succumbed to dementia, ending his days in a mental asylum at Stratheden, a few miles from St. Andrews, where he spent his time writing Shakespeare's sonnets from memory, convinced they were his own and amazed by the felicity of his pen.

The madness of all this didn't worry me, so long as it didn't interfere with my pursuit of George Mackay Brown. I determined to proceed, having decided that Falconer's dithering might work in my favor. He would not resist me, I convinced myself.

At this time postgraduates had few living options in St. Andrews—there were only a handful of available rooms in Deans Court, the single residence hall for this category of student, and I couldn't get one there. Eventually I moved into some rooms at the top of a house owned by a young lecturer in English called Tony Ashe. He and his wife, Susan, became close friends and confidants, almost surrogate parents. (Not a week goes by, fifty years later, that I don't talk on the phone with Tony, now in his mid-eighties.) But for some time during my first year back in St. Andrews I rented a damp basement flat in a Georgian townhouse on Hope Street, one of the most elegant eighteenth-century streets in the old town (as opposed to the "new town," where most houses were postwar construction). My landlady was the elderly Miss Ross, a minuscule woman with a purple beaked nose and a bun of gray hair; she wore thick woolen skirts that repelled the rain and would probably have repelled bullets. I paid her a sum of £7 each week for the privilege of occupying this dismal flat, and I was responsible for the heat, which depended on a shilling meter in a grate. This electric "fire"—a trio of horizontal bars—would blaze mightily and scorch your shins if you stood too close, though it generally cast more light than heat into the sitting room, which had a cramped table in one corner where I could eat by myself or entertain, at most, a single guest. (I often wrote at this table at night or early in the morning.) In the tiny kitchen there was a metal sink, a hot plate, a toaster, and a small fridge. In a narrow cupboard by the door I kept tins of tuna, tomato soup, beans, and boxes of Weetabix. A loaf of crusty brown bread from Fisher & Donaldson, a nearby bakery, invariably sat on the bread board by the sink, and it would disappear over three or four days.

What more did I need?

Miss Ross was a dour woman who attended a very "low" church, as she put it. It was Protestant with deep Calvinist roots. She assumed that as an Italian-American I was a practicing Roman Catholic so never tried to tempt me to her faith. (My father had in fact turned Protestant to marry my mother and was ordained as a Baptist minister in middle age. Faith, for him, had come suddenly and absorbed him fully, and I grew used to seeing him at breakfast with an open King James Bible in the Scofield edition beside his English muffin and grape jelly. He made endless notes in the margins and memorized whole chapters.) I occasionally went upstairs for tea, and we were often joined by her sister, also Miss Ross, who lived nearby in what had been the family home on Bell Street. My landlady referred to me as "my young American" and took pride in having a "postgraduate scholar from abroad" in her flat. "Don't ruin your eyes!" she would say, echoing my mother's frequent warning about the dangers of reading. "I see the piles of books in your flat, and with such fine print!"

At first the thickness of her accent posed an obstacle, but I soon echoed it back. "Do you ken?" she would ask if I looked baffled. "Aye," I would say. "I ken."

The pursuit of a research degree in English in St. Andrews was open-ended to a maddening degree. To my dismay, I learned from other students that it could take up to a decade to push through the academic underbrush to a doctoral end point, and sometimes I felt as if I had marooned myself in this unlikely spot for what might easily amount to a decade. Already I could sense that the kind of focused work necessary to attain a doctorate might exceed my patience. Complicating matters further, I didn't know if I could afford to stay for more than two years without an extra bit of help from the university, though my father was happy enough to send regular checks to "tide me over," as he put it. But his letters would often end: "I think you should be applying to law schools in Pennsylvania. There is room in Scranton for good lawyers. And your mother agrees with me."

Of course she did.

My anxieties about being sucked back into life at home increased when, after only a month in St. Andrews, I received another letter from Scranton, one I'd been expecting with dread: a notice from my draft board. I studied the envelope (forwarded by my mother) closely—even smelled the paper—and, after some hesitation, put it unopened into the top drawer of my bedroom dresser. Other letters from the draft board would follow, amounting to a small passel, which I bound with a rubber band and hid beneath my underwear. It frightened me that the letters kept coming. Did they insist I report for duty? What if I didn't appear? Could they come to Scotland and arrest me? Would a return to the States put me in legal jeopardy? I determined that I would never open those letters. Not ever.

In a gesture of self-liberation, one night I flushed my last bottle of tranquilizers down the toilet. There was relief in that swirl of water, a cleansing. I would keep myself alive and functioning without their help and deal with my anxieties on my own. (And I felt quite sure that they actually increased my panic, the sense of dread that had been dogging my days and lengthening my wakeful nights, when eternities opened between each fat tick of the clock beside my bed.)

One morning on The Scores I ran into a tutor from my undergraduate year, a woman of fifty called Miss Anne Wright, whose brisk cheer I had liked. She was Miss Jean Brodie (as portrayed by Maggie Smith in the film) come back from the dead. In her strangulated voice, pushing through gritted teeth with unbearable faux brightness, she said, "Ah, Mr. Parini! What a lovely name! I remember your name! Are you an Italian?"

"Hello, Miss Wright."

"Why are you here?"

"Where?"

"In Scotland!"

I explained that I had come back to St. Andrews as a postgraduate and would remain as long as it took to get a doctorate in the School of English.

"Oh, dear," she said. "I hear determination in your

voice. Never a good thing. But come for tea. We must talk."

She meant that I should come at once, and I obliged.

Miss Wright was the warden of Hamilton Hall, a university residence for women that, when it was built in the last decade of the nineteenth century, had been known as the Grand Hotel. Its imposing red-brick façade overlooked the Old Course and the Royal & Ancient, the oldest and most prestigious golf club in the world. She had a spacious flat on the top floor, with a dizzy-making view of St. Andrews Bay and the West Sands. On a clear day you could see the violet hills of Angus in the middle distance, with the Highlands reaching beyond to the northwest.

She served me slices of Battenberg cake (a distinctive sponge cake of yellow and pink squares covered in marzipan) and Earl Grey tea.

"Now, Jay. Or should I call you Mr. Parini?"

"Jay is fine."

"It's very fine! Is it short for something?"

"No. Just Jay."

"In which case," she said, "it will have to do."

I took another slice of the cake.

"You were not so good at English history, if I remember," she said, as if to herself, referring to my tutorials in the fall term of 1968.

"The English kings and queens," I said. "I never got them straight."

"Americans don't." She poured the tea. "Too many Georges. And Edwards! The business of James confuses everyone, as he changed numbers." She helped herself to a bit of cake and chewed it slowly, then licked her long fingers. The blue veins in her neck stood out like steel cables. "What do you hope to do with yourself? Do excuse my curiosity. I'm not polite."

"A research degree, as I said."

"I know, but for what *reason*? One must have a reason for doing things. Otherwise it's like a windmill beating the air."

"I want to write."

"Really?"

"Poetry, yes. I write poems."

"Ah, poetry. Then you must meet Alastair."

"Who?"

"Alastair Reid. He was a student here after the war. An old friend. Something of a rake, but never mind." A peculiar look overwhelmed her, as if she remembered something she wished she hadn't. "Alastair was in the Pacific war." She paused. "I've never liked them, the Japs. Do you?"

"I've never met anyone from Japan," I said sternly. "I really don't have any bad feelings about them."

"A diplomat! Good for you."

"Is Alastair a poet?"

"To his fingernails. He came back from Ohio or Iowa or somewhere a few months ago. With his son. They have a marvelous house, Pilmour Cottage. On the West Sands, right on the golf course. Shall I introduce you?"

Without awaiting my response, she lifted the telephone and called him, and Alastair picked up at once, as if awaiting her call.

"I have a young man here, Alastair, a former student.

An Italian from America. Mr. Parini. Very serious, and perhaps *too* serious. But no matter. He wants to write poetry, and I told him I would introduce you."

She winked at me, waiting for a response.

"Thank you, darling Alastair," she said at last. "I shall arrange it." She stared at me with triumph in her eyes. "Noon tomorrow. You will find Alastair at the Cross Keys, in the bar. Be careful, however. He likes his drink."

3

MY STOMACH TIGHTENED. I didn't know what to expect of Alastair when I pushed through the swinging doors of the Cross Keys Hotel that day, but I had a presentiment—the unconscious can detect these things—that my life would take an unexpected turn. I made my way to the bar, which had been a popular hangout for generations of students and staff, but there were only a few customers in evidence. A white-bearded fellow in a dirty mackintosh sat in one corner with his pint before him, smoking; it seemed that every bar in town had one of these, a lost veteran of some foreign war. There were two girls at another table, students in their scarlet undergraduate gowns, who drank half pints—this was considered the ladylike way to order—of shandy, a putrid mix of beer and lemonade. The sole figure at the bar was a man in his early forties with auburn hair above a weathered, shockingly handsome face that shone with a distinctly Celtic glow. He had high cheekbones, a tangle of blue veins close to the skin. He smoked a cigarette as he stooped over a pint.

When I stood next to him, his eyes turned in my direction.

"Jay?"

"Mr. Reid?"

"Alastair." He reached out with a fat mitt of a hand that enclosed mine easily. "Do you like Guinness? It's good for you."

"Something lighter?"

A flash of disapproval crossed his face. "Lighter" was not in his emotional vocabulary.

A pint of lager appeared. The burly bartender knew Alastair by name and habits, and he put a shot glass on the bar as well. Alastair drank the whisky quickly, then wiped his mouth with the back of his hand. There was something a little frightening about this man, a coiled viperish energy.

"Jock has been standing behind this bar since I was a student, right after the war," Alastair said.

"What was it like back then?"

A look of pain crossed his face. "It was a strange time, coming back, falling into this fantasy world. Unreal to wear a scarlet gown, to pretend to listen to inane lectures. They locked the residence halls at ten in those days. None of us were used to that. So we climbed over the walls, through open windows. I was nearly sent down, but I laughed at them. We all did. Couldn't take it seriously, not after what we'd seen. I still don't take any of this seriously. Believe nothing you see or hear, that's what I tell my son." He took a long sip. "And remember, this isn't a university, it's a film set. Don't be fooled. The lecturers, even the students, are actors. They're here to attract tourists."

His frankness scared me, but already I wanted to know this man better. And I wanted his approval, for reasons I could never articulate. I wanted a father like him: a bold and irreverent man with a natural sense of authority. And I wanted to *be* that man, too.

Alastair continued. "You're very silent. Not persuaded? Think about it. What is this place? A motley group of strangers. They come here to drink and fuck."

I had the dim sense that I'd better not let him overwhelm me, not if I wanted to be his friend. "Maybe to read and think?"

"You *are* serious, aren't you? Miss Wright warned me. Of course I was moderately serious at your age," he said. "Not a bad thing. Then again, I was standing on the bridge of a destroyer in the Pacific. There were kamikazes overhead."

"I can't imagine it."

He looked at me hard, as if peering into my heart, and I thought he must be wondering why I wasn't in Vietnam. Should I be ashamed of my draft situation? Maybe he would approve of this, but I couldn't yet be certain. Vietnam provoked odd responses in people, especially veterans, who continued to live under the illusion that we fought this war to preserve "freedom." I knew that my own uncles, the three who had landed in the first assault on the beaches of Salerno in 1943 and somehow survived, found my antiwar sentiments distasteful, if not downright treasonous. (My mother always found it deeply suspicious that all three of them had survived that horrendous battle. "What did *they* know that nobody else did?")

Alastair ordered another whisky, and Jock obliged. "Kamikazes are no fun in the moment," he continued, gulping the drink. "Later on, though, they produce the most vivid dreams. Only last night I saw one of them coming toward me. I tried to duck, but what good would that do? It missed my ship but struck another, and I watched it break apart and sink." He looked past me into space. "That happened. I didn't much think about it for years. I do now."

"Have you written about it?" I knew that many writers of his generation, such as James Jones, Mailer, and Joseph Heller, had found war a major subject for their novels. I actually worried that in sidestepping Vietnam I might have ruined something for myself. The major conflict of my generation would never be available to me as a writer.

"War is not my subject," Alastair said.

"And what's that, your subject?"

"Dear God, you ask more questions than Jasp."

"Jasp?"

"My son. You'll meet him. Everyone eventually meets him."

"I'm just curious," I said, taking a risk. "What *is* your subject?"

Alastair sipped his pint, thinking. "I'm still looking for it. Sometimes it winks into being. Sometimes, well, not so much." He opened one of his big hands and with the forefinger of the other seemed to trace his own lifeline. "Do you have a subject?"

"I'm looking for it, too."

"Looking where?"

There was an ironic edge to that question, and somehow Alastair's confidence undermined my own. Even without saying much, he assumed dominion, having a natural strictness as well, a schoolmaster's eye, and this was unfamiliar to me. My father invariably shrank from authority, preferring to have no opinion and never to question those with power over him. I, too, found it awkward and even painful to take a stance, even against the war, though I'd done this more forcefully than was typical of me. Alastair, by contrast, seemed to enjoy his stance-taking.

"You write for *The New Yorker*," I said. "Miss Wright mentioned that." That little tidbit of information had caught my attention. Here was somebody with connections and a platform.

"I'm a staff writer at the magazine," he said. "It's the best job in the world. You don't have to report to an office. I don't report anywhere, except to Mr. Shawn, the editor. I write about whatever catches my attention. And the checks don't bounce." He seemed lost for a moment, as if reflecting on his life so far. I wondered if, in spite of his confidence, he was a man of many worries, and not so different from me after all. The lines in his face had somehow been earned. "I've never held a job," he said. "Not a real job."

"You were a professor?"

"Anne Wright is talkative. Funny old thing, isn't she? Never believe a word."

"You taught at Harvard?"

"Did she say that? For the Brits, there is only one American university, and it subsumes the rest. No, Sarah Lawrence. A small women's college. I taught Latin and Greek."

"I did some classics in college."

"Arma virumque cano."

Of arms and the man I sing. It didn't surprise me that he would leap to the opening of Virgil's *Aeneid*, that song of war. Alastair was, I thought, a warrior at heart, and in this he stood before me as a contradiction of my own life.

"You seem to have avoided Vietnam," said Alastair, as if reading my mind.

"My best friend is in Vietnam. I decided not to go. That's why I'm here."

"You're dodging the draft."

"More or less."

"Good for you. It's a hateful war." Perhaps he wanted to show that he didn't mean to criticize me.

I must have looked troubled. In any case, he took pity on me and changed the subject, asking where I'd been an undergraduate. I told him about Lafayette, which he knew a little, saying that the head of the English Department there, Bill Watt, was an acquaintance.

What did it mean that he knew an old teacher of mine in Pennsylvania? Was that even possible? I sensed his reach into many areas of experience, even my own. He must be one of those people who gobbled up experiences and moved on. Again and again. Alastair, I decided without knowing much about him, had gorged on life, even swallowed it whole.

"Sarah Lawrence was an interesting place in those days," Alastair said, resuming the monologue style of speech I would come to savor. "Harold Taylor was president—the youngest president ever, anywhere. He hired me without an application. Better yet, he let me teach whatever pleased me. There was no set curriculum."

"Joseph Campbell teaches there."

"The mythographer." He seemed to approve of my knowing of Campbell and his academic whereabouts, and I realized I could play this game myself. I could become part of this if I chose. I could make associations, forge connections. Or was it just dropping names?

"*Hero with a Thousand Faces* is one of my favorite books," I said.

"Reductive, probably. But Joe's on the right track. There's only one story, the journey of the hero. It takes many forms." He looked into his beer as if something important lay at the bottom of his glass. "You're somewhere on that journey now, somewhere at the beginning."

"I've read the book twice," I said.

"Once would do," said Alastair. " 'There is one story and one story only.' Do you know that poem?"

I shook my head, feeling rebuffed.

Alastair talked on, unaware of my feelings or unconcerned. " 'To Juan at the Winter Solstice.' Robert Graves," he said. "Do you know Graves?"

"Not terribly well." Just saying that made me feel like

a fraud. What did I really know of Graves? The name graced many paperbacks in the local bookstore, and I had stood with a copy of *The Greek Myths* in my hand only a few weeks before. I had some ill-formed sense of Graves as one of those polymathic literary entrepreneurs that British culture throws up in a regular fashion. Was Alastair one of these?

"Read him carefully, especially the poems. Astonishing poems: simple, musical, full of layers. He wrote novels to pay the bills: *I, Claudius; King Jesus.*" He added, "He once said that he was breeding show dogs to support his cats."

I guessed that Alastair did not require a response. He was on a roll, exploring his own thoughts, allowing them to find a focus and form. I just happened to be standing next to him and listening. But I found him so appealing—a man who seemed more alive than anyone I'd met. His mind—and language—crackled. He knew people, interesting people. In talking, he was framing what he knew. I could learn from him, and I wanted him to want to know me.

"After the war I wrote to Graves," Alastair said, as if beginning a short story. "He was living in Majorca, in a stone villa overlooking the sea, with his wife and his mistresses and children." He sucked on his cigarette, almost swallowing it, then coughed profusely. "Every day he would clamber down the rocky path to the sea and swim. A perfect life."

"I envy it already."

Alastair approved of my empathetic powers, I could tell, as he nodded. "You write poems?" he asked. "Miss Wright has let out the proverbial cat."

"Not good ones. Not yet."

"The right answer," he said. "We're all living in the world of 'not yet.' In my letter to Graves, I said I was *trying* to write poems, and that I was coming to Spain. Would he mind taking a look at them? It was impertinent. And that's good. A young man with any self-respect should be impertinent."

"Did he reply?"

"I mentioned that I had read classics at St. Andrews, and he wrote back to say he had just begun a translation of Suetonius for Penguin. *Lives of the Twelve Caesars.* One of the great works of fiction."

"Isn't it history?"

"History is a form of fiction—you must shape the facts, find an arrangement among them. Create a satisfying narrative." He lifted the pint and drained whatever was left. "Graves offered me a job as his secretary. I was to provide a rough translation from the Latin, do the donkey work. He would refine whatever I produced. He said I could have a little hut in his garden to live in. How could I turn down such an offer?" He looked beyond me again, his eyes fixed on a high corner of the room. "Graves was badly injured in the Great War. His nerves shattered, so this was ideal for him. A peaceful limestone valley, pine trees, rosemary. A village by the sea."

"A good place for nerves to settle." I thought of my own bad nerves and the quest for them to settle.

"Well, my own nerves settled, at first," said Alastair. "But Graves ruined my composure soon enough. A long story . . ." His pause spoke volumes.

"He was a good teacher, I assume?" I said.

"I learned to write from Graves by sitting beside him, allowing him to 'correct' me, as he put it. I remember the first week, when he gave me a few pages to translate. I worked intensely for hours, making what I thought was a perfect English version. And put the pages on his desk before dinner, standing beside him. He scanned them quickly and said, 'Sit!' I pulled up a chair. Then watched him as he crossed out sentences with his fountain pen or circled them to move to another place. He crossed out adjectives but found better nouns, ones that didn't need propping up with modifiers. The same with my adverbs, which got swallowed into better verbs. If you need an adjective or adverb, you're still fishing for the right noun or verb. So Graves said. I learned this. But learning hurts, as it's ripping away something that had fit easily, that felt comfortable. All passive constructions disappeared. 'Always prefer the active voice!' he barked at me in that fucking public school manner. Elementary but useful advice. You must learn how to pare down your work, then build it up. Vision and revision. You prune a rosebush back to its roots. Then it flowers properly." He paused. "Are you a gardener?"

"No."

"That's too bad," he said. "You must take it up."

It seemed bizarre that he advised me to garden! Yet I knew he was right, that I had missed out on connecting to the physical world in the tactile way of gardeners, and if I was to be a poet, I would need to learn how to touch and see and smell.

I knew at that moment with absolute conviction that

I would apprentice myself to Alastair and learn as much as I could from him.

"Where did you grow up?" I asked. I didn't care now if my questioning annoyed him. I needed to know about this man.

"My father was a minister in Galloway, my mother a doctor. They worked at home, at opposite sides of the manse. Which is why I work at home. I've never had a job in the sense of 'working.' Can't work for anyone. Selfish bastard, my son says. Let's say I don't need much. Or want much. Wanting is the cause of unhappiness. I travel with no more than a bag or two. One for me, one for Jasper. He's nine or ten. Almost eleven? I lose track."

I knew enough already not to ask about Jasper's mother. She was conspicuously *not* in the picture. But was she still, like my own mother, present by her absence? I sensed a shell of privacy around Alastair, however invisible, and I realized that if I reached out, touched him, he would shrink. He didn't want me to probe too deeply, and I was sensible enough to resist the urge.

"It's peculiar, coming back to Scotland after being abroad for a long time," he said. "We were in Ohio last year. A teaching gig. Never liked Scotland when I lived here, and have mostly stayed elsewhere. I bought a small farm in Majorca some years ago."

"To be near Graves?"

He didn't answer. When he spoke again, it was almost with a different voice, although it completed his short story—for the moment. "After a couple of years, working with him closely, I fell in love with one of his goddesses. He had these young women—acolytes, mistresses, whatever. Mrs. Graves didn't approve, but neither did she disapprove. One of them, a dark-eyed girl, with her hair cut across her forehead, struck me at once. I began an affair with her, under his nose. He pretended he didn't notice, and I never mentioned it. We thought we'd not been discovered. Once, though, he was chopping wood, his sleeves rolled up. I stood to one side, but then he threw the ax at me! Missed my head by less than a foot. It stuck in a wall. Rather impressive, that he knew how to throw an ax. But Christ! I got the message, and a few days later left under cover of darkness, on a fishing boat, with the girl. Haven't seen Graves since the day I left."

Was this a true story? It seemed somehow unimaginable, a fantasy of some kind. But he told it with such conviction that, against my own wishes, I believed him.

Was this indeed the essence of storytelling? Did one simply have to relate a tale in a believable fashion, with the authority of the imagination?

"You're terribly silent," he said.

"I'm sorry."

"Don't be sorry. Say something."

I realized it might be dangerous to get too close to this man. He took no prisoners, and went at you directly. For a young man of my indirection, my uncertainty in life, this was terrifying. I might have to look at myself in the mirror without flinching. I might actually have to say what I meant, even find it.

"You look like you're thinking," Alastair said. "Like a child about to shit his pants."

It was time to screw my courage to that proverbial sticking place. "I was wondering if I could show you some of my work?" I asked.

"Of course. Bring a poem any afternoon. Teatime is usually good. We'll have a cup, and I'll correct your work." He took out a pen and wrote the address on a bit of paper.

Stepping onto the pavement outside, I felt an elation, the opening of invisible doors and windows. At last I had met someone who could show me a way forward. Exactly what role he might play in my life could not, of course, be known at this point. But my gut told me that this had been a good meeting, and that my life was about to shift in inexplicable ways.

Minutes later, still trying to process this first encounter with Alastair Reid, I heard a chant in the middle distance on Market Street: "Ho Ho Ho Chi Minh! Ho Ho Ho Chi Minh!"

A group of student protesters marched slowly toward me with placards in the air. Bandannas and bell-bottoms were in abundance, and I was reminded of my days of protest in Washington. I had an urge to jump in, yet withdrew. I had come to Scotland to step aside from the stream, at least visibly. The letters from my draft board were tucked safely in a drawer, and I wanted my feelings there. Unopened.

At the fountain before me, outside the Cross Keys, a sparse circle of British veterans gathered. Among them, to my shock, was Professor Falconer, who wore a kind of Napoleon-style hat. An ill-fitting uniform from his days in the Royal Navy draped his tiny frame. A ceremonial sword dangled from his belt, and there was a row of medals on his chest. But he seemed lost, dwarfed by his comrades as well as his uniform. Most of them would have fought with Falconer against the Axis powers, although two or three elderly men from the Great War joined them, one of them (in a wheelchair) wearing a regimental beret.

The professor caught my eye and a faint smile crossed his lips. And then the protesters arrived and faced off against the veterans. Falconer's right hand went instinctively toward the hilt of his sword.

The apparent leader of the protest was a woman I'd seen before. Slender and tall, she had blond hair tinged with strawberry that was pulled back tightly in a ponytail. She wore bright red sneakers and white socks and radiated self-confidence as she shouted directions to the group, modulating their protest chant into a song as they stood face-to-face with the ancient vets. "We Shall Not Be Moved," the protesters sang, although it seemed more like the old veterans who would not be moved. Indeed, I could see Professor Falconer's lips moving. "Just like a tree planted by the waters," he sang under his breath, "we shall not be moved."

4

BEFORE I DROPPED by to see Alastair with a poem, I thought I would visit the Poetry Society, a group that met once a week in a room over the bar at the Star Hotel in Market Street. Most of those who came brought copies of a poem of their own to pass around. Occasionally someone would read a favorite poem by a classic or contemporary poet. I'd been meaning to attend one of these workshops since my return to St. Andrews but had put it off. Perhaps arrogantly, I thought I was better than any of them—they were mostly undergraduates, after all. But I was afraid as well. Many of them, as I recalled from my junior year, spoke without restraint. But now, imagining Alastair scratching out my adverbs and adjectives, I thought I had better push past my reluctance.

Bella Law (as I will call her) presided over the society, running it with graceful firmness. I recognized her at once as the leader of the antiwar protest, and wheels spun in my head: a coincidence, perhaps, though one got used to expecting the unexpected in a small town. She had pale gray-green eyes that seemed to take in the whole room at a glance. I liked her fragile wrists and very long, thin legs. Her voice had a quality of throaty freshness that appealed to me. When she laughed, she tipped her head to one side. I noticed her slightly puffy lips and her long beautiful neck. She was appealing in unconventional ways. Even the way she would occasionally shudder and smile awkwardly at me cut into my heart.

Her red sneakers made her stand out from the others. I hadn't seen red sneakers in St. Andrews before this.

"Do you have a poem to share?" she asked.

I had brought the one I planned to show Alastair, but what mattered now was that it impressed Bella. Feeling tense, I read it aloud as best I could:

> *The blood-soaked jungle floor is empty*
> *Of the bodies now,*
> *Men who in valor, lethargy, or mere indifference*
> *Fell down in battle.*
> *Forces from the North and South*
> *Advance upon a blistered world.*
> *There is no factory.*
> *There is only Death,*
> *And Death is sly, is greedy and indifferent as well.*
> *It devours all comers, and returns*
> *In kind a crimson pall.*

The group offered no responses, which prompted Bella, perhaps dutifully as well as out of kindness, to comment.

"One thing puzzles me," she said. "Can Death be *sly and greedy* as well as *indifferent*? Isn't that possibly a contradiction?"

Heads bobbed in agreement like pigeons dipping to feed, and I began to regret the line. But surely there was more to say about my poem?

After the meeting, I sat beside Bella as she leafed through a folder. "I saw you marching in Market Street the other day," I said.

"Our antiwar group, yes. You should join us. Other marches are coming. I'm working on a speaker from London, a Vietnam vet. The antiwar movement in Britain is getting some traction now."

I agreed to go and invited her downstairs to the bar, where we found seats at a table by the back oak-paneled wall, and I brought her a pint of lager, as requested.

"Ta," she said.

"It's good to see these protests."

"They're probably useful if they raise awareness. But what about you? Why haven't they sent you to Vietnam?"

"I drew a reasonably good number in the lottery," I told her, "but I've got this insane draft board. Their letters keep coming. I don't open them."

"A protest of sorts."

"You don't get to ignore the draft without consequences," I said.

This caught her attention. "So what brings you to St. Andrews? It seems far away from whatever you were doing in America."

"That's the point," I said. "I needed some distance."

By way of self-justification, I told her about my thesis on George Mackay Brown, amusing her with the fact that Falconer worried that Brown was "still alive." I mentioned in passing that I had majored in English but had also studied Greek in my senior year at Lafayette—a subject I had begun at St. Andrews during my year abroad. I was currently in a seminar on the comedies of Aristophanes taught by Professor K. J. Dover, a legendary figure in the classics department.

Bella pulled a white handkerchief from her sleeve and blew her nose. "An American who reads Greek and rejects his draft board. There is a God after all."

"You must tell me about yourself," I said.

"Must I?"

"I'm one of those people who ask a lot of questions."

"I don't mind." She told me that she had gone to Benenden, a tony girls' school in Kent that her mother had attended before her. (This explained why, though she was a Scot, she spoke with an English public school accent, wherein *toast* rhymed with *taste* and *house* rhymed with *nice*.) But she was reluctant to answer questions about her school days, she said. "Not terribly interesting." Her family apparently had a "shooting lodge" in Perth, and she suggested that I should come for a visit sometime. "Daddy is always looking for someone to shoot with him."

"So is my father," I said, but I didn't pursue the joke. Not if I wished to pursue this woman, and I knew I did.

I tried to piece her world together in my head: private school in England, wealthy parents with a shooting lodge in the foothills of the Highlands. This somehow combined with her radical politics as well as a strong interest in poetry and—as I later discovered—modern art. I hadn't met any girls like her in Scranton, and to a ridiculous degree I liked hearing about life at English boarding schools, with their quaint traditions. I had visions of pupils taking cold showers, being snapped at by schoolmasters in mortarboards, and playing games into the soft dwindling chalk-light of early evenings on sumptuously green fields as church bells in village towers gonged softly in the distance. I found something to admire in the old imperial sentiments of Sir Henry Newbolt in "Vitaï Lampada," a wonderfully dreadful poem, with its stoutly martial refrain: "Play up! Play up! And play the game!"

Bella winced when I mentioned this poem, saying, "I've had enough of jolly hockey sticks."

She lived in Hamilton Hall, which I knew well because of Miss Wright, and I asked her to come back to my flat for coffee. "Ah, coffee," she said. "The problem is that I'm swotting this term. Years of neglect, and I'm having to catch up."

"All work and no play . . ."

"And," she said, glancing away for an instant, "I have a boyfriend. Angus is a medical student."

"I do want to offer you a cup of coffee one day," I said, determined not to let go of this easily. "That is, if Angus won't mind."

"We're not engaged or anything." She leaned forward and planted a kiss on my forehead. I couldn't tell if she meant this gesture as dismissive or as something to encourage me. "I'm not sure what or where we are as a couple," she went on. "We're . . . a quondam couple. Everywhere and nowhere."

A *quondam* couple? Everywhere and nowhere?

Back in my flat in the late evening, still bristling with confusion and the memory of her lips pressing on my forehead, I drank tea and started to draft a poem about what had happened—or not happened—between us. Perhaps *this* could be the poem I'd show to Alastair the next day.

5

THE SQUAT STONE house stood in a rookery, with the North Sea in the middle distance and barely visible from the front. I pushed open the rusty iron gate and followed the path to the front door, leaning my bike against a rowan hedge. From overhead came the soft thunder of a hundred rooks, those large birds of prey with sooty wings and echoing caws. Any number of cats eyed me warily.

"Bicycle clips and all," said Alastair, opening the door.

An egg whizzed over his shoulder and splashed on the steps at my feet.

"Jasp!"

His son materialized at the door. He was black-eyed, black-haired, and beautiful.

Why Jasper had tossed an egg over his father's shoulder wasn't obvious, but I quickly saw that play was part of their life, and that Jasper was a unique child: full of wonderment, mischievous, ridiculously bright, saucy, and ready for the unexpected, which his father delivered in quantity. As we moved toward the kitchen, Alastair ignored the boy, who seemed to spin around us.

The kitchen, a huge room at the back, had a bulky, coal-fueled Aga stove at the center. Through a bay of rain-streaked dirty windows I could see the North Sea churning silently, a shimmer of silver. The Old Course lay between the house and the bay, and I noticed an elderly man in a tartan hat staring at a ball that had gone into a trap.

"He's been there for a week," said Alastair. "If he's not gone by next week, I'll have him removed. Tea?"

It was a strong brew, what he called "builder's tea," the sort that carpenters in Scotland liked to drink after boiling the bags in a pan of water for extra strength. It could stand by itself without need of a cup.

As instructed, I settled beside Alastair at the table, where he and Jasper ate amid jam pots, crumbs, toast racks (with a few cold slices left over from breakfast), dishes of butter, and strange homemade biscuits that Picasso might have shaped, some of them erotic.

"Jasper was having fun with the biscuits," Alastair said. "Dicks and balls, always a classic with boys."

"I quite like dicks and balls," I said, and immediately regretted it.

"Let me see what you've got," Alastair said, "and I refer to your poetry."

I spread my crude love poem for Bella on the table. It began:

Otherwise in the wind that knows no names,
Your name alone sings out to me.
The syllables are wind in airless air.

Alastair gasped as he read those lines. Was this the sound of disdain or, dared I hope, a sign of admiration? As he continued reading, he covered his mouth with one hand. When he finished, he lit a cigarette, pondering. I could almost hear the little engines in his mind whir.

"It's not without charm," he said, and then, before I had time to respond, he took out his pen and set to work. First to disappear was "airless air," followed by others of my hard-earned phrases: all slain by quick strokes of his pen. He shifted whole stanzas from one end of the poem to the other, and a mild anger rose in me. Anger at my own stupidity, yes, but also at his clear indifference to my feelings. He obviously didn't appreciate my ear for the music of poetry. That was probably okay. But his arrogance dismayed me. The first duty of the critic, I told myself, was to read a text with sympathy and try to understand another point of view.

Alastair said, "Remember that the word *stanza* means, quite simply, room."

"I know what it means."

"A poem is a house with rooms. You are the architect. You can change the design."

I watched in horror as he cut the entire last stanza. "Never end a poem with wisdom," he said. "It never satisfies and always annoys. Let your reader imagine the ending. Let wisdom arrive, with a bit of luck." He looked bemusedly at me. "Am I upsetting you?"

"Why would you think that?"

"Good," he said. "You're not sensitive. That's the

important thing. A poet can't have feelings about his drafts. Vision and revision, I always say."

"So how do you know when a poem is finished?"

"It's never finished, only abandoned. Publication is a form of disposal," he said. "You flush it down the johnny." He pulled an imaginary cord while holding his nose. "But poems are hard to lose, rather like children. They follow you around, nudge you for a response. They want something you can't really give."

Jasper came in, as did a young man about my age with long black hair and a bright yellow bandanna.

"This is Jeff," said Alastair. "Jeff Lerner, from Ohio. He was my student last year at Antioch. He's just moved into the spare room."

"He's my babysitter," said Jasper. "Unpaid, of course."

"I'm not to be trusted with babies," said Jeff. "I eat them raw."

"Eating babies is wrong," said Alastair.

I liked Jeff at once. He cast off a glow of irreverence and sweetness, and we agreed to meet for coffee the next day in town.

"Will you read to me?" Jasper asked me in a chirpy voice.

"Go ahead," said Alastair. "I've got to peel some potatoes. Your poem is going nowhere, so let it rest in peace."

"Don't take him seriously," said Jeff. "I promise to like your poems."

Jasper led me upstairs to his small bedroom at the back of the house. All the while I felt a kind of tingle in my limbs, a lightness. Alastair had caught me on his hooks. His life, his world, compelled my gaze. I wanted this.

"Borges is coming," he said.

"Who is this?"

"Jorge Luis Borges! The Argentine writer. Haven't you read him?"

"No."

"Papa will tell you. He's translating Borges."

"So tell me about yourself, Jasper," I said. "What are you reading?"

"*Robinson Crusoe.*"

"Isn't that advanced for a boy?"

"I'm advanced. For a boy."

"Maybe you're not a boy?"

"A very short man?" he said. "Papa says you're a poet. Is that true?"

"Want to be."

"Wannabe poet. I'm a wannabe sailor. Or a tinker. Or a spy."

"What's a tinker?"

"A gypsy. Travelers. From northern India originally. But there are different kinds."

"Really?"

"Why are you so ignorant?"

"I wasn't aware of tinkers," I said.

"Or Borges. I shouldn't be shocked. Americans are ignorant."

"You think so?"

"That's what Papa says. And we lived in Ohio last year. So I know whereof I speak." He drilled me with his big dark eyes, then pulled out a volume of poems by Rudyard Kipling from a small bookshelf by his bed. He opened the book and read a stanza:

Pussy can sit by the fire and sing,
Pussy can climb a tree,
Or play with a silly old cork and string
To 'muse herself, not me.
But I like Binkie, my dog, because
He knows how to behave.

"Are you a dog person or a cat person?" Jasper asked, abandoning this poem.

"I'm not sure."

"Alastair's a cat person. They can't be trusted. They have nine lives. They distrust anything you say. They love too much, are irresponsible, even dangerous. They marry too many wives. Like Papa."

The blizzard of phrases bedazzled me. Was this really a child? And did he really call his father by his first name?

"Alastair is reading *Crusoe* to me. I want to live like that."

"Alone on an island in the middle of the sea, marooned?"

"You get to start over."

"Is that what you want?"

"We're in Scotland to start over."

"As what?"

"Anything we choose."

Suddenly Alastair stood in the doorframe. His face was bright, wide, well-wishing. There was love in his eyes. And a self-absorption that frightened me a little.

"The cat person appears," said Jasper.

Alastair sat on the edge of the bed. "You're rude."

"I'm a bird son. Tell him."

Without the slightest hesitation, Alastair began to recite a poem of his from memory:

My son has birds in his head.
I know them now. I catch
the pitch of their calls, their shrill
cacophonies, their chitterings, their coos.
They hover behind his eyes and come to rest
on a branch, on a book, grow still,
claws curled, wings furled.
His is a bird world.

6

I SAW BELLA everywhere, as St. Andrews was a fishbowl. She often walked hand-in-hand through the streets with Angus, her quondam boyfriend. He had a pleasant if rough-hewn aspect: a ginger-haired young man with an angular, thin, and often unshaven face, long muscular arms, and blue eyes. Once I found myself beside him at the meat counter in the grocery store on South Street; when he saw me staring at him, he returned a quizzical look.

He interested me only because he interested Bella and therefore must represent something she liked in men. I assumed, based on no experience, that a genuine romantic relationship could hardly survive for more than a few sensuous nights if the couple failed to relate as friends. I had a lofty and perhaps idealized sense of what this meant in real time, imagining that I would have long conversations about politics, poetry, novels, and films with any future lover. I wanted someone who would share my curiosity about the strangeness of life. I wanted everything, in fact: a highly particular response to my longings, deep passion, a sense of transcendence.

On impulse, I called one afternoon at Hamilton Hall and knocked softly at Bella's door on the second floor.

She answered and, seeing me, dipped her eyes to the floor.

"I dropped by," I said masterfully.

"Coffee?"

It was a rainy day, cold and dark, and I could definitely do with a cup of coffee. She invited me into the room, and I could see that she had been working: the chaste single bed was strewn with books and handwritten notes.

"You're working hard," I said.

"Wasting my time, reading books not on the examination list."

"Always a bad sign."

"So why haven't you come to our antiwar group?" she asked. "There's a meeting tomorrow night at the back of the Cross Keys. Some of my friends would like to meet you."

Showing up for these meetings would have been an easy way to further my contact with Bella, but I hesitated, not only because of my fear of women, but because I still needed to stay on the outside, not wanting to acknowledge my position on the war, whatever it was precisely, or to look too closely at what it meant that I'd left the United States as I had. One night I had had a nightmare about giving a speech at an antiwar rally in St. Andrews, where my uncles had come to hear me, the three who had fought on the beach in Salerno. Geno, Julie, and Tony sat in the back row with frowns and folded arms. Afterward, when I tried to speak to them, they walked away and shook their heads. Didn't I respect their courage, their willingness to risk everything for my future freedom? What did it mean to put your body on the line, as they had?

"Maybe you could say something about your draft situation," Bella said, "and how in America they tend to conscript those without resources, especially blacks and the poor? You're in a unique place to speak. It would get their attention. A few of us are going to London for a big rally next month, at the U.S. embassy. You should come with us."

"I'm afraid I've fallen behind."

"Behind what?"

"In my research. Falconer keeps casting doubts on my topic. He thinks I shouldn't have chosen a living author."

"Pay no attention to him."

Easy for her to say, I thought.

"He's proud of his war record," I said.

She pulled a copy of *Shakespeare and the Sea* from the bookshelf beside her desk. "It's just . . . so wonderfully *batty.*"

She had all the accoutrements for serving coffee on her dresser, with an array of mugs that suggested she liked to entertain. Was I nothing more to her than another in a long line of friendly, coffee-sharing guests? So far I had not put a foot forward into our "relationship," if that's what it was. She probably wondered why I had not made a pass, although her relationship with Angus gave me an excuse not to make any obvious move.

"You're quite serious about your poetry," she said. "So many who come to the Poetry Society are . . . well, dabbling."

Dabbling, to her, was not a good thing.

I told her about meeting Alastair, this impish and eloquent poet with a boy and no wife. "He and Jasper move
every year, it seems. I'd like to live in that way myself."

"It can't be good for children to move around so
much."

Unprompted, she now talked about her father, a businessman and former academic, and her mother, who
was "largely concerned with her garden." She had one
sibling, she said, a brother who had "gone down from
Cambridge with a triple first and disappeared into the
foreign service." He was eight years her senior and wrote
to her every month from Afghanistan. Improbably, he
was named Ptolemy. "After the Greek astronomer," she
said, "not the general in Alexander's army."

"I wouldn't make that mistake," I said.

"We call him Tolly."

"Tolly Law," I said. "Nice."

"Why do Americans always say *nice*? It's so bland."

"Our daily interactions are bland by nature."

"The bland leading the bland," she said.

"Do you write poetry yourself?" I asked. It struck me
that I'd never seen anything of hers and that she never
presented anything at the Poetry Society, though she
obviously ran the workshops.

"I do, but—shame—I don't like to show my work,"
she said. "One day, perhaps. There's no telling where
anything will lead, is there?"

I was curious about Angus, but she didn't mention
him, and he was nowhere in evidence in her room. Not
even a stray sock in the corner or a random medical

textbook on the window ledge. No photograph of Angus with his rugby mates on her desk. Were they lovers? Quondam lovers? I wondered if there was the slightest chance I could move onto his ground, even take his place. But how could I begin to ask about such things?

"I probably should get back to work," she said.

I took the hint and finished my coffee in a gulp, then left her room, confused but also in a state of hope. *There's no telling*, she had said, *where anything will lead.*

7

"It's NOT FOR nothing that Stevenson was a Scot," said Alastair.

"Who?"

"You're not asking me who is Robert Louis Stevenson?"

This put me on edge. Needless to say, I set my feelings aside, wanting to belong to Alastair's household, where passing allusions were obvious and abundant. I wanted to get near his flame, which could be both dangerous and warming.

He drew a tray of hot ginger biscuits from the Aga and put one beside my mug of tea, then handed me *The Strange Case of Dr. Jekyll and Mr. Hyde* in an old Penguin edition.

"Your autobiography?" I asked.

"Funny man." He lit a cigarette, as if to think. "It's must reading, if you wish to understand Scottish life."

As I leafed through it, Alastair rolled a fat sloppy joint in French cigarette paper and lit it, sucking air to make it brighten at the tip. He took in a long drag and handed it to me. The sweetly musty smell appealed, though I coughed harshly at first, trying again with a shallower inhalation. My throat burned, but I was determined to open myself to new experiences, to let in the light.

"What I dislike about Scotland," said Alastair, on his usual jag, "is that virtue is taken for an achievement. And narrowly defined. We're always judged in this fucking country. It's as if there's some blinking scoreboard in the sky. I can hear the chalk scratching above me."

"Your father was a minister," I said.

"Yes, and dour. But gentle as well. My mother was strict, caught in a busy life, with her medical practice, several children, a large house to manage. The usual catastrophe."

"You've been married?"

"Questions, questions," he said. "Once or twice. 'There's nothing in the world for us but change.' A line from Borges. Do you know Borges?"

"Not really."

"That means not at all in Jay-talk. A literary virgin."

"It's too cold for sex in Scotland," I said.

This struck a chord. "They don't even take off their clothes to fuck here. I've thought about making a special set of Scottish pajamas. The couple can tie up, open trap doors in their fronts, around the crotch areas, and . . . well, connect. They won't have to take off anything, just drop the little doors. A corridor to nirvana."

Jasper appeared in the doorway with his helmet of black hair, his beautiful wide eyes. "That was *my* idea, Papa, the fucking pajamas," he said.

"I stole it."

"You're always stealing my ideas."

"You're the next Thomas Edison, Jasper."

"So who gets rich? Me or you?"

"We share everything, don't we?"

"Fucking Communist," said Jasper, walking away.

Alastair relit the joint, sucked in a long drag, and passed it back to me. He obviously didn't care that Jasper knew he was smoking pot. This was so unlike the world of my own childhood, where everything was concealed. Where desires of any kind lived in dark rooms, where doors and windows remained tightly shut. "Don't let anybody see what you're thinking," my father had once said to me, and I'd taken it to heart.

I began to cough again and went to the sink to get a glass of water. It was late now, darker by the moment. A shadow of dread passed over me like a rook, its black wings stirring the air.

"Did you get another letter from the draft board?" Alastair said, as if, after all, he knew what I was thinking.

"I've had three letters."

"Throw them away," he said.

There was something fresh in his voice. I turned to see, and his affectionate look brought tears to my eyes.

"War is never worth the expense of life," he said.

"You fought in the war against Hitler."

"It was a different time."

"I won't go to Vietnam."

"No, you won't," he said. Opening a bottle of red wine from Bulgaria, he filled a large tumbler with the harsh ruby liquid. "Always wash down the grass with the grape." He swallowed the contents of the glass in a gulp, then poured himself another, his eyes glistening.

I had brought a poem to show him, but seeing how stoned he was, I decided not to bother, guessing that the results of such a consultation wouldn't be helpful.

"Do you have a poem? You have that look on your face."

"It's not good. I wrote it to seduce this girl, Bella."

"Remember what Auden said: 'Poetry makes nothing happen.' It has no utilitarian value."

"I can't get her out of my head."

"So bring her to Pilmour! I'll do my best for you."

"I don't think so."

"Seduction is an art, but less complicated than poetry. Think of the billions of couples who are fucking every night on their sweaty beds. Men and women, women and women, men and men, men and turtles. Making the beast with the double back, as our friend Shakespeare put it."

A voice came from upstairs. "Papa, you were going to read to me before dinner!"

Alastair ignored him. "Do you know how to cook?"

"Not really."

"I didn't think so. I'll teach you." He took out knives and a thick block of wood, and we began to chop garlic, onions, and carrots according to his highly specific instructions.

"Cooking and writing are the perfect combination," he said. "All day I move back and forth between the desk and the stove. They're elemental. You bring various and distinct elements together, the raw ingredients. You add the flame. It's chemistry."

"So poetry is soup?"

"More like a stew." He poured a tremendous amount of oil into a skillet and asked, for no apparent reason, "What about this new car of yours? I saw you in the bottom of North Street yesterday. You nearly ran over a little old lady. We could do in this country with fewer old ladies."

"It's a rust bucket," I said. "Morris Minor, 1957." I felt quite proud of this car in a way. It was a two-tone affair, with a white roof but a candy-red body. A four-cylinder, four-speed manual. Never very well looked after. I shared ownership with a postgraduate student from Australia, and the whole business had set me back only a few hundred pounds.

"Read to me," said Jasper, appearing at my elbow. "Papa promised, but he won't. He's baked."

"Read to him," Alastair said. "Otherwise he may call the police."

So I followed the boy into the sitting room, where he nestled against me on the green sofa, with its lumpy pillows and damp smell. The Indian carpet on the wooden floor showed off elephants and tigers in dark blues and reds. The room had grown dim with twilight, so I turned on a lamp.

"Let's have Stevenson," said Jasper.

"He's a favorite in this house, isn't he?"

"Papa loves him. Borges loves him."

"It's always Borges here, isn't it? Do you know when he's coming?"

"Soon."

"Why is Borges such an important man in this house?"

"Do you know nothing? Papa says you're thick."

"He says that?"

"Not thick. Ill-informed." He shook his loose and shiny black hair and crinkled his nose. "I should button my lip, that's what Papa says. He likes you. Don't worry."

"He thinks I'm naive," I said.

"What does that mean?"

"Lacking experience of the world."

"I don't lack it, do I?"

"No. You've been to so many places. More than most people ever get to see."

"We like Majorca best."

"What is there—what do you like?"

"The wine, the women."

"And the song?"

"I only like the Beatles."

"Do you really like wine and women?"

"Not so much."

"You will."

"That's what Papa says." He touched my face, running his fingers over my features. "This is how Borges sees," he said. "Did you know he's blind? He always touches your face."

"I'm glad I'm not blind."

"I'd rather be deaf," said Jasper.

"Why?"

"Papa is always telling me things. Sometimes I don't want to hear them."

"You should listen to your father."

"That's a cliché. Good writing, Papa says, means no clichés. A cliché is any word or phrase that seems familiar. It's an old printing term. I try to avoid them."

"Like the plague."

"That's a cliché."

"Right."

Alastair stood in the doorway and banged a small pan with a spoon. It was time for dinner.

"I'm hungry," said Jasper over the din.

"Well, you're in luck," his father said. And there it was again—that love in his eyes.

8

I WOULD OFTEN see Professor Falconer on the streets as he tipped forward into a blast of wind, a lonely man in a wrinkle of thoughts. A puzzled expression always bloomed when, face-to-face, I would say, "Good morning, Professor" or "It's a lovely day!" I guessed that, as with many of his generation, the war continued to preoccupy him. His sky was still full of Messerschmitts and Junkers. The all-clear signal had yet to sound.

It did interest him that an American student should wish to focus on a Scottish poet who lived in Orkney, but it wasn't easy to explain to him my enchantment. Falconer shook his head wearily one day when I was sitting in his office and said, "I hope you will find some manuscripts. A thesis must contain original research. Write to Mr. Brown. See if there are manuscripts. And go see him, if you can. I should think that's possible. Research!"

That night I wrote to Mackay Brown in care of his publishers. Within a few weeks a letter arrived from Orkney in a strange crabwise scrawl on blue paper, and he said he was "brightened by" my interest in his work, although "humbled as well." I should "most certainly" come to visit him. "I generally meet the ferry each afternoon, although I rarely know anyone who disembarks." He gave me his telephone number and suggested I call "a few days before arrival in Stromness," as he didn't "require advance notice." The letter was signed, quite simply, "George."

Cheered by this response, I took pages of my thesis to Falconer, who continued to show little interest in my work. "Ah," he said, "the thesis continues! The main thing is to continue, even with bad work."

"Is my work bad?"

"No, I was just thinking aloud," he said. "What I wish to say is, keep moving forward! Never retreat! I said this to the men aboard ship. Onward!"

That he had actually been in command of a battleship in wartime boggled the mind, and I couldn't help but wonder about his private affairs. Rumor had it that he lived with his sister and had no real life. As it happened, I got to visit him at his house after a peculiar invitation.

It was a sunny afternoon in mid-November when I met Professor Falconer walking in the cloister under its ancient bell tower in the quad.

"I say," he said, stammering, motioning me to draw near. "I s-say!"

"Hello, Professor. How are you?"

"M-may I have a word?"

"Of course." I adopted a listening air.

"There is a young man, you see. I was hoping to introduce you."

"Yes, of course."

"Ah, good. Come to my house, number 2, Alexandra Place. Do you know it? Wednesday next. Teatime, what? Shall we say at four?"

"That's fine. I'd like that."

He smiled, seeming to fumble in his drawer of memory. "He's an American, much like yourself. Interested in poetry, whatnot."

I shifted from foot to foot as he dug into himself for more information about this young man.

"What's his name?"

"Ah, yes," he said. "His name is Jay Parini."

"But, Professor," I said, "I'm Jay Parini."

His eyes widened. "Oh, dear. That's too bad. Well, do come. Come anyway!"

Before he withdrew, he asked in a plaintive voice, "Do you have two jackets?"

This was such a good story I had to tell someone, and guessed it would amuse Bella, so I turned up at that evening's meeting of the Poetry Society and waylaid her afterward. She laughed hard. She was also impressed by a couple of Alastair's poems that I read aloud that night. "I'd love to meet him," she said, and I suggested she join me the next day for tea at Pilmour Cottage.

This was going well, I told myself when I picked her up in my Morris Minor outside Hamilton Hall. The car, alas, didn't quite impress her.

"I can actually see the road under my feet," she said, lifting her knees.

My car was more like a mirage than an actual vehicle,

and the floor was indeed paper-thin. But it carried us along.

Alastair was in a distracted mood when we arrived, having somehow forgot we were coming for tea. We sat in silence at his table for an awkward time. When finally he turned a long gaze on Bella, she was unable to look him in the eye. It was the first time I'd ever seen her fazed by anything.

"Bella," he said, with a sidelong smirk. "Diminutive of Arabella?"

"Yes."

"*Ara* means altar. *Bella* means beautiful. So you're a beautiful altar on which someone might sacrifice himself one day."

This visit was quickly slumping in the wrong direction. Already I regretted bringing Bella.

"My father tells me it means 'yielding to pray.'"

"I would never yield to such a thing," said Alastair.

I had told Bella about Alastair and Graves, and she launched straight into questions. Wasn't Graves a better poet than a novelist? Why did he live in Majorca? Wasn't *The White Goddess* a peculiar sort of book? The questions poured forth, delighting me: I had brought someone with a good mind into Alastair's house, and he must appreciate that.

"Graves hates me," he said. "I stole one of his goddesses. His wife was probably relieved. Anything to thin the pack."

"Did he sleep with all of them?"

"Depends what you mean by sleep."

Bella seemed to gather strength and, surprisingly, she

held his stare in a way that impressed me. I could learn from her. "He wrote so many novels," she said.

"Nobody knows them nowadays. *Count Belisarius? Seven Days in New Crete?*"

"*I, Claudius* is good. A perfect narrator for the madness of empire. I love the scene with Caligula, where he imagines himself a god while they're hacking off his limbs."

"Ouch," said Jasper, who began to pick up the paper airplanes on the floor.

"Graves had a natural feel for the ruling classes," said Bella.

"He's a snob at heart," Alastair said. "Public schoolboy turned army officer turned author. Not the best sequence."

My flat-footed silence embarrassed me as Alastair and Bella continued to talk about the politics of the early decades of the Roman Empire. Inwardly I cursed my lack of knowledge, feeling jealous of Bella (whose British public school education had given her easy access to a wide range of information) and also of Alastair: would he, with his charisma and wild fluency in politics and literature, steal Bella's heart not for me but for himself? Would he actually poach a friend's potential girlfriend?

As they continued to chat, I knew that he would. And worried that Bella seemed enchanted now, excited by their back-and-forth.

Before long we sat on the floor before the coal fire: perfect for a Scottish afternoon as winter approached. Within moments Alastair came in with a tray of brownies, which he lifted high like the host at the altar—the kind of altar, I thought, at which even he might be willing to sacrifice himself. "A fresh batch," he said. "Hash brownies."

"I've never had them," Bella said.

"They go well with wine," Alastair told her. "Forget about tea."

He passed around the tray, and we each took one, though I did so with a hesitation that must have shown in my expression. These were potent morsels, and I wasn't sure how any of this might play out.

Bella took a tiny bite, chewed slowly, then took a larger bite. I allowed myself only a nibble and was relieved when the wine bottle appeared. I didn't want to feel completely out of control, in part because I was angry with Alastair for the ways in which he'd coopted Bella, and I wasn't sure how I might react if I got completely stoned. When you get angry, the other guy wins—that's what my father had taught me. Given my portion, the effect of the brownies was slow in coming, taking the form of a mellowness that began in my knees and rose gradually to the top of my head.

Jasper whispered, "I like your girlfriend. She's pretty."

Bella, overhearing this, smiled. "I'm not his girlfriend. Just a friend."

My skin tingled with shame and embarrassment.

Jasper made it easier, though. "You're a girl, and you're his friend," he said.

"You've got me there."

Alastair took me aside before we left, perhaps sensing my discomfort and confusion. "She's splendid," he told me. "Take her back to your place. The brownies will kick in nicely."

"Really?"

"Do you have more wine at the flat?"

"A bottle of Beaune."

"It will substitute for charm," said Alastair.

As Bella and I stepped outside, both of us weaving slightly, I asked her what she thought of Alastair.

"He's charming, though I always distrust charm." This was, I thought, discerning.

"I have a good bottle of wine in my flat," I said. "Come back?"

"Can't, I'm afraid. I told Angus I would meet him for dinner. At his cottage. He lives with his godawful brother, Jack. I'd invite you to join us, but you wouldn't have a good time. You'd hate it, actually."

My normal reserve having been eroded by the hash, I asked, "Will *you* have a good time?"

"That depends. I'm easily bored. It's a weakness in my character. I do like Angus, though not when he's with his brother. He's not often there, though, which is the best you can say about him."

I didn't know what to make of her attitude to Angus or his brother. This was a long way from Scranton, from the ways of being I had accepted as a given back in Pennsylvania. A long way from the comfortable presuppositions about how men and women behaved and what these assumptions meant for stability. In a weird way, I almost missed the certainties and simplicities of that safe if predictable world. But this was my new life, and I told myself to embrace it, to accept what came along, however strange or implausible or—at times—terrifying.

9

I SLEPT BADLY now, and half wished I hadn't flushed those barbiturates in the toilet. Even that synthetic sleep would be preferable to my current state. Vietnam weighed on me, and a part of every night was spent in that godforsaken war zone, dreaming of vast rice paddies that concealed poison spikes or booby-trapped paths I might well have been walking had I not fled to St. Andrews. My sharpest images of Vietnam came from Billy's letters. He wrote from outposts near the DMZ, where his job was to interrogate prisoners of war. "I go on walks now and then, though it's fucking dangerous," he said in one letter that I reread many times. "Not so much the Vietcong, though they're pretty awful if you happen to run into them by accident. Fucking cunts, all of them. You should see the brush: vines tangling and drooping. Stinging plants in the mud. And crazy snakes. Ask me about the bamboo pit viper when you next see me. And the ants, neurotic little goose-steppers—kind of like your thoughts—and these prehistoric birds from hell." He said he was "writing high, under a lamp in base camp, where rats run up and down the walls, big as tomcats. High is the only place to be in Nam." In another letter he told me about a whorehouse in Saigon. "Man, it's glory land. Hallelujah chorus all the way. Such bodies! Tits and ass all the way. They know what the tongue is for, let me tell you, Mr. Virgin. Hey, don't I make this sound like fun? Come out and join us! I hear they're running out of stooges. Remember: *This is our time."*

"No thanks, Billy Boy," I wrote back to him. I did my best to describe my daily work, my friends, Alastair and Jasper, Jeff, who had quickly become a friend and counselor, my longings for Bella, Professor Falconer: this strange little world on the East Neuk of Fife. Some nights I rose every hour or two and huddled in the chair by the electric fire, popping shillings in the meter, scribbling bad poems on a yellow pad or writing longer and longer letters to my friend in Vietnam. I told myself I was doing this to distract the poor bastard, but I was doing it as much to distract myself: from doubts about my thesis; from my guilt that Billy was over there in a hellhole and I wasn't, and perhaps somebody else was suffering in my place. In fact, that's what Billy had said when we had had a drink at Joey's Bar in West Scranton only a few weeks before he left. "If you don't go, somebody else is going instead. You can live with that?"

Was this true? Was war a kind of zero-sum game? Wouldn't I just be giving in to a bad version of history if I enlisted? If I went, I'd be going for myself, not my country. I'd be going to have "an experience." I'd be trying not to "miss out" on my time.

The letters from my draft board just kept coming,

ramping up my anxieties, and I waited for a knock at the door. Scotland Yard, I thought, must surely have a unit in cahoots with the FBI or some clandestine international agency that dragged deserters like me back into the fold.

Over coffee one morning, Jeff tried to calm my nerves. "I don't think they want your ass," he said. "They don't want mine, far as I can tell, so why would they want yours? You'd make a terrible soldier. The Vietnamese will jump for joy if they hear you're coming. I'll write to Nixon and tell him: *Don't draft Jay Parini!*"

I didn't tell Billy—or Jeff, of course—that I couldn't sleep, and that I felt at night as if I were sinking through layers of space, my consciousness like a roof that falls floor by floor through a burning house. I thought about death too often, and it didn't help that I'd seen a student tumbled from a bike in traffic on Bell Street. He soared ten feet into the air and landed at the edge of a curb with blood coming from his ears. (What became of him I didn't know, didn't even want to know.) One night I heard on the BBC about a crash in the London Underground that killed a nun and several others. Then one of my professors slumped at his desk one afternoon and died from an apparent heart attack at forty-seven. So much death in the world, and so little to relieve its drone in the deepest ear of my mind. How was it possible that everyone on the street shuffled about so cheerfully, as if they were not doomed, as if they didn't carry a time bomb in their chest?

My problems were not eased by the fact that I ran into Bella often, in the grocery store, in pubs, at the tea shop in South Street. One night, stepping from a dull dance at the Student Union, I saw her and Angus walking hand in hand outside the entrance to the college quad, and—like a voyeur—followed them from a distance. They turned into a gravel lane near the East Sands and disappeared into a pebble-dash cottage, which I assumed was the one that Angus shared with his brother. I stood in the garden beside the house and looked up at what I imagined was the light in the bedroom where they slept. After the light went out, I stumbled in quiet misery to the beach below and sat on a stone wall, listening to noisy surf that ground its teeth in mindless repetitions. What was the point of life? A big moon blazed on the water, but it was not a beautiful light. It was cold and unyielding.

I told this story to Jeff the next day, and he said, "You're unwell. You really should see a doctor."

The next morning I visited the infirmary, where I spoke with a nurse in a stiff blue uniform. She listened patiently to my confession of sleeplessness, which accompanied an inability to work, a sense of doom, and what I told her felt like "a crisis of existence." I told her that I often thought of death, mentioning a grisly dream I'd had about being dragged by a bus through the busy corners of some familiar intersection in an unknown foreign city. "Maybe Antwerp or Stuttgart," I said, though I'd never been to either city, as I explained.

"Antwerp has very good pastries," she said.

I told her that I hadn't slept through a night in the past week without waking in tears.

"This isn't good," she said. "You must see Dr. Gillies."

A telephone call was made as I sat there, and she handed me a slip of paper. I had an appointment the next day.

The clinic stood at the edge of the New Town, on the underside of St. Andrews, a nondescript building with the pale stucco cladding found on most recent architecture in Scotland. There was a brass plaque on the door boasting the doctor's name and professional degrees, more degrees than a thermometer. Below it was the word *psychiatry*, which cut a small hole in the mental air around me. I had never imagined myself as somebody who would need a psychiatrist.

Dr. Gillies occupied a small, antiseptic office with grim rows of metal filing cabinets along one wall. I took him to be in his fifties, a ghoulishly thin fellow with a well-trimmed gray-blond beard and a slick bald head. He spoke with what I imagined was a severe Glaswegian accent, staring at me through wire-rimmed glasses. His white jacket had a peculiar stain like red lipstick on one lapel.

After fifteen minutes of terse questioning, he diagnosed depression. "It's the curse of the northern climates," he said. "I see it every day. The lack of sleep. The doldrums, staring into space. Panic attacks are not uncommon. Do you sweat?"

"Sweat?"

"In bed, for example."

"Not especially. I don't know."

"Would you call yourself cheerful?"

"Not lately."

"Ever?"

"I don't know."

He shook his head gravely. "What would you say is your chief worry?"

"Death," I said. "There's so much death."

"The finitude we all face—limitations, the human condition."

"Something like that." After a moment I added, "I'm in love with a woman. But she loves someone else."

"This configuration, it's quite normal," he said. "Your depression turns a normal situation into something disastrous."

"I can't live without her," I said.

"This isn't uncommon, a feeling of despair, which is accompanied by frustration. Especially among young men."

"I'm a ridiculous cliché," I said.

"No, Mr. Parini, I wouldn't go so far. None of us is original."

"Can you help?"

"Oh, yes. I think so," Dr. Gillies said.

He told me with barely suppressed enthusiasm about the "exciting technologies" that had made psychiatry what he called a "brave new world," apparently unaware of the dark associations that accompany this phrase. He leaned toward me. "Have you heard of electroconvulsive therapy?"

I hadn't, but I didn't like the sound of it. "Convulsive"?

He must have read my expression. "You don't have to be afraid," he said, dropping his voice a couple of registers. "It's quite simple, the procedure. I do it here, with the help of Miss Macdonald, my assistant. We attach an electric point of contact to each side of your head, near the temples. Then we pass a current through the brain. A brief burst, and that's it. One treatment is often enough."

"What does it do?"

"Do?" He looked away. "Let's say it reshuffles the deck."

Reshuffles?

"Shall we schedule you for next week? I have several openings."

"I don't know."

Dr. Gillies came close to me. "It would make all the difference," he whispered fiercely.

I mumbled a thank-you and left as quickly as I could, then pedaled madly down the street. I had no wish to have my deck reshuffled.

10

"BORGES IS IN town," Alastair said breathlessly when I ran into him at the entrance to Geddes, a purveyor of fine wines, cheeses, and cured meats in Market Street: not the sort of place where Alastair Reid would normally shop for provisions. He explained that the Argentinian had been dropped off at Pilmour the night before by Norman di Giovanni, an American who often traveled with him these days. "Borges is a bit frail, but Norman has left him in my care for a few weeks. We're translating some new poems."

Together we stepped into the lovely shop with its rich smells, and I watched with interest as he bought a thick slice of Dolcelatte, an especially creamy version of Gorgonzola, and a bottle of dark Spanish wine. Good wine, for once. I didn't think he would normally shop at Geddes, where everything cost so much. When he asked if I would come to dinner, I quickly agreed, but I confessed that despite his exhortations, I had yet to read anything by Borges.

"The translations are mostly terrible," Alastair said, as if to excuse me.

"I must learn Spanish," I said. Spanish wasn't difficult, not compared to Greek.

Alastair of course knew I would not learn Spanish just to read Borges. He touched my shoulder as if to say, *There, there* . . .

"He's here!" Jasper said, greeting me at the door.

Jeff stood behind him, looking beatific with a yellow bandanna on his head, breathing expectantly. It was as if God himself sat in the room next door.

The old man hunched in the shadows, in the wing chair, leaning on a cane with an ivory handle, his hair slicked back. He looked every inch his age of seventy-one, even a decade older, wearing a baggy brown pin-striped suit with big cuffs, his checked waistcoat looped by a gold chain. His wide powder-blue tie was full of orange waterfalls, flying fish, and the residue of many meals. The soiled and fraying collar of his shirt suggested that it had been in use for many years, if not generations. He was talking to himself now, smiling in a twitchy way, lifting his big empty eyes to the ceiling like headlamps.

We approached him without speaking.

"This is Jay Parini," Jasper said in his piping voice.

"I'm glad to meet you, sir," I said.

"Speak louder, I'm blind!" said Borges.

Jasper made a little twirl around his ear with a finger.

"Jay Parini!" I shouted.

"Ah, Giuseppe Parini!" he said. "One of my favorites of the Italian poets. *Il giorno*. What a performance! The Alexander Pope of Italy!"

"I know the poem a little, yes." Though I was unjustifiably proud to share the last name of this eighteenth-century poet, I'd never bothered to read his verse carefully. Could Borges smell my fraudulence?

"I'm so pleased to meet you at last," he said. "Do you know Palermo?"

"I've never been to Italy."

"Not in Sicily, with the Mafia. It's in Buenos Aires. Palermo is a barrio—an adjunct quarter. Alas, there are gangsters in my Palermo, too. I will admit this. The kinship of thieves, men with knives! But you must know, it's one of the oldest parts of the city, and such lovely sad colonial architecture. Many Italians settled there, and they often speak in Italian in the streets. The best of them read the poetry of Parini."

I'd soon discover that he often spoke like this, with impressionistic bullet points, circumnavigations, and associations: a wild disjunctive manner. He seemed to chase his own tail around an invisible pole, and I wondered if this manner had something to do with his blindness, as if those who can't see can sense more than the rest of us, make daring mental leaps, sometimes doubling back on themselves to clarify and reinforce earlier lines of argument.

"Jay is a writer," Jasper said.

"I'm sure of it: Giuseppe Parini! I'd have been a better writer, perhaps more widely read, had my name been Federico García Lorca. You must know Lorca—a poet, a playwright, and a ferocious egoist? He came to Buenos Aires once, about forty years ago. Kept very bad company. Oliverio Girondo! Don't let me talk about this particular man, please!"

"Girondo?" asked Jasper.

"I wish I had never heard the man's name."

Alastair caught the end of this conversation as he stepped into the room. "Lorca!" he said. "What a good poet. I like his plays, too."

"Alastair," said Borges, "you say this only to irritate me."

"It's a failing of yours, Borges, this hatred of Lorca."

"You must know, I have worse feelings about Girondo. He stole from me the most lovely woman in the world, Norah Lange. He stole my bride."

"You were never married to her."

"But this is the problem. Let me explain to Giuseppe." The massive globe of his head spun in my direction. "The catastrophe happened in 1934, I believe. Or was it 1933? Memory is a mirror that may easily shatter. The shards would cut me into ribbons. I would bleed on this floor."

Alastair said to Jeff and me, "He's melodramatic, but he controls himself on the page."

"You don't know what I suffered at the hands of Girondo," said Borges, gazing at the ceiling.

"I do!" Jeff said. "I have suffered at his hands as well. He was last seen in Ohio."

Alastair loved this, as did Jasper, who clapped, claiming that he too had been wronged by Girondo in his school in St. Andrews. "Girondo is everywhere," he said.

"Then you will understand," said Borges.

Soon we gathered around the kitchen table for a succulent beef stew made with pearl onions and garlic, red potatoes, and capers, all cooked in a thick madeira sauce. Alastair poured wine for everyone, including Jasper. On the Aga sat a trayful of Alastair's familiar brownies.

Borges said, "I have dreamed of being in Scotland through my whole life."

"When you wish upon a star," said Jasper.

"My family had Nordic roots, but my grandmother— she was thoroughly English, from Staffordshire. She was Fanny Haslam. My great-grandfather, Edward Haslam, was a schoolmaster in Buenos Aires, which is where my grandmother met the colonel." He recited this information as if it had been printed on a card and memorized, to be pulled out for the right occasions.

"That's his grandfather, the colonel," Jeff said, and I wondered when he'd imbibed all this Borgesian lore.

"A very great man, yes. And English was my first language," said Borges, "the language of my nursery."

"So why do you speak with such an accent?" asked Jasper.

Alastair glared at him.

"It's not that I don't like the accent," Jasper added.

"It's a Staffordshire accent," said Alastair.

"He is teasing me always, dear Alejandro."

"I'm a funny man. Ask Jay."

"*Eso!* I have never been amusing in the same way. But it's a small tragedy, not a large one. My dear friend Bioy Cesares—he carries the humor for both of us."

"I do love *The Invention of Morel*," said Alastair.

"The one perfect novel in the history of novels."

"A fugitive on an island, a murderer, somewhere in the Pacific. Time dissolves. Reality dissolves," Alastair said.

"Readers become invisible, even to themselves. Only the story lives. It's the fate of the writer, yes, as well, to disappear."

"How is Elsa?" asked Alastair.

"My wife, too, has disappeared, and I'm not unhappy. Marriage has never been in my gift."

"What?"

"We are divorcing, I will acknowledge the truth. Have I failed to say this? My apologies, but—how to explain? This union which was never a union. Appearances deceive. We never really knew each other. A word of advice, Giuseppe. Do not rush into marriage."

As if rushing were my problem.

"You courted Elsa for five decades," said Alastair. "That's half a century!"

"There is truth in this, but not the whole truth. I loved her when she was a girl of seventeen. I married her when she was an old woman. Never confuse the two. Think how often our cells die, and they're replaced one by one! We lose ourselves again and again, and the worst is always yet to come. This marriage was my mistake. I loved Norah Lange, in any case. Not Elsa. My mother warned me. She said, *Elsa wants your money.* I said, *Mother, I have no money. Ay, caramba!*"

"Nobody says *Ay, caramba*," said Alastair.

"Alejandro. Did you not hear me say it?"

"Jay writes poetry," said Jasper, perhaps noticing that I didn't know where to put an oar into these swirling waters. In this I sometimes resembled my father, who could stand by the side, failing to assert himself. (I didn't like this about myself and would have to work over the years to overcome it.)

"Have you published a book, Giuseppe?"

"Not yet," I said. "I don't have enough poems, and they aren't ready for the public."

"I said as much when I was your age. But I published the book anyway."

He ate greedily, helping after helping, and we all watched in amazement the way he repeatedly wiped his mouth with the back of his hand. Sometimes he withdrew a handkerchief from his pocket and cleaned his fingers.

"He likes his food," said Alastair. "But if he stays in Scotland long enough, it will cure his appetite."

"Scotland is very dear to my heart, have you not understood me? In part, I think, this is because the greatest writer in the English language lived in Scotland."

"Who is this?" I asked.

"Stevenson, dear boy."

"I've been singing his praises to Jay," said Alastair.

"So have I," said Jasper.

"I love Robert Louis," said Jeff.

" 'Home is the sailor, home from sea, / And the hunter home from the hill.' These are, Giuseppe, the finest lines of English poetry. I would kill to have written such lines."

"They pass the envy test," said Alastair.

"In fact, I *shall* write them one day," said Borges. "I shall claim them."

"He's not much read in the States," I said.

"In the States, very little is read," said Borges. "I have traveled in your country, always to lecture. At Harvard, for instance, in Cambridge. I tell students to read the great ones: Stevenson, Chesterton, Wells. And Chidiock Tichborne. Now *there* is a poet."

Alastair raised an eyebrow. "Tichborne?"

Borges warmed his face in the spotlight of our attention. "He wrote only one poem," he said, "his 'Elegy.' An elegy for himself. He was condemned to the Tower of London, a would-be assassin of Elizabeth. A Catholic, remember. Part of the Babington Plot to bring Mary, Queen of Scots, to the throne. It's the most perfect poem:

My prime of youth is but a frost of cares,
My feast of joy is but a dish of pain,
My crop of corn is but a field of tares,
And all my good is but vain hope of gain.
The day is past, and yet I saw no sun,
And now I live, and now my life is done.

"Does it get better, I ask you? 'My crop of corn is but a field of tares.' Metaphor raised to the level of perfection. And I, you see, am an old man. I'm in my own Tower, awaiting execution. 'And now I live, and now my life is done.'"

"Are you going to die soon?" asked Jasper, who was removing the capers from his stew one by one, lining them up on the side of the bowl.

"Indeed, boy. Look at these withered hands, my stoop! Look into my eyes, which see nothing!"

"Enough," said Alastair. "Scotland is working its dark magic. Morbidity is the national curse."

"I must read Tichborne," I said. "All of him."

"Yes! And if you read Spanish, Giuseppe, I will also recommend Lugones. Turn first to his history of the Jesuits. What a masterpiece! But who reads Lugones now? He was the hero of my youth: poet and translator, theologian, historian, essayist, playwright, novelist. Does anyone write in so many genres today?"

"I do," said Alastair.

"Alejandro, for shame! Nobody is Lugones. Our age murders great writers. There are no readers for such a man."

"You're a great writer," said Jasper.

"A great *reader*, perhaps. Great readers are scarce, more difficult to find than great writers. This was not the case in the age of Leopoldo Lugones."

Alastair led Borges into the sitting room after dinner, and Jeff passed around wine in pewter goblets that belonged to the house, and the tray of glistening brownies, which reminded me of the last time we'd shared some, with Bella. I wished I could have brought her with me tonight to meet Borges. She'd have liked his talk, his thought excursions, this one-man literary spectacle!

Borges lifted his brownie to sniff it before biting into it. Then he smiled, with apparent relief. "I have, how do you say, a sweet tooth. Alejandro knows me well."

"You'll find these to your liking, Borges. My special Scottish brownies, the ones I gave you last night. Laced with stardust."

"They make me so happy."

An hour later the brownies had taken hold, and Borges was cheerily quoting reams of his favorite writers by heart, lecturing us on any number of topics, from Zeno's paradoxes to the Zohar, quoting verbatim a lengthy passage from De Quincey's *Confessions of an English Opium-Eater.* "Space swelled, and was amplified to an extent of unutterable infinity. This, however, did not disturb me so much as the vast expansion of time; I sometimes seemed to have lived for seventy or a hundred years in one night."

When we clapped for him, he said, "I'm not your John Barrymore, my grandmother's favorite actor, but I will accept your approbation." He stood, leaning forward on his cane. "We must take the air, no? I need to breathe! The North Sea beckons!"

"A walk in the dark," said Jeff. "What a good idea."

"For a blind man, it's business as usual," said Alastair.

We stepped into the tingling air under a full moon and reeled across the golf course toward the beach. Nobody but Jasper was sober.

Borges said, "You must know, I longed for the presence of the North Sea as a boy. And now here I am, too blind to see it, but I know it by its presence. Smell the salt!"

Jeff said, "It's straight ahead of you, a hundred yards or so."

The old man took off as if he could see, rushing in the direction of the water, where the moonlight splashed with a strange intensity. It wasn't an easy route, however brief, as he had to cross the seventeenth hole first, near sand traps and roughs. When he came to the sea he would have to plunge through a ridge of marram grass.

"He's going to kill himself," I said to Alastair.

"He's Borges. He can fly."

Was Alastair so high that he'd lost touch with the physical world?

I was not especially clear-headed myself, but Jeff and I followed close behind Borges, as if shadowing a boisterous two-year-old.

Borges stopped on the brink of a sweeping dune, listening to the water or perhaps the gods. He lifted his arms with his cane in the air and whirled around, but when he stopped, he was facing us and the Old Course, not the sea. In a thundering manner, he began to recite *The Seafarer* in its original Anglo-Saxon.

"Mæg ic be me sylfum / soðgied wrecan, / siþas secgan."

"Should we turn him around?" asked Jeff in a whisper.

"Let him be," I said. It was too wonderful, unlikely, and satisfying: a blind old poet beside a putting green. Alastair, Jeff, Jasper, and I gathered before him, listening to the odd recitation, the cries of gulls overhead and the nearby surf nearly drowning him out.

Alastair translated the crucial lines for us: "I can make a true son / of myself, and tell you about my travels, / and the days of struggle that I have endured."

Borges had apparently long wished to stand at the edge of the North Sea and chant this poem, which is spoken in the first person by an old salt who recalls his long years of solitude at sea, which is a symbol of life itself.

"He's consecrated the Old Course," Jeff said in my ear. "Golf will never be the same."

11

I SAW BELLA the next day at MacArthur's, the tea shop in South Street, a large room marked by the lace doilies on round tables, with a clatter of china and muted conversation in the air. She was alone, her eyes fixed on the pages of a novel, which she had propped against a sugar bowl.

I approached her warily. "May I sit?"

She was reading *Lady Chatterley's Lover*, and I knew I had disturbed her. But it was, after all, teatime, with the usual invitation to sociability that comes with this British tradition; and she had, after all, made a choice to read in public.

"As you can see, I'm taking a break from more serious work," she said. "Where have you been?"

"Lost in the library," I said, taking up a seat. I wanted to tell her about the encounter with Borges, a gift I was waiting to unwrap for her.

"All work and no play . . ."

"I have nobody to play with."

"Boo-hoo," she said.

"You seem to work an awful lot."

"You make it sound as if I were ill or unstable. Exams are coming in June, so—you know how it goes—I swot."

"Is Angus swotting?"

"Medics never let up. But he's moving to Glasgow soon. There or Manchester, to finish his training."

I eyed the tiered tray in the middle of the table, a pyramid of temptation—scones with shiny specks of currants, vanilla sponge cakes, oatcakes, and shortbread fingers. Like Oscar Wilde, I could resist anything but temptation, so I filled my plate. The waitress in her black uniform took my order for a pot of tea.

"Will you move to Glasgow as well?" I asked. "When you finish in St. Andrews?"

"Good lord, what a thing to say! My father knows a man with a gallery in Florence, a funny old chap with a Fu Manchu mustache. I'm hoping for an internship."

"Florence is lovely in spring," I said, knowing nothing of Florence. "I mean, when the flowers come out."

"The wisteria in April," she said, "huge purple tunnels of wisteria."

"I'd love to see that."

"Autumn and spring are best," she told me in her patiently informative docent's voice. "After June it's unbearably hot and crowded." She held her cup with two hands, sipping. "Florence isn't really a city, it's a museum."

"Everybody wants to see David's ass."

"An arse for the ages. And the flip side is pleasant, too. Almost perfect balls. Come to visit, if I get this internship."

The invitation tantalized but puzzled me. In fact, I

could think of nothing worse than traveling to see her if I was merely a brotherly figure who accompanied her to museums or restaurants. I already had a very nice sister, Dorrie, in Pennsylvania, thank you very much, and now what I wanted was to study Bella's features with my fingertips, like a blind man passing his hands over a text in Braille. Her lips had a fullness that struck me with force as I sat there, longing to kiss them. Her shallow eyes shone with a gray-green tint.

"Borges is here," I said.

"Ah, the Argentinian. Alastair's working with him?"

"On some translations. He's so peculiar."

"How?"

"Being blind, he talks a lot."

"Why would a blind man talk more than anyone else?"

"We're usually guided by the responses of those around us. If I ramble, you'll shut me up with a frown."

"I don't frown."

"You know what I mean."

"Why don't you get a girlfriend?"

This was a sucker punch of a non sequitur. She knew of my feelings for her—she must know—and yet she'd hit me with this question? I stared at the half-eaten scone on my plate, the pool of jam at the side.

"I didn't mean to offend," she said, "but I see you walking in the streets, always by yourself. And along the West Sands."

"I run there every morning."

"Every morning?"

"Pretty much."

"You're disciplined."

"Only when it comes to the West Sands. It's my religion. You should come with me someday."

"I suppose," she said, looking at me with wider eyes.

"It's the best beach in Scotland. Or so says Angus."

"Well, then, it *must* be the best."

"Don't be whiny about Angus. He's a sweetheart."

A small silver-plated pot of tea arrived, with a taller one of hot water for refills.

"I don't know why they give you two pots," I said.

"Then you don't know much," she said.

If the code of British teatime manners was difficult to break, the code of Bella's true feelings was more so. Was she pushing me away or leading me on? Did she actually know what she wanted, or what sort of things she implied?

"Do the letters keep coming?" she asked.

"From my draft board or my mother?"

"Which do you dread more?"

"It's a toss-up." I poured myself a cup of tea, flashing back to a letter from my mother that had arrived the day before. "You should be so careful with the Scottish girls," she said. "They all want to marry an American just to come to this country. It's a free passport." It was another of her endless warnings. *Be careful what you eat. Look out for bad company. Wear a sweater if it's drafty in the house. Don't drink too much. Don't stay up too late, as you'll be exhausted the next day.* She meant well, for sure, but she was yet another of Ben Franklin's tribe, though without his wit.

"The Vietnam thing should have stopped years ago."

"Nixon lied about ending it."

"Surprise, surprise. Kissinger's a liar, too," she said. "I'm sure the peace talks in Paris were sabotaged. Tens of thousands of civilians have died since, and keep dying, for no reason."

"The devil's arithmetic," I said. "The whole thing is a fucking botch."

Her awareness of the details of the war in Southeast Asia slightly shamed me. She wasn't even at risk, not personally, in this conflict.

"Is there any hope?" she asked.

"It gives me hope to sit here with you, in the safety of MacArthur's."

"You're an escapist."

"Exactly."

"Hence the dreams of Florence."

Suddenly desire—that mouse that can turn into a dragon—blazed into life. I wanted badly to hold her in my arms, to feel her long, smooth body beside mine between cool sheets. In my mind I undressed her as we talked, lifting her cashmere pullover, unfastening her bra. I loosened her belt and zipped down her jeans, lifted off her panties. I untied her red "trainers," as she called her sneakers. Those lovely, tantalizing, and terrifically red trainers.

"We should have dinner one evening," I said.

"Why not? Do you like Chinese food?"

"Pearl of Hong Kong?"

"Perfect," she said. She wrote her telephone number on a piece of paper.

I gave her my number as well, writing it on the first page of *Lady Chatterley's Lover*.

"Lawrence would approve," she said.

I left the tea shop in a torrent of feeling, a mingling of hope and dread. I felt like a child lying in the summer grass with a white daisy in hand, plucking the leaves one by one and whispering, "She loves me, she loves me not."

"Jay?" It was Alastair's voice on the phone, seeming short of breath. "Something has come up."

"Yes?"

"A friend, a kind of great-uncle in London, has taken ill. Nothing serious, but you never know. He's over ninety. Jasp and I need to go there. I don't think we'll be gone for more than a week. This is important."

I waited, wondering how this might involve me.

"It's Borges," said Alastair. "He can't be left alone. And Jeff has gone to Edinburgh, damn it. He left yesterday." He paused, as if to let me imagine Borges stumbling around the cottage by himself, tapping his cane against the walls. "I don't suppose you could move into Pilmour, just for a week? I can't say how many days. You can do your own work. Don't worry. He's quite independent."

Jesus. Was I now so dependent on Alastair's approval that I must respond to his every whim?

I knew, of course, that a blind old man is never independent. He's the opposite of independent. And I could only begin to imagine the ways in which Borges might depend on me.

"We're leaving in about an hour," Alastair said. "Is that possible?"

"An hour?"

"You'll be there?"

The thought unsettled me. But I could hardly say no. Not to Alastair, after all he'd done for me. Even though I had already filled my diary with appointments: tea with my new friend Tony Ashe, the possible dinner with Bella at Pearl of Hong Kong. Could I really make so many adjustments?

"Yes, I can do that," I said.

In a confused state, I threw a few things into a canvas rucksack (I had ditched *backpack* for good, and found myself pretentiously substituting *garden* for the American *yard*), including a long recent letter from Billy that I hadn't read, and a few volumes by Mackay Brown as well as his letter to me from Orkney, where he said I should come for a visit, "and come soon," giving me his telephone number. A faint resentment stirred in me as I realized that I should be going to Orkney to meet the subject of my thesis, not heading to Pilmour Cottage to look after Borges. In fact, I despaired of getting anything done on my thesis during the days ahead. Borges would talk at me, around me, and through me, scattering my thoughts like pebbles in the path. I would struggle to read or think about George Mackay Brown with Borges over my shoulder. My own poems would come out in pigeon Spanish.

Driving to Pilmour, I wondered if my deck might be reshuffled after all.

The transfer came swiftly. Alastair's recently acquired Mini, a hand-me-down from his sister, throbbed on the gravel road in front of the cottage, ready to take him and Jasper to the train station at Leuchars, and Alastair put the house keys for Pilmour into my palm. "Borges likes porridge for breakfast," he said, "with milk and three scoops of sugar. Fruit if possible. Raisins will do. Good for his guts. Likes bacon, too. Lots of bacon, very crisp."

"I'll warn the local pigs."

I watched them pull away, Jasper leaning out and waving from the open window, and went into the empty-feeling house. In the sitting room, where light pillared through a window, with motes of dust quivering in the bright funnel of silence, Borges sat staring ahead in the wing chair, his chin leaning on his folded hands atop his cane's ivory handle. The brown pin-striped suit was wrinkled like the skin of an old peach. His skin seemed translucent, thin as rice paper.

Feeling inadequate and slightly dazed, I asked, "Are you okay, Mr. Borges?"

"No *mister*, please," he said. "Borges. Just Borges."

"Very good. *Borges*. I'm Jay."

"Giuseppe, I'm not senile! Alastair has told me wonderful stories about you. Pennsylvania? The beautiful woods of William Penn? But are they so beautiful? Everything in America is exaggerated."

"We have some good writers."

"Do you like Edgar Allan Poe?"

"I do."

"A story, Poe said, should make a unified, definite impression. This is true of an essay as well. Really, there is no difference between these genres."

"Your essays are made up?"

"My work is only invention," he said. "I was in Israel last year, for a visit. I'm a great fan of the Jewish mind, which is elevated and cosmopolitan. And Israel as a state inspires me. An intractable situation, very sad, unsolvable with Palestine: competing and equally valid claims." His face seemed to close like a fist, then open again. "What I like especially is that when you walk into a bookstore in Israel, there is a wall of books in the category of *siporet*, which means narrative. Novels and works of nonfiction rub spines, even mirror each other. Anything that passes through memory becomes fiction, you see. *Fictio*—in Latin, it means 'to shape.' I am shaping things. Leaving in some facts, suppressing others." Borges surfed a thought-wave, after the briefest pause. "It is only for the gods to decide what angels will sit on whose shoulders."

"Do you believe in angels?"

"I believe in everything, dear boy. It is the secret of life. *Bileven*, in Middle English, is our belief. It means 'to hold dearly.' This is *gelefen* in Anglo-Saxon. *Glauben* in German."

I could see that I had a long week ahead of me.

"Is there anything you would like to do this week, Borges?"

"To do, indeed! Alejandro tells me you have access to a motorcar."

"I have some wheels with an engine. And a good deal of air."

"Air! In which case, let's be free as the western wind. I would like you to take me on your breeze around Scotland. I want to see the Highlands!"

"But you're blind, Borges," I said.

"Oh, no," he said. "Don't tell me that you are blind as well?"

"I'm not."

"What luck, then! *You* will be my eyes."

He told me about a man in Inverness whom he dearly wished to visit, one Mr. Singleton, who was editing a volume of Anglo-Saxon riddles. He had written to Borges a couple of years before.

"We will discover this Wonderland together," Borges continued. "I know the points on the map: Perth, Aviemore, Inverness. Loch Ness and its monster, Grendel! And the battlefield of Culloden! Just to read a map of the Highlands is to recite poetry." His eyes grew huge, wet empty globes.

I had promised Alastair I'd stay with Borges. But had I promised to be here when Alastair returned? Would he approve of my lighting out for the Highlands with his charge? As gently as I could, I asked, "Did you mention this trip to Alastair?"

"No, it has just occurred. A vision, shall I say? Let's go, Giuseppe."

"Now?"

"There is only now," he exclaimed with unstoppable force. "Act, dear boy! Do not procrastinate! It's the worst of sins. I've thought about this, you see: the progression toward evil. Murder, this is very bad, a *sin*. It leads to thievery. And thievery, dear God, leads to drunkenness and Sabbath-breaking. And Sabbath-breaking leads to incivility and at last procrastination! A slippery slope into the pit!"

I may have smiled. But Borges, of course, couldn't see it.

"I have money for the rooms in hotels, for our meals," he said. "It will cost you nothing. I will pay for the petrol as well."

"No need for that," I told him.

"There is every need. I'm an old man. You're a young man. You must save whatever you have for the future that awaits. I need to spend myself."

"This sounds like a good deal for me," I said, not yet sure if I believed the statement to be true.

To say that I had mixed feelings about this projected trip through the wilds of Scotland underplays my trepidation. I had a responsibility here, one that coupled with very little experience of the needs of elderly people. Could I really do this, whatever it was? Any number of reasons to resist Borges and avoid this improbable journey flickered in my brain. But there was a glimmer on my mental horizon, a light that seemed to beckon beyond my mental hills. I might learn something in proximity to this man who clearly knew a great deal about literature and life, a writer Alastair obviously admired. He struck me as difficult and self-involved, a man with few checks on what he said. He would no doubt test my patience. But on some deep and probably inaccessible level, I thought I might well get a story out of this one day.

"There's this wonderful thing in Britain," Borges said, "the B&B. The second B is for breakfast, and they do opulent breakfasts. Do you like bacon? And oatmeal?"

"Oatmeal is fine."

"Uncooked if possible. You will ask them for me?"

"It may raise an eyebrow."

"I no longer need to save face. This is one of the benefits of extreme age. Nothing matters much, and very little matters at all."

It would be important, he said, for me to name everything we saw, to rephrase each experience, making it permanent. "Description is revelation," he said. He would pay for our expenses, but this naming aloud would be my contribution to the trip. "Nothing exists," he said, "until it has found its way into the language."

"Should we make a plan?" I asked.

"This doesn't concern me. What is the line from Burns? 'The best-laid schemes o' mice an' men gang aft agley.' Such a ring of veracity. We're in the country of Burns, where everything is askew."

"So it's the Highlands then? Inverness?"

"*Ahora vamos,*" Borges said. "We must take the plunge. What we discover, as within any labyrinth, will always be ourselves. Wherever you go, Giuseppe, there is Giuseppe. I go where Borges goes."

12

WE BEGAN OUR journey by heading in the wrong direction, at least if our goal was Inverness. But I sensed that Borges would like to "see" Lower Largo, the home of Alexander Selkirk, the figure behind *Robinson Crusoe*. I had been there once with a friend, and the story had intrigued me. And Crusoe, I knew, meant a lot to Alastair and Jasper, so it might well be something Borges would like.

I wanted from the outset to please him. He was, I supposed, a notable literary figure in Argentina, though I had no idea what that meant. That I'd read nothing of his was an embarrassment, but I assumed there was a long important novel by him that one day I would read. I had my own vague ambitions to achieve something in literature, perhaps a poem of considerable length or even, God willing, a novel, perhaps even a novel of consequence, like *Moby-Dick* or *The Scarlet Letter* or *The Portrait of a Lady*. Only the novel could embrace the whole of experience. It was "the bright book of life," as Lawrence so memorably said.

We headed out along a stretch of rocky coastline, with my window down, as the day was surprisingly warm for early spring. The fishing villages sparkled with an unnatural brightness, coppery and clean. But a feeling of responsibility overwhelmed and silenced me as I drove. I had been elected to tell Borges what we saw, to describe it precisely. And yet how could I manage this? Did I even know the words for what I saw? Rock and water, flowers and birds. That would never do! In the meantime, Borges sat with his knees lifted high, the cane between his legs and rising to his chin.

"What is this motor vehicle?" he said, breaking the silence after perhaps twenty minutes had passed.

"A Morris Minor. Pretty old, I'm afraid. And threadbare." On cue, it coughed and spluttered.

"This is Rocinante, your motorcar."

Silence conveyed my puzzlement.

"I speak of that lazy old horse of Don Quixote. *Rocín*, in Spanish, this is a workhorse, but never a good one. *Nunca!* Lazy because exhausted, not unlike your motorcar, which may be unequal to our task of circumnavigating the Highlands." He tapped his forehead as if trying to recall something. "Cervantes took some trouble to name his horse."

"I haven't read the novel, Borges. I should have."

"Yes, and yet, believe me, you will one day read it with a profound sense of recollection. That happens when you read a classic. It finds you where you have been."

"It will become my story, is that it?"

"If luck holds, I think so." He sang a little song under his breath in Spanish. "Have you seen this before, how a beast comes to resemble his owner? Or does the owner come to resemble his beast?"

"I look nothing like my car," I said.

"Not yet."

The North Sea broke on our left, with blasts of surf in the rocks below. One could see fishing boats nearby, and on the horizon the occasional tanker.

"It's quite dark, the sea, in broad daylight," I said, fumbling to describe what I saw. "There's a surf."

"This is not specific enough," Borges chided. "Talk about the running waves, the white horses on the water. *Dark* is not detailed. What are the colors? Find metaphors, images. I want to see what you see. Description is revelation! Words that create pictures. Like the cinema, perhaps. *Moving* pictures!" He rolled down the window to feel the breeze in his face, his eyes closed and his nostrils widening as he took in the cool and salty air. "I'm in love with *Beowulf*, which is why I favor the North Sea. Beowulf swam in body armor with a sword in his belt. Nine monsters dragged him to the floor of the sea. He killed them, one by one. Swish! Imagine the bloody waters around him. Exhausted, he was carried away to the Land of the Finns."

We fell into silence, as Borges had spent himself with this memory from *Beowulf*, and I doubted I could add to his commentary. It worried me that I might buckle under the pressure of needing to "see" what he hoped to see. If my poems, which I labored over, often missed the mark, how could I expect extemporaneously to summon images and metaphors sharp enough to satisfy this unlikely passenger?

Borges touched my left arm, then squeezed the elbow. "This man I mentioned, Mr. Singleton. He wrote to me in Buenos Aires from Inverness. We share this interest in Anglo-Saxon poetry, but it's the riddles that intrigue us. Games for the mind, the origin of all plots." Borges dug a scrap of paper from the breast pocket of his jacket, then stuffed it back. "He sent his telephone number, and my mother wrote it down."

"You brought that from Argentina?"

"It was not so heavy."

"What do you know of Mr. Singleton?"

"He understands the meaning of surprise. A riddle explodes with meaning, but only at the last moment, when you stand face-to-face with it. You stand *under* the truth. And in this *understanding* we know everything. So I wish to surprise him, to say, *Borges stands before you. Did you imagine this would happen? Look at me, Mr. Singleton!*

This was, I realized, what I wished for with Mackay Brown: to stand face-to-face with the man behind the poems and stories. I wanted him to see me, his ideal reader. The exchange that takes place on the page would take place in actual time and space. This must happen, I told myself. I would take Borges to Orkney!

We paused in Crail, a tiny village, to walk around the stone-walled harbor, with its picturesque clutch of fishing vessels. The constant cry of gulls formed a backdrop to the scene, and I explained to Borges that in the sky above the bay one could see gannets as they swooped to snatch a fish, then soared back into the heavens with a meal in their beaks.

"What sort of fish?"

"Herring, I think. Mackerel? Not sure."

"This is too exciting," said Borges. "As a boy, I would sit and watch the birds over the Río de la Plata. Such colorful birds. They would arrow from the sky, killing the vipers. Zing! We never liked these vipers."

"Snakes always make me queasy."

"And we share this, Giuseppe! Even when we don't in any conscious way, we remember the snake in the garden and poor dear innocent Eve. What a thing, the serpent! And such a phallic creature, no?"

"I try not to think about the phallus, except when I can think of nothing else, which is most of the time."

"This is the fate of young men, a limited focus. One of the few advantages of my blindness has been that I no longer fasten my eyes on objects of arousal. I look inward now, though the mind has mountains, dangerous cliffs."

"'Oh the mind, mind has mountains, cliffs of fall,'" I said, quoting the famous poem by Gerard Manley Hopkins. I didn't want him to assume I knew nothing.

"Dear Hopkins," he said. "He read the Anglo-Saxon poets, and learned from them. I'm so happy you know this poet, believe me."

We took off again, passing through Anstruther, pausing briefly to absorb the atmosphere, then moving on to Lower Largo, home of Alexander Selkirk. I sprang this on Borges as we drove slowly down Main Street between three-story sandstone town houses with their orange roof tiles reflecting the late-afternoon sunlight.

"I know of this Selkirk," Borges said, foraging in his brain for details. "He was a childhood hero. Crusoe in real life! I wished, like him, to isolate myself on a remote island, but one must be careful, as they say, of what one wishes for. Blindness is my very own island."

"You seem to have set up quite an operation there," I said.

"This is the lesson of Defoe's novel—using the materials that lie at hand. I think perhaps Selkirk was more interesting than Crusoe. A terrible hothead, if I recall the facts properly. He argued day and night with his unhappy father. I don't understand this resistance to one's father. Mine was a gentle man. I respected him."

"My father usually gives in," I told him, "which makes him a second-rate businessman but a good father. My mother insists on getting her way."

"My mother, too! She is old and still quite alive, and continues to run—even ruin—my life. I will escape her at some point. My wife, who is no longer part of my existence, she has disliked her. Mother made everything impossible. She made life difficult for my sister, too. I have one sister, you see."

"So do I! Dorrie. She has a hard time with my mother. Oil and water."

"Oh, dear. This is the old tale, mothers and daughters. Mothers and sons, well, this is another familiar tale, and not often happy. My former wife and my mother, they are like cats and dogs."

"You're divorced?"

"Soon. It was never a real marriage, I confess. I never knew her. Our engagement lasted for perhaps decades, but during this time I was in love with another woman."

"Tell me," I said, wondering if this would be the important thing he might teach me—something about how to love women. God knew I could use a tutorial. Women were alien to me, another race. I projected onto them, filling in with fantasies where, if I were less intimidated, I might have discovered more compelling realities, something less weighed down by silly presuppositions.

"You wish for me to tell my story? I don't want to make you unhappy, Giuseppe. Let's think of Selkirk instead, the model of resourcefulness, this man who gives hope. He was marooned. Or self-exiled, if memory serves. He fought with the captain of his ship and was set ashore. Survival skills obsess me, and Selkirk was a genius of survival. He hunted wild goats and ate their meat, made a garment from their hides. He lived four years on a forlorn island off the coast of Chile. On the other hand, he found the most marvelous wild turnips in the dirt, and pink cabbages, even pepper berries. Rats tried to eat him, so he forged an alliance with the feral cats. He slept with them, and they loved him, and together they frightened off the rats. There's perhaps a lesson in this tale for a young man like yourself?"

"Make friends with feral cats?"

"Like Selkirk, yes. As I think of him, I glow with admiration."

"Selkirk was a pirate," I said.

"Don't hold this against him! I'm a pirate, too. Writers are always pirates, marauding, taking whatever pleases them from others, shaping these stolen goods to our purposes. Writers feed off the corpses of those who passed before them, their precursors. On the other hand, they invent their precursors. They create them in their own image, as God did with man."

It had until now seemed axiomatic to me that authors must start from nowhere, with nothing, and invent themselves, although I knew that influences mattered, that one dipped into the past and found things to remake. Had I invented my father and mother? So much of what I wrote, or thought about, was a by-product of my point of origin. Perhaps I was creating my parents? Since my arrival in St. Andrews, I'd of course been tracing the poems and novels that led to the work of Mackay Brown. But did he invent his precursors, as Borges suggested? Had he rewritten the Old Norse sagas in his mind in some way? I guessed he knew Hopkins very well, as they shared a strong Catholic vision, and their language had that intense concreteness, propelled by alliterative music and what Hopkins had called "sprung rhythm," where you lunge from foot to poetic foot.

Borges puzzled and intrigued me, and I sensed that if I listened to him keenly, I might begin to revise some long-held assumptions.

"We must have dinner, I'm so hungry," said Borges, changing the subject abruptly. (I would have to get used to these ruptures.) "I would like to visit a pub. Alastair refuses to take me to a pub. It's so noisy, he says. I want to try Scottish beer."

"The Crusoe Hotel," I said, "is beside us. Its walls have faux Tudor half-timbers, and they're the color of old cheddar. It will have a bar."

"Wonderful! We must stay there."

We had no reservations, but it was easy to book two rooms for the night, as Scottish tourism at this time of year was hardly robust. After depositing our bags, we headed downstairs into the dark bar-cum-dining room, which was below ground level. There were just two or three other patrons, silent elderly men in cloth overcoats with pints in front of them. The room smelled of tobacco and spilled beer, and there was a coal fire in the grate, next to which some cats on a knitted rug licked themselves clean. On the walls hung fox-hunting prints that seemed strangely out of place on the East Neuk of Fife.

I sat Borges down at an oak table. "It's so comfortable here," he said. "I smell the burning coals. A smell I love so much. My grandfather's house in the country, it was full of blazing wood. He was a hero in Argentina. The old men, they would often bow as he passed, whispering. This is respect!"

"What will you have, Borges?"

"Typical Scottish beer from the pump."

"The tap," I corrected.

He wrung his hands in a peculiar fashion, as if they belonged to someone else. "I don't usually drink strong beverage. Once, when I was a student, they said, *Borges is a drunkard.* Since then I'm careful not to shame myself. But I am feeling quite free of that young man, that Borges."

What a relief it would be, I thought, to feel free of my own young self.

"This Borges," he continued, "this much older man, *he* would like to drink on this journey." He slapped his palm on the tabletop. "But I am not a drunkard!"

I agreed that he was not, and soon fetched two pints of Export, the flat, warm beer with a tawny color that students drank in vast quantities in St. Andrews. Borges bent over his glass, both hands around it and lightly trembling. He sniffed the foamy head of the brew, stirred it with one finger, then licked that finger clean to taste it.

"Very good," he said. "Mild, and not too cold. This is the mistake we have made in Argentina. The beer is too cold, and it prevents us from tasting. This is true of food as well. I don't like food when it is too hot. Moderation!"

"I like moderation."

"Then you have an instinct for wisdom. Confucius said the doctrine of the mean was the highest virtue, and rare among men. The Buddhists call it the middle way. Aristotle saw moderation as the essence of virtue. I say moderation in all things, even moderation. So enough of that."

He took a long slow drink and smiled, wiping the foam from his lips on the sleeve of his jacket. The blank eyes bulged in his head. He yawned, grinning at nothing, then belched, muttering to himself in Spanish. This was going to be a very long journey.

"Alastair often speaks of your work," I said, hoping to spark something, anything.

"Alastair is always exaggerating," he said. "Remember, dear boy, that I write only the smallest of stories. Some of them only a page in length, or less."

"You haven't written novels?"

"Not a single novel," he said, with a smile that vanished as quickly as it came. "But you must know, I hoped for many decades to write an epic of the Pampas. There would be gauchos and prostitutes, and many criminals. Revolutions would come and go. It would be a saga of family life over many generations, with failed love affairs, with incest, and with spectacular achievements, too. There would be fratricide and matricide. Even patricide, the worst of sins. The volume would require perhaps a thousand pages to encompass everything I wished to say."

"So what happened?"

"It never came, this novel. So frustrating. And long decades passed. But then one day—one day!—I woke early and went to my desk. In perhaps an hour or less I wrote a one-page review of this great novel, and that satisfied the impulse."

13

AT BREAKFAST WE feasted on kippers with poached eggs and rashers of bacon: not what I would normally have consumed, but Borges had an idea about what constituted an ideal Scottish breakfast, and I felt—at this point in the journey—like making an alliance of sorts. He gobbled the food with abandon, splattering his tie, and the others in the breakfast room—commercial travelers and retirees—looked on with horror. When I went to the gents', a middle-aged man who stood next to me at the urinal said, "How long has your poor father been blind?"

It was not worth explaining.

Back at the table, I brought up our itinerary with Borges, who explained that after his time with Alastair he planned to visit Edinburgh, so we could leave that out. He mentioned in passing that he'd be traveling to Oxford later in the spring to receive an honorary degree. An Oxford doctorate seemed unimaginably grand to me, the sort of thing reserved for the likes of Mark Twain or Rudyard Kipling. And the fact that I'd probably underestimated Borges dawned on me now. Had I not been listening to Alastair? Even Bella knew about him!

Skimming a map of the Highlands in a guidebook that I'd bought in the hotel lobby, I sketched in my head a plan for our excursion. After stopping for lunch in Dunfermline, we would continue along the M90 to Perth. Then we'd aim straight for Inverness, the heart of the Highlands, moving through the Cairngorm Mountains. Borges could meet his Mr. Singleton, after which we'd take a detour to Loch Ness. The nearby historic battlefield at Culloden would appeal to Borges, too. If things went as I imagined, I could whisk us away to Orkney by ferry for a day to meet Mackay Brown, who might even like the idea that I had in tow an acquaintance like Borges, this cultivated Argentinian. Both admired Anglo-Saxon and Old Norse poetry, after all.

But I didn't bring this up yet. I needed to propose this meeting in the right terms. Borges didn't really know anything about my thesis or my need to talk to a writer on Orkney. His focus on his own fantasy journey through the Highlands was intense, and I could see in our conversations that he could easily sweep aside anything that seemed to him irrelevant. He knew what he wanted to see. Or to have me describe.

Borges had brought with him only the brown suit he wore, a single white (and fraying) shirt, and the same extravagant tie with orange waterfalls and flying fish that he'd been wearing on the day we met. None of these items was fresh. And I was not myself well prepared for this jaunt, having packed only two shirts, a pair of jeans, and a sweater that had been a gift from my mother. I wore a light brown corduroy jacket and a tie, which I wore in deference to British conventions. I wished I had a rainproof mac but didn't—probably in defiance of my mother. ("My God, it's wet there," she noted in a recent letter, "and cold. I don't know why you like it so much. Nobody likes it there. And if you go outside, remember to take a raincoat. Your lungs aren't so good. You could get *very* sick like you did at Boy Scout camp, and it wasn't even wet that summer!")

We headed for Dunfermline with Borges in an antic mood. It probably helped that we'd each had our own bedroom in Lower Largo and felt rested. I mentioned this, and Borges responded, "What luxury, yes, but I don't wish to spend so much money on beds. We should spend the money on beer. And good food. Don't you think?"

No, I didn't. Could he tell that from the grunt of my response?

"Where does your money come from?" he asked.

"I have a fellowship," I said. "And my father sends me extra." I thought about my father, who worked very hard in Scranton, often coming home late at night from the office. He sold life insurance policies to families and, despite his fragile grasp of the technicalities, seemed remarkably good at the sales aspect of the job. ("Your father could sell a cow a pint of milk," my mother always said.) In fact I felt grateful to him, and somewhat guilty, thinking that to a degree I lived off his hard work, as the fellowship from Lafayette had not been lavish. And it was hardly clear to me, or anyone, that this time in Scotland would lead to anything like a career. ("Have you ever thought of podiatry?" my mother had recently asked. "It's a good field. Think of the sore feet, the corns, the blisters and bunions. Maybe better than law school?")

"Ah, Giuseppe. I understand your silence, your embarrassment. My family supported me, too, with enough money but not so extravagant. I wasn't a rich boy. And yet I did go to a pleasant school in Switzerland. My grandmother was English, as I have told you, and she said I must go to Oxford one day. I should become a don there, perhaps. Don Borges. It sounds wonderful in Spanish. But I attended no university. Not like yourself."

"It doesn't seem to have held you back. You're very well informed."

"Ah, *informed* . . ." Borges said dismissively. "Nobody can teach you anything. This is the first truth. We teach ourselves. All my life I have lived in books, in libraries. I remember every library in my life as I remember my lovers, their smells, the texture of their skin, the taste, even the brightness in the air around them. Or the darkness. Yes, every library is for me like a woman, erotic, a creature of the dark, full of smells and textures, tastes."

Libraries were erotic? If so, I was Casanova himself.

We entered Dunfermline on High Street, passing a sign that proclaimed this town as the birthplace of Andrew Carnegie. When I said this to Borges, he beamed.

"The father of libraries!" he said. "He turned a great

fortune in steel into books and more books. Like me, he had no formal education. Not like you, Giuseppe!"

"My education has been a farce." That statement actually took me by surprise, and I wondered if indeed there was any truth to it.

I had caught Borges's attention with this claim. "Then you must sit with determination in the library of your choice," he said. "But, you see, there is only one library. The universal library."

Like so many of his Delphic remarks, this puzzled me. I loved libraries, and had found them a place of retreat in Scranton. After school and late into the evening I would stay in the old public library on Vine Street, often wandering in the ill-lit stacks, amazed by the books— especially long-abandoned novels, with their titles rubbed off or faded, the authors forgotten. Every library I'd known had been, to a degree, like every other library, with this crowd of voices, the dusty echoes of other eras, the sweet smell of moldy pages and broken spines, abandoned hopes, whiffs of glory and transcendence. The universal library indeed.

As we passed the Carnegie Library, Borges insisted we stop "for a wee snoop." It was a gloomy sandstone building, and I described the architecture as best I could, working to find the exact and imagistic details, grasping for metaphors. "It would seem to sulk," I said, "with the windows like heavily lidded eyes. The roofline is a brow that sags. There is disapproval here."

"We seem small by comparison, inadequate," said Borges, nodding as I led him into the entrance hall, where a snowy-haired man in a tweed suit with the texture of chain mail lurched toward us. He seemed startled to have visitors, and his look was faintly dismissive.

"I'm Mr. Dunne," he said. "I suppose you would like a tour? Of course you would."

He could see that Borges was blind, and this handicap earned us a degree of forbearance. "This was the first of more than two thousand and five hundred libraries that Mr. Carnegie funded," he explained.

"That is too many," said Borges. "One would have been enough."

Mr. Dunne frowned, but I resisted describing his expression to Borges.

"God was the first and only librarian," Borges added.

"The first librarian here was Mr. Peebles," insisted Mr. Dunne, quoting from an invisible script in his head. "They had over two hundred applicants for the job, but he was a remarkable man, forty years old at the time."

"I began to work in a library at the age of thirty-eight," said Borges. "So Mr. Peebles and I have this in common. My father's health had declined rapidly, and I had no choice but to find a profession. I was a librarian by nature. I'm still a librarian in my heart. But these first years were not so happy. Nine years of sadness and restlessness. A minor branch of the municipal library. I worked as first assistant to the man in charge of cataloguing. But we had few books and too much time. This is the problem of the universe, Mr. Dunne. There is so much time and so little to do."

Our tour guide said, "Idle hands are the Devil's playthings."

"Oh, my dear Dunne. Do you believe in such a

proposition? Life is propositions about life, of course. But your proposition is faulty. Idle hands are God's hands, I'm quite sure of this. God is the head librarian, and he invites us to waste our time in his stacks."

"Are you a Christian, sir?" Dunne asked.

"I love Jesus. Do you?"

"He is my Lord and Savior."

"Ah, then," said Borges, "you have much in common with your cousin, the great poet and cleric. 'Batter my heart, three-person'd God.'"

"We're not related," said the tour guide. "My name is spelled D-u-n-n-e."

"A pity," said Borges. "But let me advise you, the work of our Lord is to help us find the lost books, the ones that hold the key."

Mr. Dunne sighed, leading us dutifully into the reading room, where he offered us coffee. I could see that he was intrigued by Borges in spite of himself. "You are from where exactly?" he asked.

"I'm an Argentinian, and former director of the National Library."

With this Mr. Dunne snapped to full attention, as if a general had walked unexpectedly into the barracks. Even the curtains in the windows stiffened in an invisible breeze.

He handed us coffee, and Borges stirred the hot liquid with his finger and licked it.

"This is wonderful," he said. "Thank you! I have been freezing since I arrived in this country. My grandmother used to say that nobody in Scotland is warm." He sipped, looking around the room. "I smell the books," he said, his nostrils expanding.

"There are books on shelves all around us," I said.

"Can you see any titles?"

"There's a row of Sir Walter Scott, the Waverly novels."

"Not as good as Stevenson. But the world took notice! Even the great Russians, they admired Scott."

"And I see the *Encyclopedia Britannica.*"

"Which edition?"

I went over to examine one volume of the twenty-nine. "1911."

"The finest encyclopedia in creation! The most accomplished scholars on each subject were brought together in those pages. One could live forever in that edition, and never leave. I would happily die there. In the municipal library, I worked for only one hour each day. Then I would retreat to the basement, where they kept the encyclopedias."

He began to move toward the shelves, and I assisted him. "Here is the row of Scott," I said, drawing one of his hands toward the books.

He plucked a volume and began greedily to lick the spine, his tongue like that of a cat. There was, I thought, lust in his eyes.

"What are you doing, sir?" asked Mr. Dunne. Centuries of disapproval crossed his face.

"Some books should be tasted," Borges said. "I like to sample them." His tongue traced the length of the leather spine.

"This is impossible," Mr. Dunne said.

"Show me into the stacks," Borges said. "Take me, dear Dunne!"

I felt certain our guide would kick us out of the building, but instead he obeyed, opening the door to a room with a dizzying array of shelves. There were numerous side rooms as well, each of them opening into further rooms. Borges touched one of the shelves, as if finding his way by his fingertips, then leaned his forehead against the spines of several books, as one might lean one's head against a cross on Good Friday.

"You must not lick them, please," said Mr. Dunne. "It isn't allowed."

Borges mumbled something in Spanish that sounded like Latin, with a liturgical rhythm and intonation. A window without a curtain brightened the corridor before us, with yellow sunlight burrowing through the leaded panes. The glow lit up Borges, his large head seeming overblown. His eyes blinked rapidly.

"You must realize, Mr. Dunne, the universe is a library. When I was a young man, I searched the stacks of the branch near my house in Palermo, in Buenos Aires. My fondest hope was to find the single volume that would tell me everything I must know in order to survive. When I die, I hope very much to pitch myself headfirst over the railing and fall through the stacks. The library itself goes on forever, with no top, no bottom. There are only sides, and rows of books. But they speak to us in tongues. It's said that every single possibility of expression will be found in this universe of books."

"This is too much," said Mr. Dunne. "We can't have this confusion. Jesus wishes us to speak only the truth."

"Truth will be found in these stacks," Borges asserted. "Not one truth, but many! But there is only one Librarian, only one Director!"

"Not you, I should hope."

"I have moments of divinity. Don't we all?"

"I'm a Christian," said Mr. Dunne, for no reason I could discern.

Borges said, "My friend here is a Roman Catholic."

It surprised me that Borges would assume this. Was it once again my Italian name?

"You are Catholic?" Dunne asked, though it sounded as if he wondered if I were a necrophile.

"I believe in God," I said.

"And God believes in you," said Borges.

I thought for a moment that Mr. Dunne was about to cry. Borges was too much for him. I put a hand on his forearm to reassure him, and he quickly pulled away from me. I think I terrified him as much as Borges now.

"It's a very fine library," I said, looking for some bland capstone expression that would signal our impending exit, which could not come soon enough. "So many books," I added.

With a defeated expression, Mr. Dunne said, "There are many rooms and many more books."

"This is because the universe is infinite," said Borges. "The library is a sphere whose center is everywhere and whose circumference is inaccessible." He liked what he said so much that he paused to let his comment echo in the stacks. Then he said, "I once wrote somewhere that mirrors and copulation are abominable, as both multiply the number of men in the world!"

I felt sorry for poor Mr. Dunne, who could not fully absorb such a visitor. He kept wiping his glasses with a handkerchief, as if he might clear his vision at last.

"I'm grateful to Mr. Carnegie," Borges continued. "He was a foolish little man, so I've heard, but rich. He could multiply dollars. It's a gift, perhaps, to multiply things. I have tried, without success, to multiply Borges."

"Although one library is enough," I said, drawing a sweet smile from Borges.

Mr. Dunne stood openmouthed beside us. I think we had exceeded his capacity.

"We really must be going," I whispered to Borges.

"So soon?"

"Miles to go before we sleep," I said.

In a frantic gesture, Mr. Dunne pressed into my hands a brochure that he urged me to inspect later, at my leisure. It would, he said, "suggest the full extent of Mr. Carnegie's accomplishment."

Borges whistled as I led him to the car, then paused to pee against my front wheel, humming loudly as I looked around. This surely wasn't the right place for him to relieve himself. His urine splashed back onto his leg.

As I opened the passenger door to help Borges in, I turned back for a final glance at Dunne, who gazed into the sky as if seeking divine help. Had he encountered a demon of some kind, or perhaps an embodiment of the divine? Was he losing his mind? He shifted from foot to foot, half smiling, and finally waved to us. By now, of course, I knew only too well how it felt to be upended by Borges.

Goodbye, Mr. Dunne, I said to myself. *And flights of angels wing thee to thy rest.*

14

THAT PISSING AGAINST my wheel was par for the course with Borges. Like most men of a certain age, he peed often, and kept insisting that I stop so he could relieve himself along the roadside, often against my left front wheel, which he seemed to favor. Not half an hour further into the northward journey, he cried, "It's of an urgency! Your chariot must pause."

"Rocinante is a horse, not a chariot."

"*Whoa*, I say! It's known that gauchos will relieve themselves without getting down from their horses. Quite ingenious, this dexterity." He recited a fragment of a poem in Spanish, which I asked him to translate. "'My horse and my woman, they disappear,'" he said. "'May my horse return soon. / I don't need a woman.'" He turned to me. "I think you need a woman. Am I correct?"

"I do," I said, wondering if Alastair had told him of my romantic woes, or if perhaps he could smell my loneliness, as if it were a shelf of books. "But I have no luck."

"Nor I! Do you know this phrase *unrequited love*?"

"Too well."

"Oh, dear. We have much in common, as I'm beginning to see."

Did I really want to have much in common with this old, blind man who couldn't stop talking, who ignored everyone around him, and who seemed obsessed by some woman from a long time ago? Would this be me in fifty years?

"I was in love, deeply in love, perhaps have always and only been in love, with Norah Lange."

By now he had mentioned Norah too many times, and I wondered if he would ever get around this obstacle in his path. When I spoke of Bella to Alastair and Jeff, did I seem as stymied, as stuck in my own emotional mud? Was I looking at myself here?

Borges said, "I prefer not to speak about Norah Lange. Let's drop the subject. Tell me about the young girl who has broken your heart. I believe it was recent?"

"Her name is Bella Law."

"*Bella Law*—worthy of Dickens! Don't tell me she has red hair, too?"

"Brownish red. A tinge of blond in the sunlight."

As I spoke, Bella was almost present in the car, with her pale gray-green eyes and softly throaty voice. I had promised to call her to arrange for a dinner this week at the Pearl of Hong Kong, but what if I didn't make it back to town in time? I had dared to believe that I was making headway and that Angus had been fading as the object of her affections. Should I have stayed in St. Andrews to press my case with her instead of driving off to the Highlands with a writer whose work I had never even read? I knew that Alastair admired him without reservation, but Borges had struck me from the outset as self-obsessed, a little mad, and I didn't fully trust Alastair's appraisal. I kept thinking about George Mackay Brown and his exquisitely painful stories of lonely figures on Orkney, about his concrete, lyrical poems of place. I loved the restraint in those poems, and the keen edge of every phrase, the effect of a chiseled piece of sculpture in language.

"Dear God, Giuseppe, I must tell you, Norah lived in one of the fine neighborhoods of Buenos Aires. Tronado, that was the street. I remember its width, the shade of its plane trees. But Norah's mother became a widow too early. I loved her as much as Norah."

"And you proposed to Norah?"

"Many times, yes. She was a writer, too, which is unfortunate. For a writer to love a writer, it's a bad idea."

"Bella hopes to become a writer," I said.

Borges winced. "I can't talk about this. You don't want to hear an old man weep, am I right?"

"I wouldn't like it."

"One should avoid strong emotion, especially when it interferes with the work at hand. We have European blood in our veins, you and I. Mine is northern blood. We're cold people, you see. Warriors."

"I'm doing everything I can to avoid being a warrior," I said, eager to shift the subject from doomed love affairs, although warriors was hardly a better topic.

"You're not a warrior in Vietnam," Borges said. "I've been wondering about this."

"My draft board in Pennsylvania would like me to go," I said. "They keep sending me draft notices."

"But you've avoided their summons?"

"I don't open their . . . invitations, never. I've got several in a drawer in my flat."

"This is a protest!"

"Or cowardice. Or lassitude. Or indifference."

"I don't know. I don't see any of these things in Giuseppe." He mumbled something to himself, perhaps trying to frame what he meant, then said, "Do not hate all wars. Sometimes these conflicts are necessary, in terrible circumstances. I must tell you about Juan Perón, the dictator. Or perhaps not. It troubles me to think of him."

I kept silent, waiting for Borges to expound—or not—on Perón, and wondered again what on earth I was doing by stuffing those letters into a drawer. Shouldn't I just open them? If the draft board insisted on my reporting for service, I could make a strong statement, declaring myself a conscientious objector. If that didn't work, and it probably wouldn't (given my draft board), I could simply reject my citizenship altogether. I could become a Canadian, as they apparently welcomed draft resisters. This would, however, put me outside my American world forever. I would become a true alien, not just an inner emigré. And this frightened me, as I loved my family, even Scranton, with its familiar landscape and rhythms, the feeling of home that is impossible to find just anywhere. As much as I complained about my mother, I loved her. She cared deeply about my welfare, as did my father. The connections between us were anything but fragile.

It struck me that Borges, even with his vastly cosmopolitan mind, seemed attached to Buenos Aires, to its smells and tastes, to its familiar rhythms of thought. He could never just let go of this. It was home.

Our plan now was to push as far into Perthshire as we could before nightfall, following the M90 through the town of Kinross. I described what I saw along the way to Borges as best I could, fetching images and metaphors, noting the bright lakes, the fertile land with stone barns and hillsides smudged with white-and-gray sheep. Spring had begun to assert itself, with flowers breaking out in patches.

"What flowers? Name them. I need the particulars."

"Daffodils," I said.

"I adore daffodils."

I mentioned an impressive purple limestone church in Perth as we entered the town. The River Tay bristled in the background, running below the glebe, a field adjacent to the church where sheep safely grazed. We paused briefly to walk around the graveyard beside the church, beneath huge oak trees with crooked limbs, and I turned my back as Borges stopped to pee against one of them as he tapped its trunk with his cane. A hiss followed a grunt, so I guessed his venture had been successful.

He'd been more silent than usual, as if suddenly lost in problematic musings. I could appreciate this and left him to his ruminations, which summoned my own. I was somehow relieved to settle into my own thoughts about—who else?—Bella. It terrified me that she might take my silence over these past few days as an indication that I had lost interest, when the opposite was true. I must find a phone booth in the evening and explain how I came to be traveling in the Highlands with Borges.

It was astonishing how far away St. Andrews seemed, the dream of a dream. I had been riveted by Alastair and Jasper, but in such a short time they had vanished from my life, although Alastair lingered in Borges. I could see that so many of his ideas could be traced to this source, especially that sense of being present, taking in the world in a gulp. But Alastair was more cynical than Borges, more judgmental. I often felt criticized by him, especially when I sat down to write, feeling the heat of his gaze over my shoulder. He would mock my interest in the soul and its fate, my interest in theology. When I told him I was eagerly reading *The Courage to Be,* by Paul Tillich, he asked "To be what?" He urged me to garden and to cook. "Chop wood, carry water," he said, quoting an old Buddhist precept.

In Perth's quiet town center, we stopped for lunch at a pub called the Cock & Bull, where a lump-faced publican suggested we should visit Scone Palace. "Your old man, he will like this, aye!" he whispered to me. "History is what we sell, aye."

"Oh, yes, we must go there," said Borges. "Macbeth and Robert the Bruce stood in that holy spot!"

Before stepping back into the car, he looked up at the sky, where dark clouds had begun to gather, and sniffed the air.

"What is it?" I asked.

"There is rain coming."

No sooner did he say this than a drizzle began, though it was short-lived, with frequent breaks in the clouds. We drove on through it, and a short while later we pulled into an empty car park at Scone, a palace made of red sandstone blocks and built in the neo-Gothic style, with battlements, towers, and crenulations. I had skimmed my guidebook, relaying to Borges the elementary facts. Ancient Scottish kings had for centuries been crowned at Scone, going back to the ninth century. Some thirty-eight monarchs had knelt before the Stone of Destiny. I allowed myself to ramble a bit, offering a potted history.

Borges smiled faintly. "You say *scone* as if it rhymed with *bone*. But it rhymes with *spoon*. It's a Pictish word. Do you know the Picts?"

"I kissed one of them, years ago."

Quite sensibly, he ignored my remark. "Scotland was conquered by the Picts, who came from Scandinavia. They landed in Ireland first. That's one theory. They were Christians, like yourself, Giuseppe. They weren't pagans, so don't say that."

"I'll never call a Pict a pagan, I swear."

"They made beautiful structures, and were artists who could draw images on stone: a wolf, a salmon, a catlike creature resembling a tiger. Brilliant! I've read about them and have wished to stand here. 'So thanks to all at once and to each one, / Whom we invite to see us crowned at Scone.'"

"*Scone* doesn't rhyme with *spoon* there."

"Do you know how Shakespeare pronounced *one*?"

"I doubt it rhymed with *spoon*."

"My dear, you are in battle mode, in full armor, your sword drawn!" He reached to touch my face with his hands, carefully feeling his way among my features. It felt odd but relieving as well, and I began to believe the Fates had something in mind for me, that it wasn't happenstance that Borges and I were tracing our peculiar pathway through the Highlands of Scotland. "A stern visage, yes. I knew it!"

"I'm not stern."

"But I object! There is strength in your features."

I wished I could feel as sure of my strength as Borges did. He kept holding up mirrors, and the reflections disturbed me at times. I'd never wanted to look at myself too closely, to see the abrasions on my skin, my broad flat nose, the slightly protruding upper lip. Already my hair grew thin, and I had begun to stoop, as if the world weighed too much. Real strength was in fact a new element to witness, to see in this reflection. Was there after all a reason for this trip? Had Alastair, in some benevolent if unconscious way, engineered this journey with Borges, guessing that he could teach me something indirectly?

The rain paused, though mist hung in the air like a cloak over the grounds of Scone Palace. It was late afternoon, and a notice proclaimed the palace closed to visitors until May. When I told Borges about our bad timing, he showed no sign of distress.

"Scone Palace is not an important building," he said. "I'm blind, in any case. And I like genuine Gothic, not these pale imitations, with moats and turrets, and probably an armory inside, even a dungeon! Is there a keep in this castle? I believe so. They reproduce these elements— pure fantasy. Walter Scott would have approved."

"Not you."

"I prefer whatever is authentic, as long as it's invented."

I noticed a sign pointing around the corner to the garden at the back of the house and suggested that we might stroll around a bit. Perhaps the garden, if not the palace, would be accessible.

Borges put one arm through mine—I was beginning to enjoy, even to count on, the intimacy of guiding him—and we turned into a narrow path beside a massive beech. The gravel crackled under our feet.

"I like to walk on this popcorn," said Borges. "It's a kind of foot music. A prelude to the full choir of stones."

"And the noisy silence of heaven," I added.

A low cloud gathered around us, tangible, almost pulsating. And then, strangely, as if materializing from the wet mist, three elderly women appeared before us. Were they employees at the palace? They seemed too old for that, and too peculiar in their gray raincoats and knitted hats. One of them had wrapped her face in a long black scarf so that you could see only her eyes. Another had so much facial hair that I wondered if she were actually a man. The third was a bit younger, and tiny, with skin like crepe.

"It's the garden you're after?" the youngest one asked.

"Yes, if it's open. My friend has come all the way from Argentina."

"I speak for the National Library of Argentina," Borges said.

"This is your day," said the woman in the scarf. "And what you say is what we play."

"Is this a play then?"

"Heaven has the script," she said.

This was all too much. I wanted to take Borges back

to the car but knew he'd want to press on. "Are we allowed in?" I asked.

"Go where you go, son, and go with confidence," said the small one.

Borges mused to himself but aloud, "Such fantastic strange voices! Angels or demons? No matter!"

The one in the scarf told us they were sisters from Kinross.

"The Weird Sisters!" cried Borges. "Darlings, I've been reading about you my whole life."

"The old tree pants," intoned the one with a fuzz on her cheeks. "And the young supplants."

"This isn't good news for me," Borges said, squeezing my arm in a way that showed his vulnerability.

His comment produced a clap of harsh laughter from the bearded one. "You're already dead," she pronounced.

"I've never pretended otherwise," Borges told her, but he grabbed my arm tightly.

"Do they bother you?" I asked.

"They have nothing to teach me," he said. "Send them back into the mist."

I didn't have to do anything. They had already stepped into the swirl and vanished, whoever they were.

Borges pushed forward, as if sure of the path. Soon an iron gate swung on rusty hinges and I saw a broad expanse of snowdrops beneath the fog. A grassy pathway bordered by violets led into a row of hedges. This was, I thought, the entrance.

"There's a maze," I said.

"You will know that a bat flies by sonar. I do this as well." He rushed forward into the maze with more energy, more agility, than I had thought possible. How did he know where to go? The blackthorn hedges closed around him.

"Borges!" I called, but when I stepped into the maze I could not tell which of the divergent paths he had taken. I called out for him. His name rose in the balloon of my voice and hovered in the air. *Borges! Borges!*

Time shifted gears within this maze as the forward progress of our day ended. I was under its spell, guided by hedges and given binary choices, but these yielded only further corridors within tunnels of waxy leaves. Rabbits scurried to left and right, and the air smelled sharply of damp, piss, and piney resin.

"Borges?" I waited for him, looking around. Where was he?

Was it minutes or hours later that I turned into a corridor where Borges, winded, sat on the path, his legs folded awkwardly under him? Time had certainly become a pliant thing in this mist, in the maze.

"Are you okay, Borges?" I asked, bending over to help him stand.

"I'm grateful for this hand," he said, reestablishing his footing. "So we come to the end of the maze, Giuseppe, but this is only the beginning. It's like any good story, which has no end. A way of defeating death."

"How?" I felt sucked into his drama of ideas. He was once again playing the role of Socrates, and I was called upon to perform as one of his students, as in the *Meno*, where the Greek philosopher proves once and for all that even a slave with no education can, with a little persistence, understand geometrical concepts. Was this my role with Borges, acting as the naive young man who must learn things already present in his heart and head?

"What's the shortest distance between two points?"

"A straight line," I answered.

"A narrative that proceeds from the beginning to the middle to the end."

"That's right."

"But what if we proceed in a zigzag fashion, as in this maze, or within any labyrinthine structure? We wrinkle time, you see. Divagations! If we linger in these loopholes of history, these timeless tortuous stretches, perhaps we shall never come to the end, or if we do, we will find an opening there and start again."

"So we can hide in time?"

"Yes, but time is another fiction. It's very useful, especially for writers like us. We need the lapse of moments, even the pause between feet in a poem, or the lingering before a climax in our stories. Syntax itself is a form of time."

He was on a roll now, speaking quickly, almost whispering to himself. "Death, my dear, is a false ending. A climax that is no climax. Have you never read *A Thousand and One Nights*?"

"No."

"The centuries pass, and still we listen to the voice of Scheherazade."

"She's the narrator, right?"

"See, you know this already, even without reading it. One does not need to read this book of all books. It's part of our memory."

"She had to keep telling stories to stay alive," I said.

He leaned close to me, a hand on my shoulder. He touched my cheek in a kindly, even fatherly way. "A strategy for survival, son," he said. "We enter the maze, you see, as in any tale, and with luck we arrive at the point from which we began, which is always ourselves."

15

WE LEFT THE maze at Scone Palace, with its subtle teach-
ings and peculiar ghosts, and pushed on to Killiecrankie,
well north of Perth, into the Cairngorms. I felt better
now, getting into the rhythms of this peculiar journey,
less resistant to Borges than before. I hoped to push into
the mountains the next morning, when the peaks would
acquire a kind of luminosity that would impress even a
blind man. I would somehow have to put this into words
for him or, in a cowardly fashion, just ignore everything
I saw, as if blind myself.

Now, with the sun dropping in the skies, we crossed
the River Garry, passing over an ancient bridge not far
from the hamlet, which showed no signs of life as we
approached. I pulled in front of a house with its shades
drawn but a sign on the door: MORAG B&B. VACANCY.
I suggested to Borges that we should find rooms here
before dark set in.

After I rang the bell several times, an elderly woman
opened the door. She pushed it out only a few inches,
perhaps afraid that we might overwhelm her. Her long
nose beaked through the crack.

"Rooms for the night?" I asked.

"Aye," she said, letting us into a poorly lit hallway, where she turned on a lamp with a Tiffany-style glass shade. There was a heavy scent of perfume in the air, which mingled with the odor of cat piss.

"You will pay in advance," she said.

"If that suits you."

"The room is two pounds."

"We need two rooms."

"There is one room. It's a large bed."

"I was hoping for two rooms."

"No hope for that," she said, with a hint of glee.

"Is there a hotel in Killiecrankie? Two rooms would really be preferable."

She simply stared at me.

"Such a wonderful name," said Borges, as if pretending he hadn't heard me all but beg for a way to avoid sharing a bed with him. "Killiecrankie. One of the fine legacies of Gaelic, with vowels expanding like an accordion and the air held in place by these brisk consonants."

"Are there rooms nearby?" I asked. Surely there must be a hotel in the area, even a pub with a couple of rooms for guests.

"Not tonight," she said, with a finality that closed the deal. "What will you have for breakfast?"

"Kippers," said Borges. "Do I dare to wish for Arbroath smokies?"

"Toast and marmalade," she said.

"Eggs?"

"Aye, a boiled egg. Bacon is extra."

"I will gladly pay for bacon," said Borges. "If there are no kippers, we must certainly have bacon."

"You must use the toilet before me," she said. "There's only the one, in my bedroom. Don't take long."

Despite my dread at the thought of a long night at the Morag B&B, I filled in a form for us both and paid her the £2, with fifty pence extra for bacon in the morning. If I'm not mistaken, the money came from my wallet.

"It's a shame about the shilling," she said as I handed her the fifty-pence coin.

The country had only just gone decimal, and people of her generation couldn't adjust to a change in currency. Many of them still thought in terms of guineas (a guinea being twenty-one shillings).

"You'll probably get used to it," I said. "It's easier to count."

"Easier for you."

Borges sat in a rocker, smiling as he tipped forward and back. This drew a scowl from our hostess. A cat leaped into his lap, and he cried, "A tiger!"

"She's the nice one," said our hostess. "Pet her behind the ears."

Borges obliged, and I could hear a loud rumbling purr.

"Have you lived here your whole life?" I asked.

"Do I look so poorly?"

"No, I didn't mean . . . You live alone?"

"Since he died, my husband, Baldie."

"He was bald?"

"Archibald. We called him Baldie." She screwed up her eyes as if she might cry. "I'm Mrs. Braid."

"Wife of Baldie Braid," said Borges. He lifted his nose in the air. "Do I smell kidneys, Mrs. Braid?"

"Steak and kidney pie."

I asked her where we might find a restaurant, and she suggested the adjacent pub, The Puddock. "They do food," she said. This was a rare feature in Scottish pubs, where food took a backseat to alcohol. One was lucky to get a stale sausage roll or bag of crisps.

"The Puddock!" Borges cried. "Do you know what it means? The frog. A Scottish term for this amphibian."

"Your father is correct," she said.

"He's not my father. He's a friend."

She eyed me with suspicion. Why would a young man travel with an elderly friend? And an obvious foreigner? I could sense these questions gathering in her mind like a purple bruise of cloud, and I felt accused, as if there were something unnatural about our connection.

"I go to bed at ten," she said with a mild malevolence. "You'll want to use the toilet before I retire."

"Well before that, dear lady," said Borges. "Sleep—and dreaming, of course—these are my favorite pastimes, just behind reading. A deep pleasure for a blind man, and such a relief to enter the darkness without expectation. I see vivid colors in my dreams, the whole rainbow unfolding."

"You're blind, so how do you read?"

"There are many readers in this world, and I discover them, one by one. One reader is sublime. Two is noise."

We left Borges in the sitting room with the pets while

Mrs. Braid showed me our room. To my dismay, the bed was not as wide as most doubles, and it smelled of stale urine and mothballs. The curtains were dark navy but seemed black. A bare lightbulb hung from the ceiling.

"There are towels in the bathroom," she said. "It's the blue door at the end of the hall. If you need hot water, let me know in advance. I'll turn on the thingy." She paused. "It's extra. A few shillings in the old money."

I told her we did not require baths, giving the illusion that we might after all be decent and undemanding (if possibly unhygienic) guests. "And the toilet?" In many Scottish houses a proper bathroom didn't have a toilet, as it was used only for bathing. "Is there really only the one?"

"There was another down the hall at one time, but it's off. Just knock on my bedroom door and you can use mine. We'll get along well, won't we?"

During our dinner of barely edible fish and chips in the Puddock, Borges drank three pints of beer. With trepidation, I delivered the pints into his hands, one after the other. His frequent urination had proved awkward enough during our daylight hours; at night, all bets were off.

After the meal we returned to the Morag B&B. Mrs. Braid had provided me with a key, but the dark house unnerved me. Nobody likes a dark house. Soon I found a switch and turned on the light in the hallway, then led Borges upstairs with some difficulty, as he had drunk more than he could handle. He squeezed my arm, leaning on his cane with the other hand for balance, singing a Scottish tune a bit too loudly as we entered our bedroom. His voice was unmusical, almost a rasp, but he sang with feeling.

"There is nostalgia in Scotland," he said, "in their poetry and music, in the landscape, which I can smell. And their history is sad—a disappointed people. But I'm not nostalgic, Giuseppe. Except for the present. I'm drawn to what happens when it occurs. This is good news, perhaps, until it's not occurring, at which point there will be less to interest me."

By now I had lost my appetite for philosophy and wished only to sleep. The journey with Borges had been like standing before a teacher's desk without your homework in hand, or stepping onto a stage without a script and being told to improvise (a recurrent nightmare of mine, in fact).

Remembering Mrs. Braid's warning, I led Borges to her bedroom and opened the door without knocking, assuming for no good reason that our hostess would not be there.

She was there, however, propped in bed against the highly wrought mahogany headboard with a pillow behind her, a flannel sleeping cap tugged firmly over her ears, with a flashlight trained on a novel by Agatha Christie. A puffy down blanket rose to her chin, and a pince-nez was perched at the end of her nose, which looked even longer than I remembered it, an invasive organ that dominated the room.

"Ah, Mrs. Braid," I said. "My friend needs to use the toilet."

"I know," she said. "He's blind."

Borges squeezed my arm, needing reassurance. And for the second time that day—as with the weird sisters—I sensed his vulnerability. It could not have been easy for him to move without sight, guided by a young stranger who had shown no obvious talent for reconnoitering the world.

"This way," I said forcefully, leading him around the foot of the bed and feeling the pressure of Mrs. Braid's eyes.

I tucked his toothbrush into the shirt pocket of his pajamas and positioned him in front of the toilet, then closed the door to wait outside.

And wait.

Could it really take fifteen or twenty minutes for Borges to pee and brush his teeth? Was he also composing an epic in his head?

"I'm not so well," said Mrs. Braid. "It's the hour. I don't sleep well these days."

"I'm sorry," I said.

When he had finished, I took my turn while Borges stood outside the door. When I came back into the room, he was sitting on the bed of our hostess, who looked less than comfortable, her nose lifted in the air like the Matterhorn, the nostrils pulsing, her thin lips pursing.

It didn't surprise me that Borges had taken a seat on the bed. His legs weren't strong, and he lacked mobility and balance, even with the cane.

As he and I lay in our own bed a short while later, I thought again of the call I should already have placed to Bella. There might have been a public phone at the Puddock, and surely there must be a phone box somewhere in this town, but I hadn't bothered to look, and now I confronted the possibility that it wasn't forgetfulness causing my lapse so much as a lack of confidence. I sighed, too loudly. Hesitation was a fault of mine, a fear of making binary choices, as I had discovered in the maze at Scone earlier in the day.

"I don't like to hear a gasp from a young man," said Borges. "There will be time for gasping. Is something wrong, dear boy?"

"I forgot to make a telephone call."

A yellow glow from a streetlamp seeped through the thin curtains and tinted the ceiling. Borges, I guessed, saw just the usual nothing.

"But there's no telephone."

"Probably I could find a phone box in the village." I knew I would have to put this off until morning.

"You are having an emergency?"

"The girl I told you about? Bella? I told her I'd call. We had planned to have dinner this week."

"And now," Borges said, "you have more important plans. I do understand. Norah Lange had this same tug on my heartstrings. Even to say the name, it makes me long for her. I do not speak of the Norah Lange who is now a very old woman—although I love that version of her, too. I long for the girl of nineteen or twenty, with scarlet hair and slender hips. She had freckles on her neck."

I had an impulse to push him off the bed—the last

thing I wanted now was to hear him droning on about lost love. I needed space to think about how I would explain to Bella that I had abandoned her for a batty old man of letters. But I knew by now that until Borges told his story, I'd have little chance for sleep. So I asked, "What happened between you and Norah?"

"I can't speak of it. This is not a confessional, and in any case I'm not in thrall to priests who demand blunt confessions in return for absolution." I waited for his own ruffle of anger to subside, his large and not especially fragrant body beside me, the mattress sloping toward the center, where we met and mingled in awkward ways.

"I loved her," he said. "But so did Oliverio Girondo. A fool, a dandy, and certainly *not* a good writer. He was too old for Norah. He wore chocolate-colored suits and fedoras, and this outlandish mustache. Colorful waistcoats, too. I should have purchased a red or yellow waistcoat, but I believed, quite mistakenly, that Norah was above such things. She was a wild girl with a pure heart. So innocent. And the blandishments he could produce, these were effective, and she succumbed. Even worse, she married him, in secret, after more than a decade of fitful cohabitation. The saddest thing in the world."

How on earth had I landed in bed with an elderly, loquacious blind man in a remote village in the Scottish Highlands? This man in his ridiculous yellow satin pajamas, with a smell of sour sweat, piss, and unfamiliar lotions?

"She didn't need your approval," I said.

"Don't insult me, Giuseppe."

I felt ridiculously small, and I determined not to speak to him again until morning. The escape into sleep had never seemed more delectable.

Borges shifted to his side now, his back against me; then he swiveled, pushing his face toward my pillow. I edged as far as I could to my side of the bed, nearly tipping onto the floor, barely catching myself on several occasions. He would aggressively spin in the opposite direction.

As the night progressed he repeated these aggressive gyrations, swiveling in one direction, then the next, dragging the blankets to his side, leaving me exposed and cold. His legs twitched, and he farted loudly. He grumbled and exhaled. He hummed.

Soon a hard rain slashed the windows and drummed on the slate roof, overwhelming the sounds of the old man who lay beside me.

I had finally approached the periphery of sleep when Borges grabbed my arm. "It's nature, and she has summoned!"

"What?" I asked groggily.

"You must, please, convey me toward the little room."

I wasn't surprised. Three pints of beer sloshed in his weak bladder. So I guided him into the dark hallway, backlit by light from our bedroom, and knocked softly at Mrs. Braid's door.

"It's urgent!" Borges cried as I opened the door and led him forward. Mrs. Braid lay in the dark, silent as we shuffled past her. Easing him in front of the toilet again, I backed into the bedroom.

"What's wrong?" asked our hostess.

"My friend needed the facility."

"The wee room?"

"The toilet."

"It's not an hour since he did his duty."

"He's old. His bladder's weak."

"I'm older, and my bladder is fine."

I had no wish to play the game of dueling bladders and kept silent, listening to the rain beat on the windows.

"He's taking his time," she said. "My Baldie, he had trouble making water, at the end."

Although Borges and I had just quarreled, I didn't like Mrs. Braid's implication. "He's not at the end," I said.

Soon enough Borges grunted loudly on the other side of the door. "Giuseppe! It is finished!"

"The last words of our Savior," said Mrs. Braid.

Borges stepped through the door, smiling.

I bade Mrs. Braid a good night and led Borges back to our bedroom, where he fell asleep within moments, but I began to worry when he gulped, gasped, and rattled. His lungs were billows that had seen better days, and he groaned miserably, uttering phrases in Spanish or Latin. Feeling a million miles from the realms of sleep, I let my thoughts turn back to Bella. Was it possible that she and Angus had drifted apart? Hadn't she all but said as much? Their relationship was not happy, I decided, and I had not only an opportunity but a duty to intervene! I thought I could see Bella's features in a shadow that passed over the ceiling. Was I dreaming? The face floated toward me, and just as I reached out for it, Borges bolted up beside me.

"I'm needing the toilet," he said.

"Again? Already?"

"Scottish beer, it runs through the pipes of this old building."

"Argentine beer not so much?"

He dug his nails into my wrist. "One would not like an accidental occurrence."

I led him back to Mrs. Braid's door, wondering if I should knock. Borges shifted from foot to foot and breathed urgently, a little Dutch boy with his thumb in the dike. I pushed open the door, and holding Borges by the waist, I guided him around the bed of our snoring hostess. Once I had him installed again at the best angle, I stepped outside and closed the door behind me.

I waited, shivering.

"Borges?" I whispered.

No answer came from within, and I supposed he had decided to sit on the toilet for a while. A mild grunt confirmed this, and I resigned myself to waiting.

"Baldie didn't come out," said Mrs. Braid. Her voice made me jump. "Not the last time."

"What's that?"

"Seven years ago, he went into the wee room, my Baldie. I didn't want to disturb, but I might have saved him."

"He died in there?"

"On the crapper."

"Your husband died in there?"

"Aye. Is he dead, too, your old man?"

"I don't think so. I would say no."

"He should answer if you call."

I took this cue. "Borges! Are you there?"

Mrs. Braid said, "I might ring for the police."

"I don't think so. He's probably not dead."

"Not yet," she said.

She turned on her light and sat up, while I settled at the foot of the bed. The clock on her dresser struck twelve loud pings.

"My Baldie, what a good man."

"I'm sure he was."

"Not a mean bone in his body."

"No."

We spent a further five minutes or so on the virtues of Baldie Braid.

Finally a thin voice came from behind the door: "Giuseppe?"

It was, I had to admit to myself, a relief that he was alive.

"Where's the door? I'm inside the room."

I opened the door and extracted him, leading him by the elbow.

"You got lucky," said Mrs. Braid. "I wasn't so lucky. Sat there with his head hanging down, he did. Dead as a fish."

"Who is dead?" Borges asked.

"Baldie died in there, on the crapper," I said.

There was anguish on Borges's face. "My own father died on the crapper," he said. "Named for Thomas Crapper, as you will know. Mother found him sitting there, and the lightbulb dead as well. I shall die like this. Like Baldie. Like my father."

"Not here," said Mrs. Braid.

"In this universe, anything is possible. You will excuse me, Mrs. Braid. I recall what Sir Thomas Browne said in the *Religio Medici*. A gentleman is indeed one who gives the least amount of trouble. In this, tonight, I have failed."

"When you've got to go, sir, you've got to go," she said. "It's an old saying in Scotland."

This was, for Mrs. Braid, a bright and unexpected moment of generosity, and she opened a wide grin for the first time, revealing sharp and pointed teeth like spikes on a fence.

Borges said, "Sir Walter Scott, perhaps? That sounds like him."

16

AT BREAKFAST THE next day, an exhausted Mrs. Braid produced three rounds of fatty bacon that held no appeal for me, though Borges devoured them joyfully. He licked his fingers, catlike, and adjusted his tie in the hallway in front of an invisible mirror before we left: he was resolvedly formal, one of a generation of males of a certain class who never stepped into public view without a tie. For her part, Mrs. Braid looked almost tearful as we left—either saddened to lose the company of the sweet old man who had touched her last night or relieved to see the back of us. Probably both, I decided.

It certainly relieved me to have the Morag B&B in my rearview mirror. Though my sleep had been spotty, I felt strangely alive. The sky was screech-blue, stung with birds, and the air tingled with expectation. This journey was taking unexpected turns, and all I could think about was how much Billy Giordano was going to enjoy these stories about Borges and me. My account of our night in Killiecrankie was going to delight him. Even Alastair would, in due course, adore it—well after Borges had left.

Rocinante sputtered, wheezed, then came to life with a coarse low rumble that worried me. I'd spent very little for my part-share of the car and might soon pay for that thrift.

"The Quixote loved to get on the road each morning," Borges said. "What about you, Sancho?"

"You don't really think of me as Sancho Panza?" The name didn't strike well on my ear. Was I the foolish sidekick of Cervantes, a sounding board, more chump than chum?

Borges put his lip out, pouting, then struck an apologetic note. "You are not Sancho, unless you're my squire. Nor am I quite the Quixote. I am not mad, for example. And you, I suspect, are not fat. You are certainly not badly educated."

"Sancho was illiterate?"

"This isn't the best way to think of him. The influence of the Quixote was such that Sancho acquired a taste for literary wisdom. Such wisdom in his aphorisms! 'One can find a remedy for everything but death.' Or this: 'Make yourself into honey and the flies will devour you.' I do wish as a young man I had made myself into a honeycomb. I might then have defeated my rival, Girondo, the scoundrel. Here is another, *escucha*: 'The lucky man has nothing to worry about.' I've become a lucky man. Almost a popular writer in my sunset years."

"That's lucky, for sure," I said, wondering if I had wildly underestimated Borges. Where was he popular?

Borges said, "You see, I designed my work for the tiniest audience, 'fit company though few.' A writer's imagination should not be diluted by crowds!" After a few minutes he produced a final aphorism: "A fool knows more in his own house than a wise man in the house of another man."

"Only we can understand the context of whatever we say or do."

"You *are* Sancho after all. You've just said something wonderful."

"I was paraphrasing Sancho." Though I'd never read the book, I could guess his role in this traveling duo.

"There are no paraphrases. Only phrases."

Somehow it pleased me to have pleased Borges. I'd been wondering if he was getting what he needed from our excursion. Despite my resistance, I had already learned a good deal from my voluble companion. His way of being in the world wasn't mine, and yet I liked the freedom of association in his thinking, how he swung like a monkey in the jungle from limb to limb in the high trees of his thought. In this he reminded me of Alastair, who could have learned this from Borges—even modeled himself after his hero.

I recalled that Alastair, in addition to his work on Borges, had translated Pablo Neruda and had told me his view of how the two differed: "Neruda loves this world. For Borges, it's other worlds."

I asked Borges if he knew Neruda.

"Ah, the Pied Piper," he said. "Another friend of Oliverio Girondo. But I refuse to denigrate this man. Not the poems, certainly. They are his children, and I ask you, should you blame the child for the sins of his father? I don't think so. They are darling orphans, sad-faced, lonely in the world, innocent in their way. I would protect each and every one of them. I bought a volume of poems by Pablo once, long ago, in a used bookstore in Madrid. I thought of the book as an orphanage, and would regularly visit the pale, hungry guests there, these captives of its covers. But their father was a fool. He praised Stalin. Stalin! He disliked the United States, your country. I refuse to dislike your country, however much it disappoints me."

"I'm certainly disappointed," I said.

I tried to shake these thoughts—the U.S. seemed far away now, and happily so—as we climbed into the brown foothills of the Cairngorms, heading toward Aviemore, the small village with astounding views of the long valley where I'd once come for a weekend of skiing. I had memories of peaks and ice-blue skies. One afternoon at the crest of a mountain I saw a golden eagle, and I mentioned this to Borges, hoping to prompt a disquisition on something other than politics.

"I love golden eagles," he said. "But one has to be so careful. This is often Zeus, who takes the form of this magnificent raptor. Remember that he clothed himself in the shape of the eagle to abduct poor Ganymede, the son of Tros. Homer called him 'the loveliest boy in Greece.' Not a happy story. By the way, where are we, son? I'm not seeing anything!"

"We're rising in the Cairngorms," I said. "Foothills. Gorgeous mountains. I'm aiming for Aviemore. This is a wilderness area."

"Wilderness! Tell me!"

I dug in as best I could. "I see rocky fields, rising brown and purple hills, snowy peaks in the distance. A jagged skyline. There are still large tracts of Caledonian pine in the lower reaches, a remnant of what was once a vast forest of pine, or so the guidebook claims. Much of this region is above the tree line."

"You know," said Borges, "I lived in Switzerland as a boy, when I had my sight. I don't usually care for mountains. I'm a city dweller by instinct and habit. But I love the lichens that cling to rocks in the high elevations. I would walk in the hills near Geneva and examine them. Algae, mosses, liverworts, even fungi. The fungi—those are your mushrooms. I do like them, as they come in such colors. The blond spongy heads always seem, well, sexual in some way."

Not every object longer than its width is a phallic symbol, I wanted to say, but I held my tongue.

"My father, you must know," Borges continued, "was blind as well, or nearly so. His eyesight became a door into the dark. Think of me, a boy with this father who could not see him properly. We traveled to Geneva in 1914, in search of a cure for his vision. As ever, his timing was less than perfect. He didn't see the war coming, such was his blindness to political realities. And so I became a Swiss teenager! Whatever schooling I had was obtained in Geneva. A shy and strange boy I must have been. There was a young girl, Emilie."

"There's always a young girl," I said.

Borges sank into a reverie, thinking of Emilie. "She was beautiful, very much so. A porcelain vase. I worshipped her. She and I kissed beside the lake one evening—the singular event of my second decade."

"Your first girlfriend?"

"Don't make me sad, Giuseppe. I was innocent then. Emilie, too. So intimate, the mouth for kissing. What a peculiar activity, though marvelous. Don't you think? Make this a habit. It is my only advice."

"I quite like to kiss," I said, recalling Bella's chaste, unreadable kissing of my forehead on the night we first shared coffee in her room. Involuntarily I lifted my fingertips to touch that spot.

A phone box, I thought. I needed to find a phone box!

For a long time we rode in silence, with my companion lost in his reveries, smiling and grimacing in succession. He could never hide anything, and didn't try to, especially the sadness and happiness that coursed through him and registered boldly on his face. Was my own face a giveaway to the rivers of my feeling? Blind Borges, of course, couldn't tell me.

I wondered aloud if he had slept with Emilie, perhaps thinking more of my own situation than of his, though I couldn't hear the impertinence in my question.

"Sexual congress? Dear boy, such a question. I rarely will share these intimacies, but you and I have become soul partners. Brothers in the word! I won't conceal the truth. My father, also a shy man, called me into his study in Geneva on my nineteenth birthday. It was August, and I had recently finished my schooling. The world opened before me. My father said, in a grave voice that frightened me, *Georgie, sit down*. And so I sat in the chair in his study, fearing the worst. And indeed it came. The worst!"

"Which was . . . ?"

"*Have you slept with a woman?* This he asked. My own father!"

"And had you?"

"I confessed the truth, that I was a virgin. He sighed and told me that he assumed as much. Now I must do as he instructed. From a drawer in his desk he withdrew a card, with an address: 23 place du Bourg-de-four, apartment C. I cannot to this day forget the scene of my humiliation. A prostitute had been arranged, and my father sent me to this rude assignation."

"He sent you to a brothel?"

"It was the custom in Argentina. A father had the duty, the *responsibility*, to ensure that his son would advance into his majority with the experience of carnality. It's not a bad custom, as the human race must proceed. But in my case, a misadventure ensued. I wasn't prepared for this. She was less than thirty but seemed very old to me, almost a crone, with long black curly hair that appalled me. She unbuckled my suspenders, my trousers. She applied her lips in the typical fashion. I stood there in shock. Yes, *shock* is the only word. She pushed me back onto the bed and exhausted herself, I fear. But nothing lifted me. Nothing aroused me."

"You were impotent?"

"I dislike the word."

"Sorry."

We drove along for some time without speaking, my thoughts spiraling into areas of darkness. Would I myself be impotent when the occasion dawned? Was I perhaps one of those who must live their lives apart from others?

"It was humiliating," Borges said, following up on

some internal conversation. "My mother knew about this. She still knows everything about me. It makes life so much more difficult."

"Your mother is still alive, right?"

"Doña Leonor? She is the sun and moon. Are the sun and moon alive?"

"They are features of nature."

"*Features of nature!* My mother is this. And has never approved of any woman I have loved. She hated my Norah, whose ancestors could not compete with mine."

"And your wife?"

"My wife is no longer my wife. I love another woman. May I confess to you my deepest secret? I love Maria Kodama. She is Japanese in part—my favorite part, I shall say. I met her when she was a child. But so glorious, this child! Less than a decade later, she became a student of mine at the university. The poor girl fell behind in her work. When she came to me for help, I invited her to my apartment for further conversation, and soon after this our love—from mere kindling, I assure you, a few delicate words of conversation—became a bonfire. A bonfire!"

"You were much older . . ."

"Nearly four decades her senior, but who is calibrating? Age means nothing in matters of love."

I couldn't imagine what it would mean for a man in his late sixties or early seventies to fall in love with a woman in her twenties. Wouldn't she feel more like a daughter or granddaughter than a lover?

"The soul is eternal," said Borges. "And time plays no

role in its deepest life. I wonder if you agree. You say yes. But do you agree?"

"Why do you keep asking me these questions? I know nothing, Borges. You know that by now. I've read a few books. I'm not stupid. But what do I know? Sometimes I sit in the church in St. Andrews and let the silence teach me. This is God. I can feel the spirit moving when I run along the beach. But I seem to learn very little, and this worries me. I don't want to be one of those people who only graze the surface, who don't dig into their soul."

"Ah, your soul! I like this word."

My mind shifted back to Alastair, who had crossed out the word *soul* in one of my poems, telling me never to use it. "There is the self," Alastair said. "But no soul. That's an outmoded concept."

Borges formed a contrast to Alastair. "So many in your generation, they refuse even to use the word. I celebrate the soul. I sing its eternal existence in the present moment!" After a pause, he said, "Don't forget you are seeing for me now. So what opens before us? I see only oblong streaks of yellow and white."

A lapwing flew across the road, so I mentioned it.

"See, you know more than you think you know," Borges said. "Thank you for this!"

A mile or so later, his mind returned to the lapwing. "A lapwing is something like a plover. They have a shrill voice, and fly in irregular patterns."

As ever, his knowledge of natural details surprised me, especially for someone driven inward by blindness. In my short time in Scotland I had picked up only a smattering of local color, learning how to tell a lapwing from a rook. I could distinguish between the obvious seabirds and hawks. I knew that the red squirrels we saw rushing about in the brush were not the gray squirrels I'd known as a boy. But I also wondered what all of this meant. The connections between words and things obviously mattered, but there was an occult relationship here, and I would need to learn the sorcery required to connect them.

As we climbed into the hills, I could feel the tug of the sky, and the heathery rolling valleys and spiky peaks in the distance moved me. Now I wanted, more than ever, to write about this, to find the equivalence in language for what broke around me, here and always.

17

A LONELY RED booth by the side of the road caught my eye. Who placed calls from here, in the middle of the Cairngorms? This was a godsend, and I pulled over abruptly.

Borges startled, as if something were wrong, and I explained that I had to make a call. It would take only a few moments. He looked weirdly disappointed, as if I had interrupted the journey for no good reason, and slumped backward, closing his eyes.

After I dialed the number, a bleeping sound came on the line, followed by a vacant buzz. I tried the operator, who asked me for the number I was trying to reach, but her voice cut out, leaving the same white buzz. One more time I tried the number for Hamilton Hall, and to my relief a young woman picked up (though it didn't seem to ring): "Second floor, Hamilton. May I help you?" I asked her to knock on Bella's door.

"I'll try," she said without enthusiasm.

She came back several minutes later with the news that nobody answered her knock. If this were really true, why would she have been gone for so long? Perhaps

Bella *had* answered the knock but had told her hallmate to pretend she was away?

When I got into the car again, I sighed. My feelings silently filled the car.

"This is about the young woman?"

"Yes. Bella Law."

"She's even finer than this marvelous name. Am I right?"

"I find her quite wonderful. There's a rare critical intelligence, a sharpness. And she has a sense of justice—she leads an antiwar group in St. Andrews."

"Everything about your description sounds dangerous and appealing."

She was indeed both dangerous and appealing. Not unlike Alastair in many ways.

We resumed our journey, heading into an open stretch of road with stirring views on either side. I took in the measureless landscape, which swept upward along dun-colored hillsides to a series of mountains, one behind the other. I could only imagine the colors when, in their appropriate seasons, the mustard-yellow gorse or purple heather bloomed. It was sad to think of Borges and his blindness and how much richness passed him by. No wonder he lived so fully in the great room of his mind.

I confessed the difficulty of putting the images I saw into adequate words, and he nodded eagerly.

"This is, my dear, the work before us, always. To find a language adequate to what is revealed. I'm glad you know this. I feel the same consternation quite often, trying to attach feelings to words, to summon the image and declare it pure."

At a wayside inn at the edge of a remote village whose name I didn't know, we stopped for a lunch of mulligatawny and cheese rolls. Borges seemed uncharacteristically subdued during the meal, and I hoped his mood had shifted away from the frantic philosophizing, which had begun to wear thin. But as soon as we got back to the car, he turned back to metaphysics: always a latent preoccupation with him, and one that surfaced like a sea monster that popped its head above the black waters, looked around warily, then dived back in. It was, I thought, as if the narrow seat and low ceiling of my car forced a pressure in his head that must erupt.

"Does time really exist?" he asked. "No," he answered himself. He quoted Schopenhauer: "No man has ever lived in the past, and no one will ever live in the future; the present alone is the form of all life." He then referred to a Buddhist scholar who said, "The duration of life lasts only while a thought lasts."

"But we *do* have a past," I said, my impatience boiling over. "I remember mine pretty well."

"You think you do." Then, after a long pause, he asked, "Why did you come to Scotland? To escape this past you think you remember so well?"

"To escape my mother, that's more like it," I said. "In her mind I have no life that's not involved with hers. When she gets hungry, she tells me to eat."

"Dear brother," he said, "we confront the same issue. I'm trying to forget Doña Leonor as I speak. Every moment I pass with you is a removal from her, an excision. She will never approve of Maria Kodama. Fortunately she does not yet know about this matter of the heart." He seemed to chew his cud for a bit. "What will your mother think of Miss Law?"

"I barely know Bella myself," I said. "You're leaping ahead." The idea of my mother in a room with Bella was impossible to contemplate. They were creatures from different planetary systems who would never in my lifetime coincide.

"Bella is an object of your desire, and you *will* know her. I promise this. Borges predicts as much."

"I hope you're a gifted fortune-teller."

"Call me Scheherazade," said Borges. "*The Arabian Nights* is the source of everything I do."

"Who actually wrote those stories?"

"I did. I've written everything."

"That's ridiculous."

"No, but it's true. I've written every classic several times. This has, of course, often irritated my contemporaries."

This was a joke, I assumed. Nonetheless, it stopped our conversation, and a unique half hour of silence followed, during which I wondered why I hadn't wanted to say anything explicit to Borges about what my mother might think of Bella. I never wrote a word about Bella to my mother in a letter home. But why? Was I afraid to admit that I had dreams of sexual fulfillment, much like any other person of my age? Bella's politics would have puzzled or angered her, that much I knew. In her world, Bella would have seemed alien, inexplicable.

Borges gasped now. "Let me tell you, Sancho," he said, "these few days in the Highlands will live in my head as a lovely interval, a break from life as it normally flows."

I was an interval in his mind? A humbling thought. But it worked the other way around, too: Borges was a discrete interval in my life. For these few days he controlled my every waking moment—colonizing my life, as it were. Yet after our brief swing through the Highlands, I would never see him again. How would I? He would disappear south, to Oxford, then return to Argentina. He would probably die soon. Other than in his writing, which I must read, this would be our only encounter.

We churned upward in my lowest gear on a steep patch some miles from Aviemore. I paused by the side of the narrow road to take in the Cairngorms with a mental gasp: range after range of mountains, with a purple-and-yellow mist girdling them midway, their peaks many-faceted, glinting. Glens and corries—those deep pits in the rolling landscape—darkened in the distance. The hills bathed in the gold light of late afternoon. I saw below us an isolated stand of pines like an unshaven clump of hair on a man's cheek. Deer loped in the field below a dip in the road, moving through panels of bronze light, and the sight of them affected me strongly. The world was unspeakably beautiful as well as strange.

"Where are we?"

"There's a view of the Cairngorms. We're near Aviemore." I described everything I could see in as much detail as I could, and his ears seemed to cup my words as a thirsty man might cup water in his palms.

There was a sudden crack of thunder, with a splash of rain. Hadn't the sun just been shining?

"Let me walk here," said Borges. "The storm calls to me!"

Before I could ask him not to, he opened the door and leaped into the beating rain. I heard him shouting the famous line from *Lear*—"Blow, winds, and crack your cheeks! rage! blow!"—as he tapped his way forward and up the road with his cane. As I opened the door to rush after him, my car slipped backward, the emergency brake stuttering, unable to get a grip on the steep incline. I cursed and jammed a foot on the brakes and managed, with difficulty, to lock the car into first gear; it would not fall backward as easily now, though I didn't trust my transmission. I pulled and released the emergency brake several times, as this sometimes brought it back to life. The last thing I needed was for Rocinante to topple from this scenic perch.

Satisfied that the car would hold firm, at least temporarily, I lifted my eyes to locate Borges, and it took a moment to register that he was nowhere in view. There was no bend in the road that could have absorbed him. Where the hell was he? I found myself wondering, half seriously, if this sorcerer had somehow donned an invisible cloak.

I jumped from the car and rushed up the slope, calling for him. The name of Borges echoed in the hills, magnifying. *Borges! Borges!*

A figure lodged in my peripheral vision, a dark blur below the road. He must have toppled when I wasn't looking! He had skidded down a small slope covered with loose wet gravel.

"Borges!" I called again, and skimmed over the loose-packed surface myself, keeping my balance on the scree like a skier up to my waist in fresh powder. He had landed facedown in a tuft of thistle, with his cane a few yards beyond him. He wasn't moving.

Dear God in heaven, I thought: I had killed Borges!

I rolled him onto his back gently. There was a nearly invisible scrape on his forehead, and he groaned slightly, opening his eyes. He was alive!

"Can you speak, Borges?"

He squinted into the sun, which had burst into the open, his eyelids quivering.

"Borges, do you hear me?"

"This was not, as Milton would say, a fortunate fall," he said.

It relieved me that in the midst of this crisis he could still quote John Milton. His world had obviously not collapsed.

"I seem to have lost my balance," he said.

"Can you stand?"

He pulled himself to his feet, leaning on me, exhaling. I tried to help him maneuver onto some flat ground.

"I'm perhaps dizzy," he said. "The sky whirls."

"You'd better lie down."

"I'm a little weary, as you mention this." I helped him to lie in some soft grass and put a mossy stone under his head for a pillow.

"Just rest here and let me get some help," I said, though I couldn't imagine how or where I would find it, as Aviemore was miles away.

"We're alone in this wilderness," said Borges. "So let me die here, in the soft rain. It is not so bad. The crows, they will pick the flesh off my bones. Nature will accommodate me. I will be absorbed."

This was stupidly melodramatic. But I restrained myself.

By a stroke of luck—or Borgesian magic—only a few minutes passed before a young farmer drove by in an old Land Rover, and I flagged him down. There was, he said, a cottage hospital in Kingussie, near Aviemore, and together we managed to get Borges onto the wide backseat of his car. I followed them into town, thinking about the strange fragility of our physical lives and how tenuously we cling to these pale scraps of flesh. I thought, too, about what Alastair might say when he found out that Borges had stumbled from the road. Should I take the blame for this? Was it my fault? I imagined a glare from Alastair, with arched eyebrows, and already I resented it.

The only other patient at the hospital was a pregnant young woman who had taken a spill in her house, and she did her best to ignore us. A soft-spoken young nurse with brown hair in a bun addressed me in the hallway outside the ward, wondering if Borges was my father. Once again! I did my best to suppress a laugh this time around, and stopped myself from saying yes, he *was* my father, and I wanted to kill him. Patricide! I began to tell her that he was a writer from Argentina, head of the National Library, but then realized that this information was irrelevant, and I paused midsentence.

"He's good and lucky, aye," she said. "A blow to the head, and he's an elderly man. We'll keep him overnight. It takes twenty-four hours to tell if there's a concussion, but I don't think so. A wee shake-up. Not to worry."

Not to worry, indeed. I found a bed in a nearby boarding house, queasy with a kind of hangover from the adrenaline rush of the day. Savoring my privacy, I lay down in a big double bed, relieved to have time and space to myself. A whole room of silence! But when I closed my eyes to try to nap, I kept seeing images of Borges's motionless body in the scree and heard a voice resounding in the hills in some accusatory fashion: *Borges! Borges!*

And what if he did have a concussion? What harm would it do—headaches, confusion? Difficulty speaking? Speech was, of course, the main thing about Borges. A laconic Borges would be no Borges.

Still shaking, I remembered the most recent letter I'd gotten from Billy and fished it out of my rucksack. It was written on blue paper, crackly and thin, in ink that must have smeared in the sweat of its composition, with some passages too blurry to read. I read with amazement now:

Every day it's Russian roulette, we spin the barrel of the gun. I've been lucky so far. Empty chambers, again and again. How's that for shit-ass luck?

The guys on patrol. They pop off one by one like low little lights. I was in a village near the DMZ last week, doing some "intelligence work." Don't that sound smart?

Anyway, my friend Nicky Boose (called Bozo around here) is a medic, more like a nurse, and I was visiting him, and to say it was a fucking nightmare is too kind to bad dreams. I stood in the tent and saw a doctor dipping his head into the entrails of a corpse. He came up looking kind of sick. Get me the Medivac, he said. So we called for a chopper on the radio.

Good luck with that, I thought. The pilots, they were probably dead already.

Saw a couple of Green Berets lying on the tables, bleeding, one guy hollering loud for his Mom, next to some local militia, the ARVN, these fucking useless Vietnamese who pretend to help us but set booby traps in our tents. I'm sure of it. They're worse than enemies.

I never saw a dead body till I came here, unless you count my old dog Kisser. Even the living are dead here. We move around like corpses, waiting for the little tags on our bare toes and maybe a snug plush quiet coffin (if we're lucky). Or just to rot in the jungle.

Don't mean to drag you down, amigo. You can die in lots of ways, anywhere. Get killed crossing a street. Smacked by a fucking bus. Bang: you're a memory. Or worse, a lost memory.

So what's the moral, if I got one? Get laid. It's the only wisdom anybody gets from this shit. Get laid often as you can. Make more of us. Fuck and fuck and fuck some more. Fuck the world hollow. That's my goal now, the future I dream about. Look out, girls. Billy's coming home!

Jesus, I loved this letter, the weird street wisdom here, the army slang, the sassy tone. Billy had "a gift for gab," my mother always said. Well, he'd gone a step further here, lodging a few paragraphs beyond my forgetting.

That night I returned to the hospital after dinner with a packet of chocolate-covered biscuits, which Borges devoured, though I could see from an empty tray at the foot of his bed that he'd been fed by the staff. I felt relieved to see him recovered, more like his old incorrigible self. We talked happily, our voices echoing loudly in the ward, where Borges was now the only occupant.

"You can sleep here, Giuseppe," said Borges. He touched a finger to the small bandage on his head, which covered the invisible abrasion—no more than a scratch. "The nurse tells me there are no other patients. Only Borges."

"Thanks, but I've found a nice room nearby."

"So I will miss you."

I believed he meant this, and found myself weirdly missing him, too. In just a couple of days he'd become more to me than just an annoying task that Alastair had thrust upon me. We had begun to forge a connection.

It relieved me that Borges certainly had *not* lost his gift for speech. "When I woke," he said, "I thought I was in the hospital again in Buenos Aires. When I was a young man, not yet forty, and soon after my father's death, I stumbled into the overhanging ledge of a window. So sharp! My vision had already begun to fail me. I fell to the floor, bleeding profusely. In a pool of myself I lay there, dying! My mother found me in this frightful condition, and—you will imagine it too well—she woke the dead in the graveyard of Santa Maria de la Concepción.

I lay for weeks in the ward, with blood poisoning. Close to death, I assure you, so very close. My life changed forever."

"So how did your life change?" I asked.

"You ask the simplest of questions, which is a Socratic gift, dear boy. And yet it's difficult to answer. This was my road to Damascus. I had a vision of God, or some concatenation of images that I believed was a composite god. In any case I was lifted into the Third Heaven. This is what Saint Paul called it, when he heard the choir of a thousand angels. I heard this singing, too, and could see my friends and enemies in the audience, their wings folded. It was heaven or hell. I am not sure which."

"People close to death often glimpse the afterlife," I said. "They see a kind of glow on the horizon like at dusk, when the sun has dipped behind the purple hills or below the lip of the sea."

"You do say wonderful things," he said, though I knew he exaggerated. I'd said nothing very special. Jasper would have laughed at my clichés!

Borges continued. "After my accident, in 1938, I began to write stories, the good ones. Incredible time it was. I could not stop writing. The angels spoke to me, and I took their dictation, without volition, no act of will on my part. This magic carpet unrolled for perhaps a decade. But the good years, I'm afraid they were fewer than I should have liked."

"Why aren't the good years still ahead of you?"

He reached out for my hand, which I extended in sympathy. "You know," he said, "I remember waking after days of sleep in that hospital. I saw the nuns in their wimples, smiling and coaxing me into consciousness. They wondered if I had lost my mind. It's not uncommon, they said, for one who has hit his head with a vengeance to forget things. But I wasn't diminished in my recollective abilities but—dear God!—amplified. It was terrifying. As I lay there, I recalled the moldings and floorboards of every room in my house in Palermo. The towels in the laundry, with their intricate textures and colors. Every glass in the cupboard in our pantry, its exact size and shape. I could see one crystal goblet with a *V*-shaped chip and the bent silver knife in the drawer, every fork and spoon, some of them relics of a wedding from the nineteenth century. I could picture the faces of everyone I ever met and each leaf on every tree I'd ever met. I was engorged by these details, and wretchedly unhappy."

"That's a wild memory," I said. "Frightening. It would make a good story."

"And so it did. 'Funes the Memorious,' in which I imagine what life would be without the gift of forgetfulness. Funes was an unfortunate, you see, thrown from a horse and paralyzed. As he lay in his room, he found he could forget nothing. Nothing! He became the lonely and lucid observer of this unbearably precise world. He couldn't sleep, the poor fellow, because sleep requires erasure, turning one's back to experience. In the end he couldn't think, only recall. To think, as you know, is to disallow differences, to generalize, to make abstractions. The activity of selection."

"You've never forgotten a thing," I said.

"Don't say this! Why do you torment me?"

The nurse looked in. "Is everything good?"

"Not good!" Borges shouted. "Sancho has accused me of eidetic memory! He thinks I'm unable to discriminate among mental objects! He would confine me to a vertiginous world where every pebble has its own name. He is like John Locke, who tried to imagine a comprehensive language in which every word had only one referent. Can you imagine such a language? What library could contain these infinite volumes of expression?"

The nurse looked at Borges, then at me. "Are you accusing him of this?"

"It was more or less a joke," I said.

"Once," said Borges, "I imagined a total map of Argentina. It contained every mottled shadow in the landscape, each rock, bush, or brisk and rushing stream. The map withheld nothing! Every inch of every river had its corresponding mark on the map. The city of Buenos Aires wasn't a crosshatch of streets and alleyways, parks and squares and hidden gardens; instead, every square foot of every street found a corresponding footprint on the map. The map was like a photograph that has resolved into such detail that nothing disappears. Not one leaf on any tree was missing."

Puzzlement doesn't begin to describe what befell the face of the nurse as she listened to Borges.

"The problem," he said, "was that it unfolded to the exact size of the country. A perfect mirror of reality. It was useless."

"You are not well," said the nurse.

"On the contrary, I've never been better," Borges said to her. "I have almost forgotten the cruel machinations of Oliverio Girondo. I recall only a handful of the many slights administered by Norah Lange over many decades. My mother's insults fade into one large insult, which I have put into a drawer and locked. I can move forward, but only because so much has been abandoned and willfully forgotten. The weight of the past becomes light in the amnesia of my living. I move into the present unencumbered."

"Are you all right, sir?" the nurse asked me.

"Yes." I sipped a glass of water from the tray beside Borges's bed.

"May I have a word with you?" she whispered in my ear.

I followed her into the hallway, beyond his hearing.

"Your friend seems very confused," she said.

"This is just the way he talks."

"He doesn't appear to know what's happened to him, even where he is."

I assured her that Borges knew exactly where he was and what had occurred. I would collect him in the morning. If the doctor found no evidence of a concussion that required further medical attention, we would continue our journey northward, then return to St. Andrews in a couple of days.

"I would alert his family to the issues," she said.

"Oh, I think they're aware of his issues."

18

IN THE MORNING I met with Dr. Brodie, a fair-haired woman in her forties with sharp features.

"He's had quite a stumble, your old one," she said. "There may be a concussion. I don't think so, but I don't know. He does appear confused."

"He seemed lucid yesterday," I told her. "And he's got a hearty appetite. Can we keep going?"

"In what sense?"

"The plan was to visit Inverness and maybe Orkney, then return to St. Andrews."

She stared at her clipboard. "He's not a young man," she said.

"No," I said. "But vigorous, for his age. And strong-willed, so I doubt we could change course abruptly. I'll look after him."

Dr. Brodie studied me, as if trying to assess my suitability as a guardian. "There may be headaches. I would expect the confusion to continue."

"I'm getting used to confusion."

We went into the ward, where Borges was eating a bacon sandwich, with a mug of tea on the tray. He looked a good deal better than he had the previous night. He'd changed from his hospital gown back into his suit and tie.

I explained to Borges that Dr. Brodie would allow us to go.

"Brodie?"

"Yes, sir," she said.

"Aberdeen?"

"My grandfather was from Aberdeen."

"Was he a missionary in Africa, then in Brazil?"

"Yes, but how did you know this? My grandfather wasn't well known. He wasn't even my grandfather. My great-grandfather, I believe."

The sorcerer was at work again, and I sat back to watch him plying his craft.

"He left behind an abbreviated account of his travels," said Borges.

"This is true?"

"I would never make anything up. Unless, of course, the world failed to provide sufficient material. We need reality, as you, being a physician, must know. These are the coals we put into the grate, that we light. One day in a library in Buenos Aires I found something written by your great-grandfather in a volume of *The Arabian Nights*. It had been stuffed between the pages. Have you read *The Arabian Nights*?"

Once again *The Arabian Nights*.

"I don't read so much," she said. "It's a wee problem. One gets busy in my profession."

Borges shook his head. "One who has failed to read *The Arabian Nights* is, well, an innocent, and this is dangerous."

She released us quickly after this fusillade, handing me a packet of what she called "pain pills" for Borges, warning me that they were strong and should be used only if necessary. When I asked what this meant, Dr. Brodie said with a conspiratorial look, "I will leave this to your judgment."

Back in the car, I asked Borges how it was possible that such a coincidence could occur, that he had actually read something written by the grandfather of Dr. Brodie. He was surely making this up?

"The story of two dreams is a coincidence, like horses or lions in the sky in the shape of two clouds," he said. "Her dream and my dream coincided. Now *your* dream, which is what you call your life, has features that coincide with mine. That's the more astonishing coincidence. Two lives occurring in different zones, in different bodies. I have gone before you on this planet by a few decades. It's not so long in the grand scheme. I wonder who will come after us, describing these same circles?"

As we drove on, I considered our parallel lives. My car and the horse of the Quixote, my Italian ancestry and his childhood in Palermo—not the "real" Palermo, but its distant refraction in Argentina. I thought of his imperious mother, with mine in her shadow. His sister and my own sister. Our sweetly passive and predictable fathers. Our erotic frustrations, with the dream of a sassy and brilliant partner with perhaps a tinge of red in her hair. Or red sneakers? And then there were my literary aspirations, so blatantly unrealized—a handful of poems, none of them quite right or in my own voice. My endless journals, which amounted to little more than scribbles in the margins of my life. My rough chapters on George Mackay Brown . . . Perhaps, I thought with a shudder, I would go blind one day as well.

I couldn't begin to fathom this.

"Did you reach Beatrice?" he asked.

"Bella? I left a message."

"So she will know you care."

"Not if nobody passes along the message."

"Women are not so cruel as men. But I've noticed this, that women rarely care so much about beauty, not as men do. They marry a soul, not a body. The problem is, they often misread a soul. They see profundity where in truth there is a shallow ditch." Of course he could not resist a tirade about Oliverio Girondo, whom he called "a second-rate hack."

"Tell me about Girondo's writing," I said, knowing nothing about his work. In a strange turn, I began to worry that everyone in the world was a writer, which left very little space for Borges or me.

"The avatar of ultraism," he said, "one of the fraudulent strains in Argentine literature. Such excess! He once compared a woman's hand to a dead ostrich. Had he actually *seen* a dead ostrich? I've been to the zoo, at least. There's nothing worse than the smell of ostrich piss. Have you smelled this?"

"No."

"When you're next in a big city, go to the zoo. There's always a zoo, and there's always an ostrich. And where there is an ostrich, there is ostrich piss."

—

We motored along the narrow road into Inverness, the putative goal of our journey, where Borges would at least meet Mr. Singleton to discuss Anglo-Saxon riddles, their shared passion. I had yet to mention my specific hope of visiting George Mackay Brown, thinking he might not like the idea, his mind being so focused on his own preoccupations. But soon, *soon*, I knew I must plunge into this matter, asserting my own needs, seizing this opportunity to visit the subject of my thesis. It would be a pity to lose this chance, with Orkney within a day's easy travel from this part of the Highlands.

Soon Inverness glowed in the pale afternoon sunlight. I said to Borges, "It's a beautiful city, with bright stones that catch the sun and give it back. An orderly place, too, with wide streets, very little traffic." We paused before St. Andrew's Cathedral, called a "must-see landmark" in my guidebook, and Borges insisted that we go inside. "We have been negligent tourists," he said. "I shall have nothing to tell my mother!"

I led him into the church, where the purple stones of the exterior gave way to a nave of five bays made of stern, immovable granite. The pulpit was green marble. We stood before an angel of white stone, and Borges insisted on feeling the sculpted figure with his hands. "My angel," he said. "I'm always surrounded by angels, but they aren't usually so palpable."

"Do you believe in angels?"

"I believe in everything," said Borges.

A man with short white hair appeared at the bottom

of one aisle and drifted in our direction as if walking on a cloud. He wore a black cassock and stopped beside us, looking at us with curiosity, as if we'd landed in a space capsule. He introduced himself as William Burns, "a priest of the cathedral."

"Ah, Burns!" said Borges. "I like the poems of your dear cousin, Robbie Burns. Are you a poet as well, Mr. Burns?"

"I'm just a priest."

I envied this, with its simplicity. I thought I might have made a good priest and had once entertained fantasies of life in a monastery. I often sat in empty churches, not so much praying as floating, letting my feelings attach to the stones of the building, letting the light of the sun break in its prismatic way through high windows. The idea that God should dwell in particular houses intrigued me. It couldn't literally be true. But it wasn't untrue.

"A priest is a poet, sir, and a poet is a priest," said Borges. "*Hieratikos* in Greek. Both are vessels of incarnation. The Word becomes flesh on your tongue."

"I'm not so special."

"Oh, never underestimate your powers, Father Burns."

"I fear that I do." As he said that, a blade of golden sunlight slashed through the window above the altar and cut across the priest's face. I stepped back, almost in fear. The man appeared shockingly humble, stooped, probably underconfident, with large red arthritic knuckles on his hands that suggested years of praying in cold northern rooms.

"Tell me the truth about yourself," said Borges.

"I was unsure of my vocation. It's the only truth."

"How long have you been a priest?"

"Forty-two years and three months."

"So you persist! This is all we ask. You made a choice, and continued in the faith. *Felicidades!* The stream gabbles along. You are the burn, the blaze of water on the landscape, a blister of love. You remain true to the Word."

The priest shuddered, then smiled. "Thank you for saying this."

Borges reached for him, and the priest dipped his head forward. With his hands on the forehead of Father Burns, Borges intoned, *"Si quaesieritis eum, invenietur a vobis; si autem dereliqueritis eum, derelinquet vos."* If you don't abandon the spirit, the spirit will not abandon you. Borges had given the priest a blessing.

Tears rinsed the man's cheekbones. And I thought these were my tears, too. He wept for me, and for all those who engage, or fail to engage, with the spirit that courses through us, throughout the universe. Exactly how we deal with our souls was at this moment the only question I thought worth asking.

Back in the car, rather weirdly, I missed Father Burns and wished we could have talked at greater length with this gentle man.

"Where are you taking me?" Borges asked.

"Into the center of Inverness." I noted the Inverness Palace Hotel, which mirrored Inverness Castle across the river in its russet-tinged stonework. I guessed it had seen better days, but it remained impressive, with turrets and leaded windows, a massive façade. I did my best to describe this architecture but didn't have a wide vocabulary for such things.

"It's the Gothic fantasy!" Borges said. "We shall stay here in this great palace. I feel a little tired, with so much rushing about. And my stumble in the mountains has set me back. There's a throb in the back of my skull. A quiet room is required, and I shall pay for two beds this time. And extra bacon."

"The room may be expensive," I said.

"There's no need for cash in the corridors of oblivion that await me."

We checked in, as he wished, and they gave us a high-ceilinged room on the top floor, with Greek figures on the frieze that crawled in white plaster around the walls. The florid wallpaper with a chartreuse background was so offensive that blindness afforded a blessing to Borges. We had, at least, a single bed for each of us, separated by a chipped wooden table and a dusty lamp. There were fading prints in gilt frames on the walls of legendary Scottish kings: Alexander I, Duncan II, Kenneth II, Donald III, Lulach, and Robert the Bruce. I recited the names to Borges, whose eyelids quivered as if he were trying to push through the gauze of blindness to see the regal faces with their eyes outstaring history.

"Is there a telephone in the hotel?" asked Borges.

"I would guess so."

"Ah, splendid. Wonderful!" Borges handed me the slip of paper from his jacket pocket. "It's time to call

Mr. Singleton. I've waited patiently for years. Invite him for breakfast tomorrow. And when he comes, you must allow us time alone, as we shall burrow into the riddles."

The idea of a breakfast reprieve from Borges sounded good, and I took the slip into the lobby to find a telephone. When I told the manager it was a local call, he invited me into his office to use the phone. "I'm glad to assist," he said.

I dialed the number, but nothing happened. It did not even produce a ring: just a dead silent space. I tried again, without luck.

When I showed the number to the manager, he said, "It's not a Scottish number, sir. Let me see what I can find out." He rang the operator, who told him this was a number in New Zealand. There was apparently an Inverness on the South Island.

With vicarious disappointment, I returned to our room and gave the sad news to Borges, who let out a sigh. "My mother is never clear about these things. And I shall never get to New Zealand. I'm sure you won't drive me there. This encounter is lost, Giuseppe. But I feel I know this man, in any case. His absence registers a kind of presence, perhaps more profound."

"Perhaps."

Borges and I had dinner that night in the gloomy dining room at the hotel, where the wallpaper had the appearance of splattered mud. We were the only diners, apart from a large elderly woman in a purple dress, who kept staring at us. Did we create such a spectacle? Throughout our nondescript meal, Borges said nothing, eating little of his gammon, barely touching the turnips and potatoes. He slumped in his seat, wearier than I'd seen him before, with gravity tugging on the lines in his forehead and cheeks. Was this an effect of his head injury or perhaps his disappointment about Mr. Singleton?

"I feel on the order of woozy," he said as I was about to say how interesting it might be for him to meet George Mackay Brown.

I led him back to the room, making sure that he found the toilet in the hallway outside, then helped him into bed.

"You would make a very good nurse," he said.

I mentioned that Walt Whitman had been a nurse during the Civil War, tending to wounded soldiers, especially his brother—so the vocations of nurse and poet weren't mutually exclusive. This appealed to Borges, who surged back to life.

"Whitman! How I have loved him, your Walt, whom I have translated. Yes, a nurse he was. His brother lay wounded near Fredericksburg. And he devoted himself to the dying young men. He read letters from their mothers, from loved ones. And helped them to write letters home. He bathed their wounds, changed bandages. Some of them died in his arms." He wiped tears from his eyes as he spoke.

"What I most admire about Whitman," Borges said, "is that he created Walt Whitman, an ideal projection, not of himself but someone like him, a character every reader could find in his heart and admire."

With this, he slipped into a sleep so deep it was almost death. As I lay beside him in the adjacent bed, listening to his faint, persistent snore, I wondered if my own work in life was to summon an invented Jay Parini, one who was not me. Or if maybe the person I should try to summon was in fact the *real* me, the truest version of myself. And if I should learn to stand behind this self, this persona, the voice sounding through the mask.

I felt a call to honesty. To say how I felt. To declare myself. And to Bella.

Slipping into the hallway, I sat before a desk in an alcove overlooking the river, which gleamed in the moonlight, and wrote a letter:

My dear Bella,

I hope you don't mind this affectionate opening. I feel such a warmth for you, which is a kind of sexual attraction, I know. A purely animal thing. But I hardly know you, and you don't know me. How many times have we talked? Have we ever really talked except superficially? I love you in ways difficult to explain. I should probably not say such a thing, as perhaps I don't understand fully what the phrase means. Though I think I do.

I felt a fondness for you, an attraction, from the first time I met you at the Poetry Society. (And it was more than your lovely red sneakers!) Even before that, at the protest in Market Street, when I caught a glimpse of you. There was something in the reserve you projected that appealed to me. And the firmness and fire of your convictions. Can one project reserve? I think so. The fire is the fire.

I don't mean to be intrusive, or to sound foolish.

I know I can be ridiculous at times. There's a foolishness in this letter, and a bravado. And I'll say frankly that the circumstances of your relations with Angus are unclear to me. I know that you feel affection for him, that you perhaps love him, and to love anyone is a good and wonderful thing. I don't want to interfere with that.

I wanted to talk this over with you and did try to call from a phone booth in the mountains but didn't persist. You must think I'm a hopeless and unreliable friend. I promised we would have dinner at Pearl of Hong Kong. And here I am in Inverness at the Palace Hotel!

I'm here with Borges. Alastair suddenly had to go to London and left me in charge of the blind old fellow, who is snoring in our bedroom. I'm escorting him through the Highlands on a kind of weird circuit. I have stories to tell. He's not easy. And yet Borges has more stories in his head and heart than anyone alive. He talks incessantly but is rarely boring, though I'm sometimes lost in his chatter. It's like trying to cross a violent stream from one shore to another over stepping stones where it's hard to find a footing. I fall into the icy water but climb to the surface again and continue to the other side. Every day is a crossing, and every day I stumble and fall. But I think I'm learning from him. He takes an otherwise dead universe and animates it, brings everything to life in his blindness, which is a kind of vision itself.

Dear God, I'm chattering like him. I'm under the influence, not only of a couple pints of Export but of Borges himself.

You can be sure I will come to see you when I return in a few days.

I signed the letter "Love, Jay," folded it, and placed it within an envelope I found in the desk, feeling the intense satisfaction of having begun to tell a story in my own way and words. I took the letter downstairs to the front desk and asked them to post it for me in the morning. And damn the torpedoes!

19

AFTER BREAKFAST WE returned to our room, where Borges lay fully dressed on his narrow bed and groaned.

"You're in pain?"

"My head is not perfect," he said. "I feel like Admiral Nelson at the end."

"The Battle of Trafalgar?"

"Ah, Trafalgar, yes. Think of dear old Nelson, hit by a dastardly French sharpshooter who hid in the riggings of a nearby vessel. He said to his lieutenant, 'Hardy, I am shot through. My spine is shattered, and I shall die.' And he died, not an hour later, saying, 'At least I have done my duty.'"

"You have not been shot through," I said.

"Do you challenge me?"

"To a duel? If you like. There are swords in the lobby. Why not?"

He rubbed his temples, crinkling his brow, and I saw that he hadn't quite recovered from his fall into a ditch by the roadside near Aviemore. With reluctance, I handed him one of the potent blue pills that Dr. Brodie had provided. Then gave him another, vaguely recalling the doctor's warning. I myself had had a version of these pills, of course, but they only made matters worse for me, producing nightmares that left me wandering the streets of St. Andrews at night in misery. Which is why I flushed them.

"I shall just close my eyes for a few minutes, and then we shall proceed," he said. I watched him drop, as ever, into profound and childlike sleep.

I went back into the lobby to call Mackay Brown through the hotel manager, who was happy to oblige, having disappointed us with the bad news about Mr. Singleton. It was time to arrange a visit to Orkney, where I would get a sense of the physical place, meet the man himself, and actually hear the human voice behind the words. I might even lay my hands on some original manuscripts, thus pleasing Professor Falconer.

The writer picked up on the second ring. "Hellooo? Is anyone there?" He sounded defensive, cramped, and fearful, and the line was scratchy.

"Mr. Brown, this is Jay Parini. From St. Andrews. We exchanged letters, and you sent me your number. I'm writing a thesis on your work."

"I've only just had the telephone," he said. There was a long pause, with a windy noise on the line. "Can you hear me?"

"Yes, it's working. I hear you."

"Aye, good."

"I'm wondering if I might stop by, Mr. Brown. I'm

in Inverness with a friend, an elderly Argentine writer, a poet, a writer of stories. Like yourself. He's blind."

"I'm not blind."

"No, my friend is blind."

"Oh, dear. This is very bad news."

"I'm guiding him around the Highlands."

"Ah, good lad. And where are you?"

"Inverness."

"Not so far! Then take the ferry."

"The day after tomorrow?"

"Yes, good. There's a ferry in the afternoon from Thurso Bay. I'll meet you at five."

"Where?"

"Stromness, the pier head. How will I recognize you? There are sometimes other passengers, whom one docsn't really see."

It was like a dream ferry, which sometimes deposited ghosts, or fluttering empty sleeves.

"I have longish brown hair. Glasses. My friend is a blind man with a cane." I didn't want to say to Mackay Brown that I would surely recognize him—the scrunched, sun-blasted face I'd seen in photographs, his unruly brown ringlets of hair, and a lower jaw that lunged forward like the bottom drawer of a dresser extended to its full length.

"God has a special place in his heart for the blind," he said.

"Will we find somewhere to stay in Stromness?"

"Of course! I shall ask Hamish at the Strom for a couple of rooms. He's a generous man, especially when he pours a drink. There are rooms above the bar. No need to book."

It worried me that there was no need to book. Such rooms could not be comfortable, but then, this was research. I might learn something!

"I'll see you on Thursday!" he said, and after only a few seconds he shouted, "Can you hear me, sir?"

"Yes, I hear you! The day after tomorrow!"

Borges was animated after a short sleep. "I'm newborn," he said as we got back into my car late in the morning. "Remounted on Rocinante, so we must visit Loch Ness, the home of this terrible and sad monster. Grendel!"

"Nessie," I said.

I noticed that Borges had more than recovered. His skin looked clear and less wrinkled. His high spirits swelled the car, exhausting me slightly.

"These are the same beast, I assure you. Nessie is Grendel."

I seized the moment and put forward my plan for a visit to Orkney to Borges, and he didn't object.

"What a splendid idea," he said. "I want to meet your man, this illustrious poet of the north world!"

Was he mocking me? I gripped the wheel tightly as I drove, my mind drifting to Bella. Had I overstepped the mark in that letter? She might think I'd lost my mind, and she might be right.

We would spend a day at Loch Ness to satisfy Borges and then head to Orkney the following morning, after finding a room at one of the many lodgings by the lake; the guidebook listed several of them. At this point all I wanted was an initial meeting with Mackay Brown, and if things went well, I'd return in a month for a full interview.

"After Orkney," said Borges, "we must stop at Culloden, field of that sad battle. This will provide a climax for our lovely excursion, I'm quite sure."

The site of this ancient battlefield had been calling to him, and I knew we must stop, however briefly, on the way back to St. Andrews. I would keep the visit short—a quick look at the bare field, a place once drenched in blood. I'd read a little about the site, which didn't appeal to me. Enough of battles and blood. It was lucky that Borges was blind and easily distracted and I could elaborate in ways that would satisfy him. "A windswept moor, with the ghosts of dead soldiers." Phrases gathered in my head in advance of this visit. All the while, my eagerness to get back to Bella only grew. I must set things right there.

Stopping for petrol, I looked around nervously at others at the filling station, especially a tall man in a mackintosh. Scotland Yard? I couldn't shake the fantasy that at any moment a policeman might tap me on the shoulder, arrest me, and ship me back to Pennsylvania to enlist in the army or go to jail. (Both of these options were preferable to the little bedroom in my parents' house on South Rebecca Avenue, where a rat-faced stuffed monkey from my childhood still crouched on the headboard, waiting to pounce.)

"I think of monsters quite often," Borges said as we continued on. "They mirror my deepest self, which swims in cold depths, usually at night."

I looked at him sideways as I drove. He seemed

oblivious to everything but his own dreams. I said nothing; yet he had summoned these monsters just when I felt that my own beasts were in need of slaying. I could imagine the jaws, the fine sharp teeth, the long greasy slide into the dark belly of a whale. Yet I would not, like Jonah, be spit up onto dry land in three days.

As I'd read over breakfast, Loch Ness was about twenty miles long and as deep and cold as Borges imagined. Geologists speculated that underground channels may well have run into the Atlantic in former times. In such dark fathoms the myth of Nessie emerged.

"The monster exists, I feel quite sure," Borges rambled to himself more than to me. "Her presence was reported by Saint Adamnan in the seventh century. She attacked one of his fellow monks. The poor soul had fallen from a boat, and she tore his arm from his body and swallowed it whole. I believe she ate his ears—quite tasty, the ears. A delicacy among cannibals."

His straightforward and uninflected tone and apparent lack of irony made me want to challenge him.

"Nessie is a myth," I said.

"*Mythos*, in Greek," said Borges, "is not a story that is false, it's a story that is more than true. Myth is a tear in the fabric of reality, and immense energies pour through these holy fissures. Our stories, our poems, are rips in this fabric as well, however slight. Think of *Beowulf*. The prototype for Nessie lies there, in the figure of Grendel, a fallen angel. Envious of the light, he lived with his difficult mother in a cave. You and I have lived in this cave as well, with our difficult and exacting mothers. We bear the marks of our captivity, but we survive."

"I hardly feel like I'm surviving," I said.

Though I tried to shut it out, my mother's voice sounded in my head, with its random warnings. I could imagine her now: "Don't even *think* of going to that lake. Loch Ness! It's deep, and it's cold. There's a monster? Even Nello wouldn't swim there." Nello was my father's oldest brother, the black sheep among the five brothers. I hardly knew him, but even glimpses in childhood sent a shock through my nervous system: that face like an ax blade. I thought of him and sighed.

"Oh, Sancho! You exhale, again and again! This sadness! Don't question survival, mine or yours. More powers lie at your disposal than you realize." There was a faintly beatific glow about his head as the eastern light wrapped around him. "I recall those lines in *Beowulf* where Grendel emerges from the fens. The sky glowers, in contrast to the shining mead hall, where light and music blast out. This is the eternal city, the mead hall. A place of singing—and this is what we have at our disposal, you and I. Song!"

I found him annoying, with this blithe enthusiasm.

"Grendel was a monster," I said.

"I'm a monster, too. You're a monster. There are no human beings who do not have Nessie or Grendel in their hearts. We swim in dark waters, especially at night. I wake trembling. Don't you?"

I did, but I didn't want to think about that now. Borges had found me where it hurt, and I resisted the intrusion. I didn't want to think about anything except, perhaps, getting to Orkney. That must be my goal. If I could actually get some original manuscripts from

Mackay Brown, I had a chance of surviving Falconer's skepticism. This would be "research," and nobody could claim otherwise. If the manuscripts were interesting and helpful, revealing something of value about the poet, so much the better.

Yet Borges refused to let go. His lips moved silently, a prelude to his next rhetorical volley. "You were a god once, as Emerson has reminded us. And then envy arrived in the world. You thought, as did I, that others possessed more of everything. More love, more talent, more affection from their father on the throne."

It was true enough. Others exceeded me in talent, in potential.

"I just don't know enough," I said.

"Nor I," said Borges. "But we all proceed on insufficient knowledge."

What an idea, I thought. Helpful, encouraging.

As he would, Borges slipped into reverie, allowing me to listen to his thoughts. "I had Eden once," he said, "as a young man. Back in Palermo, I would stop by the villa of Norah and her family. Her mother was Eve before the Fall: Señora Berta Erfjord de Lange. She presided over three beautiful daughters, Haydée, Chichina, and Norah. Each of them reflected her red hair, but Norah's was fire itself. Fire! I was singed, then banished from paradise. I fell for decades into the solipsism of my own passionless existence. I lived on what I call Tlön, the ideal and dreadful world of perfection, where there's no love." He twisted his lips in a way unfamiliar to me, more than a mere wince. "No love, only the cold symmetry of perfect ideas."

I tried to absorb this blizzard of facts and fantasies. It wasn't easy to follow Borges, but his anguish was unmistakable. And I felt sorry for him. He was an old man, and time had flown over his head. He stared at death, and must have wondered about all he had missed, especially in his lost love for Norah Lange. I could, I think for the first time, appreciate the agony of this.

When we got to Fort Augustus, a village at the southwestern tip of Loch Ness, we pulled over and sat together in front of the Viking Arms Hotel, with its heavily leaded Tudor-style windows and oak doors. It looked out over the indigo water from a slight prospect. Above us, gulls sliced the air, their cries like warnings.

"We can probably find a room for the night," I said. "Or two."

"Where?"

"The Viking Arms. It's behind us."

"I want to fall into the arms of a Viking," said Borges. "They have beautiful women, so tall, with clear porcelain skin. Their hearts are brave."

I left Borges to his Nordic fantasies and stepped into the inn, where a woman appeared at my elbow and introduced herself as Ailith McTaggart. She was strong-limbed and blond, with a hard exterior and cornflower-blue eyes. Her jaw had firm, clean lines, and she had a coiled energy that appealed to me. A brave spirit shimmered through her flesh.

"Are you needing a room then?"

"Yes."

"So," she said, "we have one."

"Only one?"

"Yes. But it has two beds. I saw you through the window, with your grandfather."

"He's a friend, an Argentine poet."

"Aye."

I guessed she was the same age as me, although her steadiness and firmness added about a decade to her frame.

"You're an American?"

"From Pennsylvania, yes, but I'm living in St. Andrews." I gave her my concise biographical spiel, perfected in the past few months. I was "doing research on a Scottish poet" and hoped "one day to teach." I added, with a measure of bravado, that I also hoped to make my living as a writer.

"A writer! My da' has written a pamphlet," she said. "You should talk to him. It's about Nessie, the monster in our lake. It's available in the bar for a quid." She rummaged in a drawer in the desk and found one. "You can have this. A gift."

She appeared glad to chat, telling me about her time as a student in Edinburgh at Heriot-Watt, assuming (rightly) that this would interest me. She studied at the university for a year, she explained, but then her mother died unexpectedly and she moved back to Loch Ness, where she helped her father to look after the inn.

"What was your subject?"

"Geoscience. I'll get back to it, one day soonish. There's a research branch of Heriot-Watt on Orkney."

This seemed too coincidental. But with Borges in tow, I had begun to take the uncanny for granted. "We're going to Orkney tomorrow," I said.

She smiled at this, with a touch of envy. "It's so close, and yet I never go there. My father says, *Ailith, I'll take you.* But who would look after the inn?" I liked the way she talked so openly about these choices. Her father obviously meant a great deal to her.

"While we're here, if it's possible, we'd like to take a boat ride," I said. "My friend is keen to go onto the loch."

"So you're lucky. We've a motorboat and a rowing boat."

"A rowboat is better," I said, knowing Borges would prefer that.

Soon Ailith walked us both to the shoreline, with her father behind us. Mr. McTaggart was under sixty, but the skin of his cheeks and forehead had cracked and splintered, and the backs of his hands resembled the shell of an old tortoise. A scar zigzagged across his cheek under his beard, and I wondered if he had a past that required concealing.

"Here you go," Ailith said, untying a boat from a frail dock, a little anxious about our marine adventure. "You've done this before, I would assume?"

I assured her that I'd had lots of experience in rowboats back in Pennsylvania. There was very little to know, in any case, and I didn't worry about my skills. I helped Borges onto the dock, gripping his free hand firmly, then settled him into the aft of the wobbly boat. An inch or so of water pooled around our feet, a leakage from the keel, which had known fresher times. Borges rolled up his cuffs, but his shoes would need drying out overnight.

Ailith pushed us off with worry on her face. Her

father hovered behind her with a grim look, his arms folded at his chest.

"You're a magus," Borges said to me as we slipped into the loch, "finding this boat."

"Keep it steady," Ailith called from the dock. "Slow, smooth strokes are best!"

As we slipped into what felt like a stream below the surface, Borges tilted his face upward, allowing the radiance of the late-morning sun to soak in, his lips moving as they often did when he felt excited by his thoughts, as if reading something from a page in his head. Soon he began to hum, a low discordant sound that played against the dripping oars, the click of the oarlocks. Water curled around the bow.

"Tell me what you see. Speak! I see only a blur of light."

"The shore is nearby. Ailith's father stands with his arms folded. She herself is watching us carefully."

"Ailith is an Old English name. She's a warrior. Does she look belligerent?"

"No. Slender, strong. There's a confidence there."

"She's tall?"

"Rather tall, yes. Thin."

"Androgynous?"

"A touch of the masculine."

"As with many beautiful women." He let one of his hands dangle in the water. "Tell me," he said, "is she as beautiful as your Bella?"

"I think so," I said. In truth, I found his conversation oddly disembodied. Borges hadn't lived in his flesh and bones, had not moved through the seasons of the skin with much awareness. The vast library of his mind pre-occupied him. Women for him were mythic creatures, and he clung to a code of courtly love, with the man as knight in love with an inaccessible (and often married) woman; this passion would rarely be consummated. He frequently mentioned Beatrice, Dante's female spell-binder, one who leads a man into the light.

"Don't be silent, Giuseppe! Talk about the setting today," Borges said. "You are my eyes, remember. You're failing me!"

"The setting?"

I looked around, fetching images. "The hills run down to the lake," I told him. "They're steep. No houses in sight. Some sort of vegetable life on them. Bracken? There are trees nearer to the water, tall pines with a red-dish bark. White rocks at the shoreline."

"A bright smile of shingle," said Borges. "I hear the lapping of waves. 'Doom is dark and deeper than any sea-dingle.' A wonderful line from Auden. He is fond of Anglo-Saxon verse. That alliterative voice, the play of consonantal rhyme. *Maravilloso!* The *Beowulf* poet was master of this method, too. So difficult to replicate in Spanish. Impossible, really."

"I've read very little Auden."

"You'll love him, Giuseppe. He's a very intelligent poet, and the language is brisk, witty, mixing high and low."

I rowed for a few minutes, slowly and with care, seeing that our soft glide pleased my passenger. The lake whirled about us, and Borges touched his forehead with wet fingers, as if blessing himself in preparation for a mass.

As if summoned, a fish splashed in the water nearby.

"Nessie approaches," said Borges.

"Some kind of trout, I think. They leap for bugs." I looked over the oarlocks to see the bottom of the lake perhaps eight feet below. We weren't far out.

"Let's drift, dear boy. I have keen ears, and will hear things you won't hear."

I rested the oars in the locks. It was astonishingly calm now, with gulls hanging in the sky like tiny kites. Ailith stood on the dock with her eyes on us, not twenty yards away. Her father stood behind her.

Rashly, Borges rose to his full height, making the boat rock.

"Be careful, Borges!"

He shifted his weight from side to side to keep his balance, then raised his cane to the sky. In a full-throated voice, he bellowed some lines of what sounded like Anglo-Saxon verse, which doubled back on themselves in the form of echo.

"Sit down, and carefully!" I did my best to steady the boat.

"This is the Song of Creation," Borges said. "It celebrates the music within us, how we can in dark moments sing! It caused such fury in Grendel, who was mad that men could sing like this, could soothe and inspire themselves and others. The song is about origins, how the Almighty shaped the earth with his hands, laid out the fields, bounded them by water, hung the skies with the sun and moon, lamps for his poor creatures. He lifted the trees, spread them with limbs and leaves, and breathed life into every turtle, frog, lizard, bird, and beast! The men and women of the world shivered with joy."

"Sit down, please!"

"Then Grendel arrived, the fiend from hell. This is Nessie, dear boy! And now, yes, Nessie approaches!"

He swung his cane with two hands like a claymore.

"Borges, no!" I shouted, but too late. He lurched forward, his knees quivering, his lips in a pout, and toppled into my arms. I could smell the stale sweat of his armpits, and his rough cheek brushed against me. I tried to push him away without destabilizing the boat, which in a crazy, blurry instant capsized.

I had no time to absorb what had happened, or to feel fear. The water dazed me, and I wanted only to bolt for the shore. But what about Borges? I opened my eyes underwater and frantically searched for him. Though underwater, he lifted his face to the surface and smiled enigmatically—a child caught with fingers in the cookie jar. I'd been trained as a lifeguard and reached for him, gripping him by the collar just a couple of feet below the surface. With my free arm I pulled us up the water's frosty ladder.

Somehow Borges still clung to his cane with one hand, grasping me with the other.

"Try to float on your back," I said, putting a hand under his wet jacket. I could see his leather shoes dragging his feet down.

The rowboat bobbed nearby, upside down, and I

dragged Borges toward it, needing something for us to hold, even though it wasn't so deep, and my feet touched the bottom. Soon I saw Ailith and her father churning in our direction in the motorboat, and within moments they hovered beside us. Ailith crouched at the tiller while her bearded father scowled, shaking his head. Our little stunt had not pleased him.

I felt like an idiot, knowing that one should never take an old blind man who can't swim in a rowboat, especially when this person is childlike, irascible, and unpredictable. Where was my fucking mind?

Borges proved surprisingly agile, and he managed to get one foot onto their rope ladder. Then I helped to lift—*heave* is a better word—his bulk into the bow of the waiting boat. McTaggart used his muscular forearms to help, and before long Ailith wrapped the soaking Borges in a woolen blanket and pulled a cloth cap over his head. "You'll be fine, sir," she said. "We'll dry you out at the inn."

Borges muttered something to himself, his lips blue. The whiteness of his cheeks suggested a state of shock, as did his labored breathing. The blank eyes rolled in his head as he clutched at his cane. And I regarded him as sorrow itself, a man whose venture into the Song of Creation had, at least this time, unmade him.

That evening the four of us sat in the bar by a fire. Because neither Borges nor I had brought a change of clothes, I wore a pair of trainers and a shirt that a previous guest had left behind, and Borges was forced to wear

McTaggart's castoffs—a pair of twill trousers and a baggy sweater. He didn't even look like Borges.

Ailith assured him that within hours they would dry and press his suit and shirt, even his tie; a woman at the inn would like the challenge, she explained. She herself would dry and shine the leather shoes. "We'll make you a new man," she said.

"The old Borges will do," he said.

As I watched him, safe and snug by the fire, it struck me how rarely the physical aspects of reality impinged on his daily life. Even his walk—splay-footed, gingerly, as if he were stepping over blazing coals with bare feet—suggested a hesitance in his attachment to this earth. Loch Ness had been for him an idea, not a body of icy water that could easily drown a man.

"What happened out there?" asked McTaggart, who lit a pipe and settled in a captain's chair.

"Grendel," said Borges.

This produced hardly a flicker of interest from McTaggart, whose eyes lifted to a corner of the room, but his daughter brightened. "I read *Beowulf* in school," she said.

"The Song of Creation, this is my favorite part," Borges said. "I was reciting this passage when the monster approached and overturned our boat. Do you still like poetry?"

"Oh, I do," she said. "I write a bit of it myself now and then."

I could see him perking up in the presence of this beautiful Nordic woman, an after-echo of young Norah Lange. And one who wrote a bit of poetry!

"I know a tune from the Song of Creation," Ailith said. "We have a folk club here on Sunday nights."

"Oh, do sing! I will become your fan."

Almost as if she'd been expecting the request, she pulled a guitar from a nearby cupboard and delivered a lyrical folk version of the Song of Creation, drawing on a Celtic melody that I vaguely recognized. Her father nursed a pint of ale and listened with his mouth open, as if tasting the words his daughter sang.

When she finished, Borges clapped with boyish abandon.

"She wants an audience," said McTaggart.

"She's found one," I said.

"Do you have another song, my dear?" Borges asked.

"I should be delighted. I could even dance!" He stood now, with the blanket around him, and did a kind of sideways shuffle.

His unabashed and complete recovery shocked me. Was it possible? Hadn't he nearly drowned in Loch Ness that morning? Was he just used to pratfalls and lunges? Was this, bizarrely, par for the course as he motored or soared through time and space? Was it somehow even part of his poetic life, how he created the world with his own longings in spite of everything that conspired against him, including his blindness?

It had been a long day, and we'd have to make it to the Pentland Firth by early afternoon to catch the ferry to Stromness. So I bid Ailith goodnight and thanked her for everything she'd done for us.

"I've always wanted to go to Orkney," she said.

"Then you shall be my guest," Borges informed her. "I shall pay for your ticket, your meals, and lodging as well. But I shall not be accompanying you and Giuseppe."

"You're not coming to Orkney?"

"No, Giuseppe! This adventure on the loch—I do not wish to get into another boat with you. And in truth, I'm weary. The throb in my skull returns."

I felt a flicker of disappointment, even annoyance—I had genuinely looked forward to seeing what would happen when Borges met George Mackay Brown—but the feeling was snuffed by a bigger one: relief.

"Thank you, sir. I shall go with your friend," Ailith said. "Da' will look after you. He's a sweetheart."

This remark drove her "da'" from the room, though Borges remained unaware of anything awkward. His blindness allowed him to live within his circumference, excluding noxious elements. A gift, in its way. For me, I could only tremble with a kind of giddy anticipation. Ailith and I would be going to Orkney, the two of us.

After Borges had gone to bed, I sat in a parlor downstairs and preemptively wrote to Bella, riddled with minor guilt about my upcoming adventures with Ailith, however they might unfold. I gave her a florid account of our hapless tour of the Highlands, taking up where I had left off in my previous embarrassing letter, trying to talk over that, asking, "Can this be happening in what now passes for 'real life,' or have I wandered into a land of unlikeness?"

I pushed the envelope into a pillar box outside the Viking Arms that night with the usual misgivings.

Maybe I should have kept my mouth shut and let the relationship with Bella unfold as it would or—more likely—wouldn't. Hadn't I been stricken by self-doubts after sending the previous one? Then again, I needed to write to her. Why shouldn't I tell my story, find my own way of talking?

20

I took Borges his breakfast on a tray: a plate of burnt bacon, boiled eggs, toast, a mug of tea, and a couple of blue pills, which I warned him to parcel out carefully.

He swallowed both of the pills at once, downing them with a gulp of tea. "I don't need to parcel. You nearly drowned me yesterday," he said. "I felt as if I floated through the night. I woke this morning like a beached whale."

"You look fine." I reached for his wrist to feel for his pulse. "It's ticking."

"It is Big Ben. *Gong, gong, gong.*"

"Will you be all right here by yourself?"

"I savor a quiet night without interruption," he said. "One should realize I'm far too old for dangerous boats, for monsters like Grendel!"

I looked out the window at the lake, trying to collect my patience. "I've gone out of my way for you, Borges. I put aside a full week of my research. You might have badly hurt yourself when you fell off the road in the mountains or nearly drowned yourself—or me," I said.

"It's a good thing that little accident happened close to shore."

"I must apologize—you're quite right. You were valorous in the lake, reaching into the depths to retrieve me, though you nearly strangled me." He touched his neck with one hand. "Are there marks from your fingers?"

There was no way around him, I realized, and sighed. At this moment he reminded me of no one so much as my mother.

"I worry about you, Giuseppe," he said, turning the blank yet burning headlamps of his eyes toward me. "Is something wrong? I can't see you, but you look terrible."

In truth I'd had a wretched night, feeling guilty about Bella for no reason, and instead of being excited about the trip with Ailith or the meeting with Mackay Brown, I had begun to rummage through a number of pathetic old poems in my notebook, most of them about unrequited love. "My life is fucked up," I said.

"Nothing in Spanish quite conveys the tang of this American phrase, its thoroughness of feeling."

"Sometimes I'm lost. I don't know . . ."

"*Una selva oscura.*"

"What?" Would I never stop asking what?

"I refer to the opening lines of the *Commedia*. We find ourselves in Dante's dark wood, again and again. We must each of us, one by one, descend into hell through layers of blackness. Of course, I admit to envy of Paolo and Francesca, the whirling lovers. They feasted on the body of the beloved. Let me confess I have never had this pleasure. The banquet of the gods was never offered. My marriage, it has been a sham."

Oh, Borges, please stop! I wanted to say.

"I've had no physical pleasure in this union."

"I'm sorry. That's sad."

"Sad, yes. And you are a virgin, too, I believe."

"Yes," I said, too ashamed to say more, being (as Alastair had wryly noted) the last twenty-two-year-old virgin in the Age of Aquarius.

"This is purity," said Borges. "It moves me. My own virginity and yours, but mostly yours."

I picked at the lint from my trousers, a result of its recent spin in the Viking Inn's dryer. "I hate purity."

"You'll be a fallen man before long, I assure you. Miss Law is your revelation, your path," said Borges. "Climb her ladder to heaven, as Plato suggested." He paused to nibble on a burnt length of bacon. "But I will admit, dear boy, that it's probably not with Bella that your life will become . . . unfucked up. Is this an expression?"

Before I could respond, a knock came at the door. It was Ailith. She wore a colorful tam with blond curls streaming below it, a thick Arran sweater, and black jeans. Her work boots needed a polish. I didn't especially like the rough tomboy look but admired her ease of being, the insouciance.

"You must have a good day and a wonderful night," said Borges, raising his hand like a bishop to bestow a blessing.

"He'll be fine with Da'," Ailith said when we stood outside the hotel. "He's responsible. More or less."

"I'm not worried."

"You look worried."

"I'm not."

But I was. My caretaker instincts quickened, and I didn't want Borges to feel abandoned. I hated to abandon anyone, as when I had left my mother that first time in New York in her bewilderment and grief. I felt guilty then. Now I felt guilty about Borges! ("If you were a Jew," Jeff had recently said, "it would be Yom Kippur every day.")

"You're too good to him," Ailith said. "I want a husband like you."

"I'm available," I said.

This drew a wry smile, and I felt a lightening. We would get along well.

"I know your man, by the way," she said, "George Mackay Brown. I read a book of his stories last year."

"Really?"

"I can read, yes." She put a hand on my arm to say, *Not to worry.* "It will be good to meet him. Even better to meet Orkney."

As we drove off together, there was a feeling of freedom combined with a delicious anticipation about being alone with Ailith. I'd never been in a confined space with an attractive woman—not in circumstances as intimate as this. And Orkney beckoned, with the prospect of meeting a man I had admired from a distance for several years. The deeper I'd moved into writing my thesis on Mackay Brown, the more I had idealized his life on a bare and beautiful island. And the more I had grown to envy the way he'd managed to cut himself off from the greater world and its distractions. It buoyed me to think that within hours I would stand beside this man who until now had seemed like a character I'd brought to life in the accumulating pages of my thesis, not a flesh-and-blood person.

"Are you nervous about meeting Mr. Brown?" Ailith asked.

"I guess so."

"You're afraid of him. I can tell. Remember, he's only a man."

"Jittery and skittish. That's me," I said.

She reached across the front seat and seized my hand, which had settled on the gearshift, and I felt a mysterious thrill. Was she only being kind? Did she wish to comfort me? She withdrew the hand but looked quite happy beside me throughout the trip to Thurso Bay, where the Orkney ferry would set off. I'd have given more than a penny for her real thoughts, but I didn't want to interfere with the sweet happy silence filling the car like sunlight as we drove north. The fine balance between us was an applecart I had no wish to upset.

By early afternoon we had arrived at the postage stamp of a harbor, with its cluster of activity around the ferry. Leaving Rocinante in the car park above the docks, we filed onto the ship with half a dozen others. I didn't like the look of the sky, however, with violet-and-black clouds pushing from the northeast. A low-voiced driving wind ruffled our hair, the flag on the ferry snapping.

"Expect weather in the Firth," said Ailith.

It would be a journey of about two hours on this rusty

nautical bucket named the *Saint Ola,* which had made this crossing a thousand times, in every sort of weather. We stood on the high aft deck, where we could wave to the crowd on the pier below, if there had been a crowd. This afternoon only a single old man with a peaked cap signaled to a jowly woman in a slicker who wept beside me.

"Parting lovers?" Ailith whispered.

"He's a bit old for that."

"So the urge vanishes? I don't think so."

The remark was frank and unabashed, and it surprised me. Her blunt cheerfulness was appealing, too, creating an atmosphere of no-nonsense affability. That she had chosen to live at the Viking Arms and look after her father was in its way admirable—a sign of character. I thought of her as a woman with firm, clean, inviolable lines.

In the bar on the ferry, off the aft deck, Ailith seemed quite excited by the prospect of our little adventure. "I've wished to see Scapa Flow," she said, "where fleets have anchored for centuries. During the Great War, the Germans scuttled their ships rather than let the British have them. During the last war, the Germans sank the *Royal Oak*—a huge defeat for the British navy."

"You know your history," I said.

"Don't patronize me," she said.

"I didn't mean to do that."

"*Didn't mean* isn't good enough."

The sea darkened suddenly, with a black wing overhead, and the waves began to churn. According to the bartender, who gathered glasses and cups into a basket for safekeeping, we were in for "a rocky passage." The waves, he estimated, were already at six to ten feet.

Almost at once I felt decidedly unwell.

"I should wander to the rail," I said to Ailith, flashing a look of worry.

On the back deck again, I leaned over the rail and puked into the sea. Some of the vomit splashed back onto my shoes and trousers: a rank smell. Ailith stood beside me with a hand on my back.

"Can I help?"

"I think I should go below," I said. "It might be steadier."

"Are you sure?"

I was quite sure, and climbed in a wavering fashion down a metal stairway to a large public room, where two or three liverish passengers slumped at wooden tables. I joined them, burying my head in my hands, trying to absorb the shock of the ferry's side-to-side roll, which had grown more exaggerated. Cups of tea or coffee spilled onto the floor, and a young woman at the next table heaved into a brown bag. A rancid smell hung in the air, and one large woman wept loudly in a chair beside me. "I want to die," she said.

This crossing could not, in my opinion, end soon enough.

The sky still looked miserably dark as we approached Orkney, a scowl on the horizon, with the ship edging past a stone breakwater into the well-protected harbor at Stromness. Any number of vessels lay at anchor, and it was a relief to see the smooth surface of the water. I could feel the backwash of the propellers as our ferry slowed and docked with a thud. A dozen men in blue overalls and boots leaped into action, and lines were tossed and tied. Chains rattled, and the gangplank was lowered into place.

Once we were in dock, my seasickness disappeared, so I'd not be retching over the rail in front of George Mackay Brown. The stench of vomit rose from my jeans, and my shoes were stained. I couldn't hide these signs of my recent distress, but at least I was returned to the world of the living. Maybe this was me in the Jonah role, coming back to life? But how many times must I be swallowed and spat out?

"You sure you're okay?" Ailith asked as we disembarked, stepping onto the solid pier.

"Is anyone ever sure of that?"

I tried to wipe the worst of the vomit from my shoes, but no amount of wiping could erase that odor.

21

I STOOD AWKWARDLY on the wharf between Ailith and George Mackay Brown, who met us as promised, stepping into my world as if from nowhere: the spirit made flesh before me.

"Aye, you're here," Mackay Brown said. "They don't often come. A lot of chatter, but they don't come."

I was glad not to have to count myself among their shameful company, though I wasn't sure who "they" were.

His silvery eyes looked at me searchingly, as if trying to discern something. There was a faint smell of old beeswax about him. The leather boots he wore looked two sizes too big for his feet, and his trousers didn't fit well either.

It was just too strange, talking to the subject of my thesis and seeing the face and ringlets of wild hair that I'd studied in photographs. I extended a hand, which he reluctantly took in both of his big ones—the hands of a farmer or fisherman, not a writer, with stiff white bristles of hair on their backs. His nails were dark brown, probably stained by tobacco, chewed and uneven.

"And where is the blind man," he said, "your writer from the Argentine?"

"He wasn't feeling well," I said. "We left him to rest at the hotel."

"What a shame. He's Borges then?"

"Yes. How did you know?"

"I made an assumption, because he's from Argentina, I suppose. And Alastair has translated him. One of the finest writers of our time, with a speculative mind, those labyrinthine ways."

This unsettled me. All the world seemed to know more about Borges than I did.

He put a hand out for Ailith to shake. "And your name, my dear?"

"Ailith, from Loch Ness. Your friend fished me from the loch."

"With a strong line, no?" He laughed at his own joke. "You bring cheer, which is welcome here. The tourists usually fetch diseases. Summer colds are the worst—although in a way I like a good illness, an excuse to stay home with the hot toddy and so forth."

"But you stay home mostly, don't you?" I said.

"You think you know me because you're my chronicler, my devoted critic, is this so? My very own Boswell. I shall be careful of what I say, as you will record me for posterity. Very dangerous to repeat what others say. My mother's first and last lesson. And what a gossip she was, the old lass!"

With an inaudible whoosh, the clouds parted above us, the sun breaking through and sharpening the sea, its harsh edges glassy in late-afternoon light. The waterfront acquired a rose-and-gold tint.

"I'll take you both to Hamish later to get your rooms, but for now you will come for tea," said Mackay Brown.

A cold wind swept the pier, upending a bin for litter, and Mackay Brown rushed to stand it up again.

"I'm sorry for the north wind," he said, "a knife at the throat in these parts."

"It's colder here than on the mainland," said Ailith.

"Than on Loch Ness, I'm sure of it. You get the western breezes, the gulf air." Now he recited a poem from memory:

O western wind, when wilt thou blow
that the small rain down can rain?
Christ, that my love were in my arms
And I in my bed again!

The famous lyric burned a hole in the air, as he must have hoped it would; I only wished that Borges had been with us. He'd have loved to hear this recital in Mackay Brown's lovely and precise Celtic voice, and would have added something of his own, probably in Anglo-Saxon or Old Norse.

"Quite perfect, the little poem, would you agree?" Mackay Brown said. "But it's rarely a small rain in Orkney, and my bed is empty."

The lyric's deep, lonely cry of need, at once beautiful and painful, had somehow evaded me until now, however many times I'd read it.

As we followed along the harbor road, Mackay Brown talked with a kind of random energy and natural lyricism that excited me. I wished I could simply write down everything he said in my journal, but that would have overwhelmed him. The idea that I could somehow miss something worried me. This would all be pure gold when I sat down in St. Andrews to resume work. And Professor Falconer would at last believe in what I was doing. I had gone to the source.

The council house at Mayburn Court was not far, part of a block of whitewashed cottages that huddled together: the usual bleak postwar construction that had become a blight in Scotland. Mackay Brown hadn't bothered to latch the door; this was Orkney, after all. We stepped straight into the kitchen, which was cramped. Jam pots and butter, with bits of leftover toast, were scattered on the tabletop, with an old Bible in the center of the table. (I flashed back to my father's King James Bible in Scranton, with its busy marginalia and underlined passages, and wondered if Mackay Brown liked to hover over the Bible's pages with a pen in hand.) A notebook lay open beside the butter dish, with the writer's easily recognizable crabwise scrawl in bold azure ink.

"A poem?" I asked.

He blushed, closing the notebook. "I'm as always in the middle of something. Or nothing," he said. "One does or doesn't respond to the music of the world with a competing music, note upon note. It's a bit insolent even to try, is it not then?"

He spoke with a quiet purr, a lilt, a melody in his syntax. One could have set what he said to music.

"Please, do sit, both of you," he said. "We do not stand on formalities in Orkney. I'll put on the kettle."

I watched Ailith watching him, and I could see that he compelled her attention. She listened to him with her lips slightly parted, sometimes grinning.

The writer shuffled around the kitchen, obviously at home in his self-enclosed world. Again I thought of my father and how he occupied the kitchen from dawn till he left for work. He commandeered the stove, scrambling eggs. He produced endless pieces of toast and would slice apples and bananas into my cereal bowl, as if I needed help.

I liked to think that here, at this actual table, Mackay Brown had probably written many of his best works. (I had copies of his recent book, *A Spell for Green Corn*, and a volume of his *New and Selected Poems* in my rucksack, hoping he might inscribe them for me.) An early volume of his poems, *Loaves and Fishes*, lay on a counter beside the bread box. Could he have left that out on purpose? It's the kind of gesture I could imagine myself making, were I ever lucky enough to be in his position, but I didn't think he would do it, as he seemed a modest man without a strong wish for affirmation.

"This was my mother's place before me," Mackay Brown told us. "She only recently died, poor wee thing. Bronchitis it was that swept her to sea."

"You've stayed close to home," I said.

"Aye. Home is good. What does your man Frost say? 'Home is where they have to take you in.'"

Home *was* good, I realized, and thought again about my family in Pennsylvania. That had been a reassuring world in many ways. My father's kindness and modesty suited him well, and was a gift to those around him. Even my mother's madness had a giddy edge of self-parody about it, and she told stories with relish. I'd loved sitting at the table of my Italian grandmother on the weekends, eating her hand-cut linguine with ragu. I'd seen her meticulously cutting the strips with a razor blade on big sheets of waxed paper the day before and had always admired the patience and skill of her work. "Who's a-gonna cut the pasta if I don't?" she would ask.

"I tend to live between the house and the harbor," Mackay Brown continued, "between Ness Road and the pier head."

I thought of Thoreau, who had "traveled much in Concord."

Soon there was tea and toast, with plenty of marmalade, and a plate of knobby shortbread fingers baked by his neighbor, whom he called "the widow Duff." To add to the amplitude, Mackay Brown unwrapped a roll of digestive biscuits and put them on the table with a packet of onion crisps. "Help yourself, please," he said, waving a hand in a gesture of bounty. "There's more where this came from."

Ailith took a handful of biscuits and grinned like my sister used to grin when my father handed over fig cookies. He always said without irony, "The figs will make you regular." The greatest terror that swept all of Scranton was the fear of "irregularity."

Mackay Brown was wildly different from the unstoppable Borges, who would say whatever he thought whenever he thought it, running along siderails of speculation with a kind of signature compulsiveness. No feeling went unexpressed for long. No thought searched in vain for matching words. If anything, Borges was language itself. "What are you thinking, Giuseppe?" he would say, almost shouting at me. "Tell me what lies below! Speak!"

Breaking an uncomfortably long silence, Ailith mentioned her time as a student in Edinburgh. "I love the city," she said, recalling that Mackay Brown had been a student there as well. "The view of the castle, it's fine."

"Fine, yes. You've heard about my student days?" he asked.

"I read this about you in the papers."

"Oh dear. I like to think I'm anonymous. I should never have put a name to my books. Anonymous would do. He or she was the greatest writer of all time, Anonymous."

"But you liked Edinburgh?"

"Is anything more beautiful? Princes Street and the Scott Monument, and, as you say, the castle on the hill! I was a young interloper on Rose Street, in the pubs where the poets met to drink and argue."

"Did you meet Hugh MacDiarmid?" I asked.

"And I did," he said. "A difficult wee man. Gifted in his way. Not my way."

I had actually met MacDiarmid myself in a pub in Edinburgh, after a literary gathering where he had read aloud from *A Drunk Man Looks at the Thistle*. We had talked for a brief while in an unsatisfying, incoherent way. He was probably lost in a haze of alcohol. Any number of pretty young women gathered around him, eager for contact with the great man, which I was certain, if I could trust the expression in his eyes, he'd be only too happy to provide.

When the last shortbread finger was gone and we had each finished a second cup of tea, Mackay Brown announced that it was "time for the Strom." I could see that, unlike Alastair, he didn't like literary chitchat. There would be no ranking of poets or novelists in this kitchen, no casual dropping of names.

On the way to the Stromness Inn, I couldn't help but wonder about the sleeping arrangements ahead of us. Would Mackay Brown, a passionately frugal man, really have asked for two rooms?

As I watched Ailith walking ahead of me, the alluring Ingibiorg in Mackay Brown's "Viking Testament" flashed into my head. She was the "tallest of women," as he said. I thought of pulling him aside to make an inside joke about this but restrained myself. It would never do, in his austere company, to make an ingratiating gesture—which in any case was not required, as he must already know of my allegiance. Was there another student in Britain who had chosen him as a doctoral subject? I was breaking ground with this work, despite Falconer's worries.

Being in Mackay Brown's presence thrilled but also disconcerted me. He was an unlikely creature, with his distorted features and inwardness, his self-possessed attitude bordering on contempt for the outside world, his blunt, pervasive kindness. I could tell even from our limited interaction that his natural sternness combined with an impulse to generosity that had no bounds, as signified by the digestive biscuits and shortbread fingers, his overflowing teapot. I could imagine the beneficence of his soul and found myself loving that quality in him. What I admired most about his stories, and the secret to their charm, was that he invariably shined warmth on his characters, loving them unreservedly—even the dissolute and desperate ones. Perhaps especially those.

We rounded a corner where, on a bench, several witchlike creatures sat with pinched faces. One of them berated Mackay Brown, as if he were persona non grata in Orkney, calling him a "radge wee shite" and a "hackit Jessie." He waved off these insults, which must have been familiar, and I couldn't help but think of "Old Women," his peerless sonnet, which begins:

Go sad or sweet or riotous with beer
Past the old women gossiping by the hour.
They'll fix on you from every close and pier
An acid look to make your veins run sour.

He had surveyed the local scene with a curious eye, a generous ear, and drawn from this rich material a trove of verse and story. That some might find him too inquisitive didn't surprise me. He was, after all, a loner, a man at the edge of his own small circle. He was also its judge, psychoanalyst, and priest. As I realized this, ideas for my thesis began to spark, and I knew I must make notes after dinner. It would be easy to lose these insights in the din of travel, with its dislocations and lack of creature comforts. It frustrated me to have only a single evening with

Mackay Brown, and I considered staying for a month next time, becoming a student of this universe. I must cut these strips of linguine patiently and skillfully!

We stepped from the mist-filled dark of dusk into a warm, fire-lit bar, where the publican beamed. He had been expecting us.

"This is Hamish," Mackay Brown said, gesturing.

Hamish was an oversized elf from the North Pole who stepped forward with a fantailed beard and mottled nose, which seemed to have been laid on for effect: a tangle of flesh and blue-red veins. He wore a tattered shooting vest with a leather patch on one shoulder and drooping pockets that could hold shotgun shells. In keeping with the aura, he sported a pair of plus-fours, which one rarely saw these days except, presumably, on old-fashioned golf courses or hunting estates: tweedy trousers that billowed at the thigh and pinched just below the knee. Pea-green socks covered his calves, and he wore maroon brogues. He wrapped his arm around my waist.

"Call me Hamish," he said.

"What else would they call you?" Mackay Brown asked.

"I'll no have your sass," he said.

"Ignore Hamish," said Mackay Brown. "He means well, but he slips on his own snot."

"What a brilliant phrase, and for a poet," said Hamish. "I only read Georgie on his birthday."

"Enough of the critique now. Have you room for the girl?" asked Mackay Brown.

"In my house there is always room for the girl," Hamish said.

"I'm Ailith," announced Ailith, probably miffed at being called "the girl." She had no time for this patriarchal nonsense, though feminism in Scotland flourished only in little resistances, hot small fires of rebellion.

"Whisky or beer?" asked Mackay Brown.

"Any beer is fine, thank you," I said.

Ailith asked for a pint of dark ale, and the three of us settled in chairs around the fire with drinks in hand. The temperature outside had dropped precipitously, and I shuddered to imagine what the dead of winter must be like here. St. Andrews was bad enough, with bleak wet winds sweeping across the waters from Norway.

"It's good to be here," I said. "Like walking into your stories and poems."

"Jay is among the partisans of my work," Mackay Brown said to Ailith. "And they're relatively few."

"I know your work," said Ailith.

I'd almost forgotten this. She had liked *A Time to Keep*, a fact she had brought up once or twice in the car, though my attempts to talk about these stories hadn't gone far. Why did she like them so much? I knew so little of her inner life, her hopes for herself, her longings. I shouldn't have been surprised that a young woman who wrote poetry and lived in northern Scotland might know something of George Mackay Brown or admire his work.

"You flatter me, lass," said Mackay Brown. "I tend to forget that what I write may have readers. But perhaps history is the only reader who matters."

"And what do you mean by history?" Ailith asked. "Isn't that a generality, an abstraction?"

Good for her, I thought. She refused to sink into the background. In fact, she was doing my work for me now!

"History is what we Christians call God, I think," said Mackay Brown. "He holds us in his large mind, within the totality of time unfolding there. It's not old calendars tucked in a drawer. Do you know the line in the letter to the Hebrews? 'Christ the same today, yesterday, and forever.' I do love that."

"You're a Catholic, I believe," she said. And it surprised me that she would either know or intuit this. Had I just wildly underestimated her?

"By conversion," he said.

"It's always the converts who take up the collection," she said.

"But I prefer to sit quietly in the back. The soul is invisible except to God. I don't know if even the Great One sees me. Or perhaps he's the silence inside me." He turned to me directly. "Jay, sir. You're a Catholic yourself, being Italian?"

"Italian by heritage, yes. My grandparents are Catholics. My father has fallen away into the arms of Calvin. But I admire the sacrament of communion," I said. "I used to go to the Sacred Heart in Pennsylvania with my grandmother. I often attend the Anglo-Catholic masses in St. Andrews now. There's something very moving at the altar." Saying this, I surprised myself. I didn't talk about my religious predilections much, not in public. This was something I considered private. But it felt good to say this aloud, declaring myself. What did I hope to hide?

"It's called Real Presence," said Mackay Brown.

"Meaning?" asked Ailith.

"We believe . . . we do, in my church, that God—that Jesus himself, as part of God—is present in the host. It's not symbolic. It's the spirit becoming flesh. And the cup is filled with his blood. And we who come to the altar, poor wee creatures each and every one, we're broken, too. But restored. We fall apart, and we're restored. Again and again."

"It's a symbol," said Ailith.

"Yes, true enough, but we're present when the host is present, and all of eternity advances toward us in this moment. It's our way of entering heaven while marooned in this sorry state."

Ailith leaned toward him. "Sorry state, aye. You know, there's something I don't understand about the Christians—their hatred of women."

"We admire the Blessed Virgin," he said. "And I love women, I surely do, though I've been unlucky in this part of my life. There's been no attachment."

"Women must be whores or virgins," said Ailith.

"Oh dear," said Mackay Brown. "I feel ashamed, I do. This is why it's good to step out into the public sphere. In Mayburn Court, I live too much in my head. I need other voices."

"You have your reading," I said. "I've wondered, who means a lot to you? What writers have mattered?"

Mackay Brown's face tangled in its own features. "As I get older, you see, fewer writers cast a spell. It's a sadness."

I couldn't help but think how Borges would have responded, with an encyclopedic answer, dazzling us with a quotation from Tichborne or Lugones.

I pressed him further. "Why did you make a profession of letters?"

"Is that what I've done? It seems I was unfit for anything else," he said. "I never felt I could leave Orkney for long, because of my health and probably my temperament."

"You love Orkney," said Ailith.

"It's like any marriage."

"You've been married?"

"No, no. There was a girl once, in Edinburgh. I fancied her, yes, and I think there was some responsiveness on her part, but time passes, as we know, and, well . . ." He dropped off a verbal plank into the cold sea below.

We waited for him to resume, but he didn't. His features sagged, and I regretted having lured him in this direction.

"I write a little bit of poetry," said Ailith, stirring the pot. How did she know the exact questions I felt I must ask? "I do wonder, sir: what *is* a poem? I mean, how would you define it?"

"A poem is the next best thing to silence," he said.

"So why bother?" Ailith asked.

"I feel a surge of joy most days, fleetingly. The light and dark that one sees on the water in the bay. My work is this, to re-create a part of that happiness with marks on the page. The exaltation can be felt, I hope. Here and there."

"And the sadness," I said.

The ill-shaped globe of his head—with its protruding forehead and jaw—craned in my direction, and I saw a filmy wetness in his eyes, which glistened like oysters.

"My mum, she worried about me," he said. "*You're too sad, Georgie,* she would say, God bless her soul. A marvelous woman! We do love our poor mothers, don't we then?"

Ailith asked for another glass of ale, and with a lifted finger from Mackay Brown, the pint appeared on the table before her. She held the glass like a chalice in two hands and drank far too quickly, her eyes teary. Was she thinking about her own poor mother, who had died the previous year?

Mackay Brown finished another glass of whisky, washing it down with beer, and we all devoured the warm sausage rolls that Hamish put before us on platters. There was no sign anywhere of payment being required, even expected. The usual din of the commercial world was absent here, replaced by a kind of silent affectionate bartering.

A young man with a guitar sat down in the corner and sang a number of old songs of Orkney.

"That's young Douglas," said Mackay Brown. "He's the son of the cobbler on the Hellihole Road. He'll go far."

"Perhaps to Edinburgh," said Ailith, teasing him.

Mackay Brown looked at his watch in an obvious and embarrassing way. "I'm afraid I must go," he said. "Tomorrow is a work day. As with every day except Sunday, when I take the bus to Kirkwall."

"For mass," I said.

"Aye." He finished the dregs of his final pint with obvious satisfaction. "I remember my first pints, many years since. Such a revelation! They flushed my soul with such a song—exhilaration, buoyancy—and washed sorrows away. I remember thinking to myself, *If I could have two pints of beer each afternoon, life would be a blissful thing.*"

"It's not a solution," said Ailith. As the daughter of an innkeeper, she spoke with authority here.

"I'm sure you're right," said Mackay Brown. "I've not had an easy time with the drink. The early promise of paradise failed in its delivery." He touched my hand gently and whispered, "Your girl is a sweet lass. Lovely as the first wash of spring. Good luck to you both." His wink did nothing to ease my uncertainty about my relations with Ailith, such as they were. She was definitely not my girl, but this wasn't the right moment to correct this. I would perhaps say something to him in the morning, if that seemed appropriate.

Before he left us, Mackay Brown kissed Ailith on the forehead and looked me in the eye. "I will read whatever you write about me," he said, "and will never object, as long as you're honest. Say only what seems true."

"I'm honest," I said.

"So I'm in good hands! Will you come again, now that we're friends?"

"I will."

"Ah, this is fine. Goodnight to both of you," said Mackay Brown. "This has been splendid. And, dear Jay, what a pleasure to meet at last. We shall say goodbye at the pier head on the morrow. I look forward."

"On the morrow," I said, feeling like an Elizabethan.

I walked him to the door of the Strom. So far, so good, I thought. We'd met, and the meeting had been good. But I hadn't gone as far as I might have done, hadn't pushed deep. He remained, for me, a mystery. Next time in Orkney, I would sit with him until revelations began to pour, no matter how long it took. He would eventually let me understand his fears, what gave him pleasure, what wrung his heart. He would talk to me about the writing process, and how he had managed to create his poems and stories, and what he felt as he wrote them. I wanted to learn more about him, and a brief visit such as this one could only be unsatisfactory, a whetting of the appetite.

Ailith had a room across the corridor from mine, and this was probably just as well, I decided. It would have been awkward to have to share a room with her, even with twin beds. I bade her goodnight with some hesitation, pausing at her door, drawing close but not overly close. We had been attracted to each other, I felt quite sure of this, and our glancing gestures of affection had been signals, lights flashing across dark and distant waters. But here we were, retreating into solitudes of self-enclosure— for me that most familiar zone.

She looked at me with attention, as if trying to gauge my feelings.

"It was a good day," I said, feeling like an idiot. Could I not muster the strength to say what I meant? Couldn't I just pull her into my bedroom?

Ailith nodded in a neutral way, and she waved shyly before stepping into her room. I assumed that the several pints she had consumed would settle her quickly: I'd seen her yawning in the bar. I had certainly missed whatever chance I had. And this was probably for the best, I told myself. I would preserve myself for Bella. The passing alliance with Ailith meant nothing. A benign flirtation. We hardly knew each other, and this would remain so. The pathway to paradise had a ROAD CLOSED sign at the entrance.

Propped against the bedstead, I turned back to Mackay Brown, his *Spell for Green Corn*. I'd been through it many times, this eloquent if odd play in incantatory prose, influenced by Brecht and set in seventeenth-century Orkney. In six scenes it tells the story of Sigrid Tomson, a young Orkney girl, who falls for a wanton fiddler, Storm Kolson. Kolson summons his courage and, with a mad inspiration, hurls himself upon her.

Just saying that to myself, I knew what I wanted.

In my boxer shorts and a T-shirt, I hovered outside her door, listening. Was she humming a tune?

I knocked quietly, hearing the drumbeat of pulse in my throat. There was no answer, so I knocked more loudly, looking around the dim hallway. Was anyone else within hearing?

Ailith opened the door, standing in a cotton nightdress, white with pink flowers.

"Hello," I said.

"Did you forget something?" she asked.

"You," I said.

I pushed through the door and led her to the bed with one hand. Then I kissed her, chastely. She smelled of hyacinth, I thought, a light floral aroma that may have been entirely in my mind, though I saw a number of dry flowers in a vase on a nearby table.

"You can do better than that," she said.

Feeling summoned, I took her face into my hands, eager to study her features, to look into her eyes with a deep, complete affection. Bright gold flecks in her irises caught my attention. When I kissed her again, this time more passionately, our teeth clattered like ice. I let my tongue explore her mouth, my hands dropping to her ass and pulling her close.

When I felt her hand dip into my boxers, I knew she was not a novice. And that she meant business as much as I did.

"I'm afraid I'm inexperienced," I said.

"Aye," she whispered. "I'm more observant than you think."

22

THE PASSIONATE NIGHT with Ailith in Stromness would take time to absorb, especially as my thoughts returned—as they quickly did in the morning—to Bella. Ailith's confidence in bed had astonished me. She had led me through the antique dance of sex in ways I could never have imagined. And yet I had a whelm of feelings I couldn't easily name. Was this love? I didn't think so, as my feelings for Bella were more distinct, more powerful and nuanced. To be fair, I hardly knew Ailith, and love was certainly more complicated than one night's entanglement in the bedsheets. So was this lust? The notion didn't thrill me: I was a romantic, and dreamed of something finer. But lust, as the first of the deadly sins, was not easily dismissed.

I wondered if I would see Ailith again. When I suggested the next morning that she might wish to visit me in St. Andrews, her response was not a ringing endorsement.

"It's the busy season coming at the Arms," she said.

I wondered when the "busy season" might end, telling her that I would write from St. Andrews.

She smiled sweetly. "I have no plans to leave the Viking Arms, and so letters addressed to me there will find me. I'll write back, as time permits. No promises."

No promises? Hadn't our night in Stromness implied something of a promise, however inexplicit? It should, I thought, have warranted at least a postage stamp and, however cursory, a reply. Then again, I may have overestimated whatever had happened between us. I didn't put this past myself.

At breakfast, I wondered if there was not a little sadness about her as she scraped butter onto her toast and complained about the runny eggs. "We do better eggs at the Viking Inn," she said, making sure our conversation bobbed on the surface. An emotional distance swelled between us like some invisible balloon and kept inflating, as if she wanted to make sure I didn't read too much into what had happened in her room the night before. Perhaps she had traveled farther with me, physically and emotionally, than she ever wished to go.

"We need to catch the ferry at ten," said Ailith. "My father will be wanting me home. And your Argentinian, he'll be chomping at the bit. He loves you."

"I doubt that's the word for it," I said.

What a thought! For the last twelve hours or more, Borges had remained in the margins of my consciousness. And yet he had continued to travel with me. I could hear him, obliquely, in the back of my head. There he chattered away, asking me to lean into the world as he did, to have faith in myself. That came home to me now. Borges wanted me to find myself as he had found Borges, this peculiar mask which had in time become his face.

Mackay Brown appeared, as promised, at the pier head to say goodbye. He looked older and smaller in the morning light, in his brown mac and floppy boots. A big waterproof hat shadowed his brow.

"It's been a short visit, son," he said. "You must come back to Orkney, so we can talk for days. There's always room at the inn, unlike in Bethlehem."

"You'll not tell King Herod I'm coming?"

"Ah, we're baby Jesus, are we?" He made the sign of the cross on my forehead with his thumb. "I'll take you with me to mass in Kirkwall next time."

"I'd really like that."

"Good lad," he said, blinking as he smiled at me. From the pocket of his threadbare mac, he pulled out a paperback of *Labyrinths* by Borges. "I suppose you have this?"

"I don't." I held the book in my hand, a lovely and well-thumbed Penguin, with a noticeable sticky spot of jam on the spine. It had done its time at the kitchen table in Mayburn Court beside the Bible.

"I had two copies," he said.

"You admire him?"

"Read the ones that I've marked with an *X* in the contents."

I opened to the contents and saw that nearly every entry had an *X* beside it.

"He is Jorge, I am George. But we're very different. He travels in the heavens. Out of time, mostly. But I'm here, rarely more than a few miles from where we linger. The clock ticks on my mantel. It's too loud, aye." He leaned over my shoulder with a hug, much as my father often did. "Will you pass a greeting to your man, Señor Borges?"

I assured him that I would, but it puzzled me, this turn. Did everything come back to Borges in the end?

"In particular," Mackay Brown said, just before we parted, "read 'Borges and I.' It's important for us."

"I'll read it on the ferry."

"If it doesn't roll too bad," he said. "I'd say it's calm and you're lucky."

I'd forgotten about the way I had puked on the last crossing and looked down at my shoes. The vomit was still evident. But I had, happily, not dwelled on it. I must have smelled of vomit, too. But it hadn't mattered.

"Be good to your Miss Ailith, aye, there's sunshine there. She lights the sea," he whispered.

There was wistfulness in the way he said that, and I detected depths below depths of regret as he kissed her goodbye moments later.

"I'll come back soon," I said.

"So you will," he said. "And be careful of the wind's direction when you spit over the rail. There's no telling. You stink a bit, you do. And don't we all?"

I decided not to overthink his remark. So much in my life now felt beyond deciphering. Or not worth dwelling on self-consciously.

As I stood at the aft deck and watched the pier recede to a smudge on the horizon, I remembered the books by Mackay Brown in my rucksack that I had forgotten to get signed. This would ensure another visit, I told myself. There was so much unfinished work for me in Orkney. In fact, I had unfinished business everywhere.

In the lounge on the ferry, I settled into a chair by a window to read "Borges and I," a little piece about the differences between the man and the writer. The writer keeps intruding, taking over the life of the man. "Borges" apparently had this "stubborn habit of falsifying and magnifying things." In the end, the internal voice and the public voice blend, the one informing the other. And the author of the story can't really tell which Borges has written the page, as Borges and "Borges" coincide.

I saw my reflection now in the window and wondered if indeed I might dig into Jay Parini, finding within him someone who was me and not-me, a transgressive voice hauled out from the vast inarticulate jumble of voices in my head. I wanted to say something, to burrow into this unspoken area, to find a place where poetry became a kind of restoration of the self, giving as Shakespeare said a "local habitation and a name" to "airy nothing." I knew I must say whatever I saw, looking around as well as inside of me. Description was revelation.

Feeling the pressure to write something, anything, I opened my journal and scribbled a few lines about Orkney: "The island burns all night, / a blaze of rock and water, / riding near to the sun on the rim of the earth."

Yes, that was it. A beginning of sorts. Opening a vein I must follow.

As we drew near the mainland, I found Ailith where she stood at the aft rail. I put an arm around her waist and pulled her close, and she tipped her head reflexively to my shoulder. This was perhaps her way to say, *Yes, it was fine what we did. We loved each other as we should have in the moment when we found each other. And there is no need to do this again.*

This was in any case how I read the silence between us as we swung into Thurso Bay, inhabiting a near-silence that lasted until we drove up to the Viking Arms in time for lunch.

Borges sensed my presence in the lobby before I spoke. "Giuseppe! They have freshened my suit in this hotel. It's clean and sweet! I smell like a daisy, dear boy! But you—when you walked into the room, I winced. Have you been rolling in the shit?"

"I got sick on the ferry."

"I've the most acute sense of smell," said Borges, aware of Ailith and McTaggart. "The nose of a hound! It's often useful, but distracting as well. Giuseppe will smell of this excrement—this vomit—as we travel through the day. No matter. All is forgiven."

I assumed he was forgiving me for abandoning him, or for throwing up on the ferry, or for letting him fall into a gully in the Cairngorms or topple from our rowboat into Loch Ness.

"Go forth and sin no more! I'm absolved," I said. "I like this feeling!"

Ailith grinned now, but McTaggart said nothing. I'd stolen his daughter for a night, and he wasn't stupid. He could easily guess what had happened on our brief excursion.

"You must worry about this monster in the lake below," Borges said to McTaggart. "Think of the loneliness he or she must suffer."

"She's a monster, aye," he said. "But we're kindly toward her. She brings visitors from abraid. They come from Japan and Ohio! From Timbuktu!"

"I pity the monsters," said Borges. "They're chosen by all readers for revilement. I don't revile the beast, you must realize. Is there not a beast in you, McTaggart?"

"A beast?"

"A monster."

McTaggart looked unhappily at his daughter, wondering how much longer they must suffer our company.

"Rocinante is pawing the dirt," said Borges, and I was grateful, ready to pack the car and carry on. "We've a battlefield before us!"

Before we headed out, I asked Ailith for an old wet rag to wipe the vomit from my shoes. She obliged, and whispered in my ear, "You're a right good fuck."

As we headed out, I waved goodbye over my shoulder, taking a final look at her. She had a rare if unlikely beauty, one that startled me, and it wasn't just a physical beauty or even mostly that. It was, I told myself, the beauty of character.

To myself I said, *Aye, you're a right good fuck as well.*

23

"You're a little sad," said Borges as we drove toward Culloden, the infamous battlefield, which would be the final stop on our tour of the Highlands.

"I don't know, Borges. I wonder about myself, where I'm going."

"We're going to Culloden!"

"In my life, in my heart."

"*Confide tibimet,*" he said.

My Latin was shaky, but I could translate this: Have faith in yourself.

"I've faith in you," Borges added. "We have been battle-tested, tried by circumstance. Fire and flood!"

This may have slightly overstated the case, but I had grown used to these extravagant statements, even gestures. Even to prize them. It was not Borges who spoke and gestured, I realized, but "Borges."

After a less than an hour's drive through the soft green air of early spring, with bays of daffodils by the roadside, we pulled into the car park at Culloden, where in 1746 the Jacobite army of Bonnie Prince Charlie was routed, leaving thousands dead or wounded. Charlie himself—a self-centered cad more than a hero, in my view—had evaded capture, despite a bounty on his head, slipping out of the country on a French vessel from the Isle of Skye. From what I had gleaned from the guidebook, Culloden was the last pitched battle on British soil, and it signaled the end of a way of life in the Highlands, squashing the dream of Scottish independence under a Stuart monarch.

There was a tin-roofed shed with a hand-painted sign that read CULLODEN WELCOME CENTRE. An elderly man in a cap sat in a cane chair and smoked a pipe. He eyed us with suspicion as we approached.

"Visitors?" he asked, narrowing his gaze.

"We've come to see the battlefield," I said.

Borges brightened on my arm, with an inane grin. "You should know, good sir, that I harbor Jacobite sympathies."

"It's fifty pence," said our gatekeeper, "and that's for each. A pound will do."

The full car park confused me, as I didn't see other tourists—an oddity that didn't quite register as we proceeded on foot, with Borges gripping my elbow tightly as we crossed the windswept Drumossie Moor, where the battle took place. I did my best to describe the landscape, pleased by my language. I had the hang of this now. "I'm seeing marram and thistle, the rose-tinged furze beginning to come to life and some kind of white moss over stony patches like doilies. Hawks hang in the sky above us, as if ready for a further feast of corpses, and I feel the presence of slaughtered Highlanders clamoring for revenge."

"Oh, this is good! Moving pictures! A private cinema!"

The battlefield saddened me when I thought of Billy in the jungle near the DMZ and remembered his last letter, with the badly wounded or even dead soldiers lying on stretchers. I thought about the hopeless, frantic work of the medics, and Billy's efforts to radio for help. Was there ever a more foolish or cruel war? All the dead young men, on both sides, depressed me. What was the point?

Battlefields had figured in my dreams since childhood. I had taken a trip to Gettysburg with my father when I was very young, not yet twelve. That experience cut a blistering hole in memory, with the thought of blood-soaked corpses, some of them boys only five years or six older than I was. One would have guessed that Americans had learned something about the futility of war by now, and how it rarely advances the cause of humanity. Wouldn't slavery have petered out in a few years? Weren't the decades of so-called Reconstruction as bad as slavery itself, creating battle lines between the races that had yet to fade? We had recently suffered the bitter blandishments and compulsive lies of George Wallace, a sociopathic fool who had forged a political career from the populist scraps of resentment that continued to plague Americans more than a century after the Civil War.

When I mentioned this to Borges, his lips began to move (as often happened) before the words emerged, as if his voice must leap onto a conveyer belt already in motion. "The American Civil War, a frightful tragedy, my dear," he said, breathless. "It has played in my mind since childhood, too. Gettysburg unfolded over days and days, with how many casualties?"

"Maybe fifty thousand," I said.

"Horrible numbers. And one did not long survive the wounds of these battles, not with infections. This is what nearly killed me in 1938, when I hit my head, as the bacteria ran wild in my bloodstream for months. Before penicillin was a remedy. There must be a God."

"You prayed for assistance?"

"I pray for assistance each day of my life, but who listens? This is the question, and yet I pray."

I prayed as well, nearly each night before falling asleep, speaking to a God who seemed to live inside more than above or outside me. I mentioned this to Alastair once, but he knocked aside my "religious delusions" as "so much poppycock." Like so many of his generation, his opinions had somewhere along the way hardened into a stance I considered simplistic, a literalistic atheism that was no more interesting to me than literal-minded Christianity. Neither of these opinions felt open to the mysteries of being. They were two sides of the same coin.

Now the wind came rasping from the northeast, scraping along the ground, and Borges turned up the collar of his jacket—though this could hardly have helped.

"An ill wind blows. The pity of this place is evident," he said. "It overwhelms Borges." He winced, leaning on his cane. "Do you have more of those pills? My head!"

"We should be careful. They're strong."

"These restless natives, they're pounding a large invisible drum at the base of my skull."

I handed over two of the pills, taking them from the pocket of my corduroy jacket. It wasn't possible for them to work so quickly, but relief flooded his face at once after he swallowed them (without water). He looked up into the sun, and the light bathed his face, a liquid radiance that dripped from his cheeks onto his collar and coat. Did the fish on his tie begin to swim as well? His eyes closed, the lids quivering rapidly. I realized that he was, in his way, quite handsome, with a masculine beauty, his features hewn from marble. He might, like his revered ancestor, have led men into battle.

"They came with nine thousand men under an English duke," Borges said. "'The Butcher Cumberland,' a formidable man but vain as well. The redcoats had trained in hand-to-hand combat in Aberdeen, in preparation for a Highland charge. By mid-April, I believe, these troops had reached the Nairn. Cumberland gave his men the day off to celebrate his birthday. No, he would not fight a bloody battle on his birthday! And this vanity deceived the Jacobite army and their prince, who let down their guard. On this moor, where we stand, some five thousand men fell prey to ambush. Think of it, Giuseppe: the armies of the duke on horseback, wielding swords and guns. The clans had their bagpipes. This is a terrifying sound, agony turned into music. But it will not hold back a vicious army."

He raised his cane like a pikestaff, letting out a wail of shocking amplitude. How could an old man who usually spoke in soft tones summon such a shriek?

"Get down, laddie!" he shouted, curling to the ground.

I lay beside him, smelling the peaty dirt, the tough heathery groundcover. Why did he care about Scottish independence? I thought of Vietnam again, especially those who resisted the American charge, the bombing raids from on high, the poisonous sweep of napalm, which obliterated whole forests. All for a fantasy of liberation, as if the Vietnamese required liberation from what the majority of Vietnamese wanted: a unified (and socialist) country. They had somehow resisted our well-financed onslaught, our technical might. Ho Chi Minh was more like Borges's heroic Charlie than Charlie himself.

"See them coming! You're eyes, Giuseppe! What's the view?"

On the other side of the field, if I was not mistaken, were dozens of warriors, clansmen in tartan kilts. The bleating of bagpipes and the clatter of drums drew closer.

"We must stay low," whispered Borges. "The dream will pass."

The drumming only grew more intense, and the thunder of feet, with horses beating over bridges, a fife-and-drum corps hard by where we lay. It felt as if I had myself swallowed several of those blue pills.

"They will not defeat Charlie! Not today!" Borges cried, lifting himself to his feet, raising his cane in the air again, his flag of defiance. He rose and rushed forward, moving over uneven ground in springy steps, skirting a patch of thistle. I could see a boggy pool in the distance, a blister on the landscape. I must stop him!

"Borges!" I called, chasing this full-grown toddler on the loose. A troop of soldiers looked my way, and

somebody waved a flag. Was I seeing things this morning, sucked into some sort of folie à deux? When my
charge disappeared over a ridge, I followed and found
him, moments later, on his back in some heathery grass,
a mossy stone not three feet from his head. A couple of
jet-winged crows landed nearby, as if inspecting the scene
for a possible meal.

"I think we've lost this battle, dear comrade. My
clansmen, they are scattering." The bagpipes drew closer.
"The English have routed us again."

A small band of Highlanders in checkered black-and-
red kilts moved toward us, and one of them came forward
from the others. He stood beside us, arms akimbo.

"Your grandfather?" he asked.

"My father," I said—the only answer that made sense
today.

This man of perhaps fifty, with a beard like cotton
wool, stood close. Below his kilt he wore high socks
fastened at the top with an orange ribbon. His blue vest
was open at the bottom, not quite able to latch over a
huge paunch.

"You're a ghost," Borges said, pointing his cane toward
the man as if he could actually see him.

"No ghost, me!"

"Who are you, sir?"

"Robbie Makgill, son of Rab Makgill."

"Are you a warrior, sir?"

"I'm quite benign. Don't fret yoursel'."

"I will not let you pummel me with musket balls!"
Borges cried.

"I shoot no one."

"You see that I'm blind, Robbie?"

"Aye."

"I can't see you. May I touch your face?"

Makgill looked around and winked at me, obviously embarrassed. But he stepped forward, unable to resist the force that was Borges. He knelt beside him, took his hands, and drew them to his fluffy beard. Borges explored the weathered face, the wiry beard, the woolen tam.

"He's real," I said to Borges.

"I commend you, Robbie," said Borges. "You've done well, an auld-farrant lad, I would say!"

"Auld-farrant? You can speak our language?" He seemed in awe of this peculiar foreigner.

"The language of resistance, yes. It's tasty on my tongue."

A dozen of Makgill's comrades in arms looked on without comprehension.

"We're Fraser's Dragoons," explained Makgill. "We do the reenactments."

The pennies began to drop. History buffs. I had heard of these enthusiasts who put a great deal of time, thought, and money into their re-creations of life on famous battlefields, mimicking the actual movements of troops. Gettysburg and other Civil War battles had legions of men—they were mostly men—who spent their weekends reliving the hell of long-ago furious engagements. It was the defeated armies who apparently garnered the most avid replicators, as if they hoped, in the mirage of reenactment, to find victory at last.

Borges tried to understand. "Reenactments, you say?"

"Aye, we replay the past."

"And for what reason?"

"Pleasure."

"What a marvelous answer. You mirror reality! And this is what I do for a profession. Hold little mirrors to the world, I do, but they're untrustworthy. Like all mirrors, prone to distortion." He paused, perhaps aware that he had lost his audience.

"He's well enough, your father?" asked Makgill, looking at me instead of Borges.

"Well enough," I said.

He didn't trust my response, but our fate no longer concerned him. His friends readied themselves to charge Cumberland's men in the middle distance, and he must join them.

"What's this again?" Borges asked, sitting. "I didn't quite follow the chap."

"Reenactors," I said. "Groups who replay old battles."

"I've found a name for myself. Borges the Reenactor! The problem is, one never wins old battles. The losses only mount."

Borges reached for my hand, and I helped him to his feet. Slowly we made our way back to the car.

"Our heroes," he said, as we drove away, "they disappoint and frustrate us. Charlie was impossible, arrogant, obsessed by himself. He caused so many deaths, fighting out of vanity, ruining his army and himself. The Jacobite cause fell to his madness. Probably a delusion in any case. Most wars are fought over delusions. I will agree with you there."

I hadn't said anything, but he could read my thoughts.

"But you mustn't give up, or lose your idealism," he said.

"That's not in the cards, Borges. I feel pretty determined about this. Americans are, I think, idealistic by nature. Think of our Declaration of Independence."

"You are declaring your own independence!"

I remembered how, when I had first arrived in St. Andrews, I had copied a line in my journal from *Walden*. Henry Thoreau had moved to his cabin in the woods on the Fourth of July in 1845, to "live deliberately." I had not quite taken that on board when I wrote it. But I would.

Borges continued to think about the Jacobite cause. "Culloden failed on nearly every count. So much was lost."

"And the little people who fight these wars, they lose the most."

Borges seemed to think about this deeply. "You wish to write, I know," he said at last. "Remember that the battle between good and evil persists, and the writer's work is constantly to reframe the argument, so that readers make the right choices. Never work from vanity, like our Bonnie Prince. Or the Butcher of Cumberland, for that matter. What does Eliot say? 'Humility is endless'. . . We fail, and we fail again. We pick ourselves up. I've done it a thousand times, Giuseppe."

As ever, he circled in his head, where he found—or created—a reality that to him was obsessively present.

But there was reality in the hard lines of the world, upon which the imagination depends. I recalled a line from Wallace Stevens: "Soldier, there is a war between the mind and sky."

Borges liked this quotation. "Yes, a war between the mind and sky. Marvelous, your poet! We fight our battles over and over. For us, it's the effort to express reality. It's a battle. I feel sad at times, lonely and detached from reality. But the sky overwhelms me, even though I'm blind. The sun is too bright, blinding a blind man! This is the reality we encounter and wrestle into words. This wrestling is our life. But it's impossible to win. There's never a total victory. That would be death. The victories of the living are partial at best. We vomit on ourselves, but we wash our shoes clean. And begin again."

Though I didn't know it consciously, this was for me a beginning. I could find somewhere to go from here. *Confide tibimet* indeed!

I couldn't wait to tell Billy about Culloden and its reenactors. And I might try to say something about my subsequent insights, though I wasn't sure he'd understand. Billy had landed in the most literal sort of war. And my theorizing about any of this might feel unhelpful, if not infuriating. He used to laugh at me when I'd go philosophical, saying, "Don't talk out of your ass, amigo. It's noisy and smells bad, and everybody wants to leave the room."

Uncannily, Borges continued to read my mind. "War is always unfortunate, even evil, yes. That's an argument one could make. But you, son, haven't been conscripted. This is lucky. Rejoice, and let it rest there."

"It's an immoral war," I said.

"And this is somehow an argument? Isn't every war, in a most basic sense, a meaningless exercise, a cruel and pointless one that rarely changes much for the better?"

"My uncles landed on the beach in Salerno in 1943. That war meant something." I could feel the presence of my Uncle Tony behind me, and he was pleased. Had I, his pigheaded nephew, suddenly understood him?

"The stench of Hitler had to be erased, yes. This is true."

It might take years to sort through these thoughts, which probably couldn't be sorted. War was always the last choice for any nation, an admission of defeat. One should never enter a conflict with a sense of triumph, with the slightest jubilance. A war is an enormous funeral, and one should proceed sadly into battle, in humility, with a bowed head, fully aware that one might never be forgiven. I knew I'd never for a second approve of any rhetoric about war that verged on the exultant. There was no glory in war, only shame for having lacked the imagination to prevent this stumble into the abyss.

Borges asked again about the letters from my draft board, as if needing to push into this wound a little, to make it bleed. Was he being cruel? Or did he have a benign motive that eluded me? I decided to assume the best.

"It's much like I said, Borges. I don't know if they want to draft me. But I don't want to know."

"Then you should burn them!" he said. "The letters will plague you if you don't. I destroyed the letters from Norah Lange that I received as a young man, though

I waited too long. By that time, alas, I was completely blind, so there was no point."

This was a thought. Just fucking burn them. If I wasn't going to war, and I wasn't, I should make my point—at least to myself—boldly. The idiotic notion that I should enlist had flickered in my brain like heat lightning over distant hills. I'd wondered if I shouldn't, like Billy, do something heroic. Was it actually true that somebody else fought in Vietnam in my place and therefore my evasion of the war had moral consequences? Culloden had unexpectedly forced me to face the truth that war is always destructive, and one should not, under *most* circumstances, fight for somebody else's grand illusion. Uncle Sam might want me, but at this point in history, I didn't want him. He wasn't worth it.

24

DRIVING SOUTH, I saw such staggering vistas, which I did my best to describe to Borges.

"The sky goes on forever here, reaching to the west, leaping over invisible islands," I said, ramping up my poetic affects to the point of nonsense.

"My favorite islands, Giuseppe. Whatever is invisible rests easily with me."

"Being blind . . ."

"Poetic vision is better than mere sight. What color is the sea when you catch a glimpse, if you do?"

"Wine-dark?"

"An unfortunate phrase, so I approve of this interrogative mode. Homer has turned generations of sailors into drunken fools."

"It's a formulaic expression," I said. "Homer wanted to make a line easy to memorize. A cliché, probably. Alastair would have crossed it out."

"But I adore clichés. Would you like for the air you breathe always to smell of roses? I don't think so. You would be desperate for clean, unpopulated air. I like to read novels that don't keep grabbing me by the collar and shaking loose my teeth. A rose is more fragrant when rare."

"You should talk to Jasper. He's against clichés."

"And he's still a boy. When he matures, he will be grateful for them. When he meets his first girlfriend, he will reach into the vast treasury of clichés for language, and it will carry him through into adulthood. Shakespeare, I'm sure, impressed no women with his conceited phrasing."

"I see a blue valley, with blurs of white sheep on the hillside."

"A happy or a sad blue?"

"The happiest of blues. Like a June sky on your wedding day."

"*Your* wedding day, perhaps. Mine was purple-blue. More like a bruise. Even the roses smelled foul, of death, in vases on the long tables. My mother wept through the ceremony, but this was not joy. She understood that I had put an obstacle between myself and poetry."

We entered Balmaha, a tiny handprint of a village on the moss-and-mud shores of Loch Lomond, and stopped for sausage rolls sold from a caravan overlooking the harbor, where small boats lay at anchor, with miles of indigo water opening to the islands beyond. The sky was shock-blue, almost sapphire, with only a few clouds floating in the middle distance.

"The lake is long and skinny, very long and very skinny," I said to Borges.

"And deep!"

"I can't see the depth," I said.

"Have you not read Mark Twain's book on the Mississippi? He was a riverboat pilot—his first profession. He learned to read the surface of the river and could tell by the ripples what depths moved underneath. It was a text, you might say. The surface of water is always a text. A trained eye will know what obstructions hide below and how to navigate the currents. As a young man, I learned how to read books with a peculiar alertness to what remained out of sight, in the margins, between lines. Even between the words and between the syllables!"

"I see islands, lots of them."

"More! Populate my vision!"

"Crannogs, built by human hands. Green tangled jewels, I believe. Islands fetched from the imagination!"

"This is good, my dear. What a fine touch, *crannogs*."

We listened in silence by the roadside, our ears open to the sounds. An oystercatcher called, strutting in sand at the water's edge, while gulls cawed overhead.

"I haven't heard such lovely cries from the birds in many years. Too much time in libraries, I fear. I've missed nature's music."

"But you had a wonderful position. National librarian!"

"A wonderful title. But I was demoted by our ruffian president, Perón. I was made inspector of poultry."

"Poetry?"

"Chickens, dear boy. Poultry!" He made a clucking sound, pumping his elbows like chicken wings. "I was allowed to inspect the rabbits as well. Being blind, I was not terribly good at this work and resigned."

"*The Art of Poultry*," I said. "It would make a good title."

"It occurs to me, Giuseppe, that I've never read a word of yours. Why don't you read something? My ears are open."

"There's something in my journal," I said. I'd both hoped for and dreaded this invitation.

I shuffled among a handful of poems in my rucksack while Borges closed his eyes to listen, his lips slightly parted.

I read in a slow voice:

Your forehead, with its silken widow's peak, enchants
   me now.
I would lie beside you,
Touch that brow, and kiss your oval almond eyes.
I would solve the mystery of you, my love,
enfold you in my arms, a nightlong vigil.
The night would never know us as we are,
Not two but one, a fabled creature.
And at dawn I'd see you—almost in the way that God
   himself
Could see you now, his full creation,
And beyond mere time, so free from everything
That holds us, harrows us, that keeps us lonely
In ourselves, our separate skins.

" 'Our separate skins,' " Borges said. "There is isolation in that phrase, a yearning. One often reads this line, this sentiment. It's common, but not any less painful for its very ordinary pain."

"It's a cliché, you're saying."

"No! It's poetry, but poetry that moves in circles we have all traced. My Norah had this widow's peak as well! A coincidence? Longing is a useful emotion for a poet, as we know. But may I tell you something?"

"I think you are," I said, annoyed that he had turned my poem into another story about himself. I was actually more than annoyed. Anger rose from my heels, working its way up through my spine, and broke over my head, a silent splatter of indignation.

"Dear boy, something quite surprising must be said. Believe me. I have written the same poem. *This exact poem*, I must say. It was called 'Anticipation of Love.'"

"I've no title for the one I read you."

"Then use mine! The same words, the same title."

"I don't think so." I had keenly felt the originality of my poem as I read it, and could sense my own voice emerging, however imperfectly. I didn't need his title, nor his poem.

"It's the same words, I'm quite sure," he said. "In another language, of course."

"I've never read a word of your poetry, Borges," I said. "I should avoid this, or you'll accuse me of copying."

He didn't take offense but came back at me another way. "You must read my story 'Pierre Menard.' I will insist that you read it, the tale of a man who rewrites *Don Quixote*, word for word."

"He copies it?"

"No, he *writes* it, for the first time. In doing so, he liberates the idea of originality from the prison house of Romanticism. Every word is original in the mouth, in the fresh context of what is uttered. In its own time and space."

"I'm lost."

"Your poem and my poem, as with our anticipation of love, move in the same sphere. It's a poem I copied from elsewhere, no doubt. I became a reader of this great poem of love, which nobody could find in the original, as it exists only when refashioned and re-created. You have every right to this poem, as I have every right to it. The difference is only the context. Your lovely Miss Law, she has inspired you, as I was inspired by Miss Lange. They may well be the same woman, alive in different times, in different countries. We understand little about how life unfolds."

"As I said, I've never read your poem, Borges."

"No matter. Think of this: Leibniz and Isaac Newton each discovered the calculus in the same century, but they never knew each other."

"What does that mean?"

"Ideas arise independently from the same mysterious source."

What Borges said was beginning to make sense, although it would take some time for the truth of it to settle. I couldn't admit this then, of course. I wanted to cling to what I had written. I wanted to believe I had said something fresh, added something, however small, to the stock of English poetry.

The engine sputtered into life without enthusiasm. This poor vehicle had seen better days, and Borges had managed to get under my skin in unexpected ways. I would *not* read another of my poems to him, I told myself, as he would surely lay claim to it.

"I shall write *King Lear* soon, you know," he said as we began to drive away. "I feel it coming on."

Along the road, forty minutes later, I noticed a paper mill, a rude intrusion on the otherwise blissful and bucolic landscape. Its putrid smell, like rotten eggs, nearly blew my car off the road as we approached, and my unhealthy engine responded with a low coughing noise. The factory loomed on the left side of the road, its smokestacks huffing, with massive lorries backed up to its loading docks. This unhappy structure, made of colorless blocks of concrete, had few windows, only a handful of doors. It rose to a surprising height, with a flat roofline. I slowed to a crawl and then, feeling an inspiration, stopped by the wire fence not a hundred feet from the mill itself.

"What is it?" asked Borges, his nostrils wide. Puzzlement stitched his brow.

"It's such a lovely scene," I said. "Wordsworth would have found this moving."

"Yes? A perfect idyll? Let's step outside, please. I need to stretch my legs and breathe more deeply."

We stood together at the roadside in the shadow of the mill.

"Speak, Giuseppe. Let your eyes widen for me. Summon the poet in your breast."

"There's a velvet cover of grass on the hills, which are low and rolling. A brook is nearby, a bristling strip of water, and the water weeds follow it into the deep countryside. There are trees, willows, letting down their long braids into the stream."

"Other trees? Only willows?"

"Alders, I would say. Alders adore wet feet, I believe. But it's definitely willows that droop beside the brook."

"Do you see cows or sheep?"

"Both! Brindled cows. There are strings of spittle coming from their mouths. The sheep obviously need shearing. They are shaggy, overblown."

"A pastoral landscape! Worthy of Theocritus, who wrote the first memorable poems in this vein. I remember the poems of Bion, Moschus, and Longus as well. Virgil brought this rich tradition to Rome. But a pastoral poem isn't about the sheep and cows, the fields and flowers, the gabbling streams. It's about contrast. The rude, sad world of politics hovers nearby, however invisible. Beauty and ugliness live on the same page. One isn't possible without the other."

"The flowers have a lovely smell, I think. I don't know what to call them."

"I would call them putrid and disgusting egg-flowers," he said. "There's nothing quite like sulfur to quicken the lungs."

He doubled forward now, laughing so hard I thought he might do himself an injury. He was almost weeping.

"I wish you could see this," I said.

"Oh, dear, I do wish. What I would give to see a factory like this one."

—

We continued along a narrow road through the undulating countryside in a happy mood, though my car showed increasing signs of stress, and I began to wonder if we would make it back this afternoon.

"How long before St. Andrews?" Borges asked.

"Two hours or less, unless we stop."

He would have to pee, that was certain, and I wanted to look for a phone box. It was time to see if Alastair had made it back from London.

"Rocinante is not sounding healthy," Borges said.

In fact the car's indistinct rattle had magnified throughout the late morning and become a miserable cough by midday; even more worrying, the wheel pulled repeatedly to the right, once or twice almost tipping me into a ditch. Could there be a problem with the bearings as well as the motor? I should have had the car checked over by a mechanic before I left St. Andrews, but there hadn't been time, and I suffered from an innocent trust in engines. My father drove relatively new cars, his most recent being a bumblebee-yellow Ford LTD with a black vinyl roof, and these rarely broke down if one changed the oil every three thousand miles. At least that's what he had taught me.

Borges rapped the handle of his cane on the dash, as if to provoke it.

"It needs a tune-up," I said.

"You're good with the rude mechanicals, I can tell."

"Engines are a mystery to me."

"Internal combustion! Remember that I began my life in a world of horses and buggies. My father as a boy rode through the streets of Buenos Aires in his grandfather's barouche. Now I have flown thousands upon thousands of miles above the clouds to lecture in distant places, such as Iceland and Israel, where I talk with people— lovely people—I could never have met had I remained at home. But I should never have left my city. I'm a shy man, you see, and have no courage." He paused to wipe his brow with a handkerchief, which he returned to his breast pocket. "And few convictions. Though I admire bravery in others. You mentioned that we shall pass through Stirling."

"Very soon."

He drew a breath of anticipation. "Stirling Bridge! The name sings in my heart. A key victory for Scottish independence, led by William Wallace. Blind Harry the poet wrote about this great battle very well. Such a tradition, the blind poets. Homer, Milton, Harry . . ."

"And Borges," I said.

He touched my forearm. "Thank you, dear boy."

I paused twenty minutes later for a view of Stirling Castle, which I described as best I could. There was a nearby café, where we sat for half an hour: Borges needed a cheese roll and tea. Through the window I saw a fire-engine-red phone booth by the road and excused myself to call Pilmour Cottage.

Alastair picked up at once and asked me where I'd been.

"I took Borges on a little tour of the Highlands."

"Mercy."

"We've had a few days on the road."

"I'm trying to absorb your phrase 'a little tour of the Highlands.' It's a hurdle, and I doubt my horse will jump over it."

"He was hoping to meet Mr. Singleton, an editor of Anglo-Saxon riddles, in Inverness. Something went amiss."

"You're describing the next episode of *Monty Python*. No spoilers, please!"

"I'll have him back to you soon. Before dinner."

"Good! I did a big shop this morning. I'll have shepherd's pie and a bottle of wine, and whisky if necessary—a single malt from the Highlands. We'll celebrate your 'little tour.'"

In just a few days I'd lost track of Alastair's voice, his way of being the world, with its sarcasm and whimsy. He lived on the other side of the looking-glass, and I felt quite sure now that Tweedledum and Tweedledee would join us for dinner.

25

"ALASTAIR IS BACK," I said as we drove out of Stirling.

"*El magnífico* returns! Our adventure, Giuseppe, has ended. There's a melancholy in these endings, don't you agree? I dislike the last pages of any good book, as I anticipate the coming losses, the vacancy."

A loud snap of thunder surprised us, and a rainstorm swept the road, almost tropical in its density, with flowing sheets of water. There was zigzag lightning in the fields and occasional blasts of sunlight as well. My old wipers could barely combat the rain that lashed over us, and I strained to see the way ahead, ignoring Borges, who rattled on with further thoughts on the demise of William Wallace. A slippery road meant nothing to him, of course, as he'd never driven a car.

At one point, when I failed to respond adequately to his running commentary on Scottish history, I said, "You know, it's very difficult to see!"

"You tell this to a blind man?"

I'd have liked to end our journey with elaborate descriptions of the countryside, but my goal was not to crash. Nonetheless the latent glory of our surroundings flicked by, with fields of beetroot and soft grass on either side of the road. I saw a bright yellow tractor in one muddy rut as it grumbled along in the downpour, tilling the soil. Even quicksilver bolts of lightning hadn't sent this intrepid farmer into the barn for shelter, and I felt inspired by a man who plowed forward despite inclement and possibly dangerous weather. The task at hand absorbed him.

As we approached Guardbridge, I could feel the unseen presence of St. Andrews behind the scudding mist a few miles away, imagining the chapel tower and the broken ribs of the cathedral. I visualized the stone pier that pushed into the sea below the castle. And knew that before long St. Andrews would absorb me into its labyrinth of alleyways and cobbled streets, its hedgerows and hidden gardens. My travels with Borges in the Highlands would recede in memory. The work on my thesis would press upon me within days, and I'd resume my quiet argument with Professor Falconer about the value of George Mackay Brown. I'd probably look for Bella at her residence hall or pass her in the street with an embarrassed nod. We might even dine together at Pearl of Hong Kong as planned! Time would bite its own tail.

As we reached a familiar turn just above the broad plain of Eden Estuary, only a few miles outside St. Andrews, what had been a mere clatter of distress in my engine became a full cry for help, with metal grating on metal, bone on bone. Then I heard a kind of low whistle, with a foul odor rising through the floor.

"The Quixote blamed his defeat on misunderstanding

the strength and resilience of his horse," said Borges. "I will not make this mistake."

He was right. It wasn't possible to go another mile in my rusty Morris without risking its mortality, and possibly ours. There was no choice but to stop. So I pulled over by the side of the road at the gravel lead-in to a bus stop.

"We're finished?"

My grunt answered him. "I'll have the car towed to my garage in St. Andrews. I don't know how long it will take."

"It's how far, St. Andrews?"

"A few miles. I suppose we could walk."

"You must know, Sancho, I'm too old for such perambulation." A weariness in his voice seemed new. "The idea upsets my feet, which sometimes refuse to accommodate me. It's important not to ask too much of them."

Standing in the rain, I lifted the hood to stare at the tangle of hoses, belts, and unfamiliar mechanical parts. Their configuration meant nothing to me, but I pulled on one black hose that seemed loose. A slight wheezing sound followed. An exhalation of steam from the radiator gave off a strong chemical smell, and I knew for certain that the poor beast desperately needed expert attention.

I could manage by myself, but what to do about Borges?

As if summoned by bells, a taxi stopped beside us, and the driver, a ruddy man of sixty with a handlebar mustache, offered to help. When I explained the situation, he quickly agreed to take Borges back to St. Andrews, allowing me to stay with Rocinante. "I know Pilmour

Lane," he said. I would remain with the car to call a tow truck.

"The captain goes down with the ship," Borges said.

He stepped close to me, reaching a hand to my face. His fingers played gently across my forehead and cheeks, and he held both ears in his big hands. His eyelids quivered, and he smiled, his breath oddly sweet.

"You'll be fine, Borges," I said.

"Oh, I'm sure of this. We shall meet up at Pilmour. But release all worry. Go back to Miss Law. Do not neglect your affections or 'lose the name of action.'"

"I consider myself the name of action," I said, glad to recognize the phrase from *Hamlet*, recalling that in Orkney I had found in myself a capacity for action.

"'In thy orisons, be all my sins remembered.'"

Hamlet, and *Hamlet* again. Of course, it hadn't gone so well for the Prince of Denmark.

"*Your* sins, Borges, lodge in my memory. I won't easily forget them."

"Ah my sins. . . . Dear boy, you have no idea."

He let go of my ears, and I helped him into the backseat of the taxi, which soon dwindled into the mist.

I called the garage from a nearby phone, and the mechanics agreed to rescue my car. But I should have guessed that when the tow arrived, after an hour or more, there would be no room for me in the cab, as two mechanics had come.

I told them not to worry, that I would walk to St. Andrews.

"It's a fair mass to cover in the rain," said one of them,

in an accent so thick I thought he had instructed me to cover my ass in clover.

It felt good to walk, even necessary now. The low plains stretched to the sea along the estuary, calming, and the rain had thinned to a translucent spray, almost imperceptible, with an early-evening sun pulsing behind it. In the distance I could see the pink West Sands and the town itself, its towers visible in a misty gauze. As I drew near St. Andrews, I felt grateful for the protective walls of the city, with the hush of centuries gathered in a ring of old stones. And I thought of that maze at Scone and how—after a mysterious and disorienting time that my watch could never track—I'd circled back upon Borges, even back upon myself, sensing that I'd been somewhere and that everything would feel different from that point forward.

Standing outside my flat in Hope Street, I heard the bells of St. Salvator's chiming seven.

Descending the several wet steps to my flat, I felt hesitant to unlock the door, even scared. But why? When I opened it, a rank and musty smell overwhelmed me. I might have been gone for months, not days. On the table across the room a copy of Mackay Brown's first volume of poems lay open—I owned several copies—with a pad of scribbled notes beside it. Having met the author, I had a better sense of the voice behind the words, though I wasn't convinced that my trip to Orkney had shifted my understanding in significant ways. At least a few of the geographical sites were no longer abstract names on a map. I could visualize the harbor, the pier head, and the flagstone main street of Stromness, which Mackay Brown nicely described as uncoiling "like a sailor's rope from North to South." I could approach my work now with a quickened sense of place.

I knew, however, that I must return to get a fuller sense of the island and the writer. Who was this little man who'd reminded me of my father, with his simple manner, his forthright optimism, his quiet shrewdness and lack of pretension? I had barely begun to understand the mystical core of his writing, and the link to Roman Catholicism I'd somehow missed. I would attend a mass with him in Kirkwall, as he had suggested. I sighed loudly, hearing myself in the still room. So much work lay before me, and I wondered if I could actually complete this thesis within four or five years. And if I didn't, what then?

A passel of letters had been pushed through the slot onto the tile floor of the entryway, and I glanced at them, almost afraid to look too closely. A fresh one from my draft board sat on top, as if defiantly welcoming me home. How many times would they send the same letter to my house in Scranton? Did my mother never tire of forwarding them, always with more postage than was necessary? I assumed it was the same letter; not having opened any of them, I couldn't really know. My ignorance was certainly not bliss.

I carried them into my bedroom, propped myself against the wooden bedstead, and read the letter from my mother first. She wrote with the same complaints. "It's such a long way to Scotland, as your Aunt Irene keeps reminding me. And why are you there? Everybody asks me. There is no good reason. Have you been thinking about law school like your father suggested? He wants to know. Did the letter from the draft board arrive? They keep coming, as you might have noticed. Don't they know you're not here? Shouldn't I give somebody a call down there? It strikes me you don't say much about any of this. Your letters, they never comment. All you talk about is the weather. Rain, rain, mist, rain. What do I care? I know the weather over there. I've seen the movies! It's what I do these days, with you and your sister gone. I go to the movies once a week by myself. *Dirty Harry*, now there's a picture!"

Dirty fucking Harry. I felt sorry for her, trapped in a small circle of fantasies. My father had his own busy worlds of business and religion, and these didn't include her. My departure had added to her isolation. The usual recitation of illnesses and events filled many paragraphs here: Aunt Ann was suffering from gallbladder attacks and "it was just like her." One cousin had hepatitis, the result of "bad seafood at a restaurant in Pittston and he doesn't even like seafood." A distant uncle—actually a cousin of my grandfather—had gone into a nursing home in Altoona, suffering from "a case of the shingles and gout as well, two illnesses for the price of one." As usual, her blood pressure was "not what it should be," she said, adding, "But who am I to complain?" Her sister, Helen, rarely came to visit, though she lived only half an hour away.

Of course I knew why Helen didn't come, as did

everyone. My mother didn't listen, and it's not fun to hear someone talking nonstop in random fashion. Her stories had no beginnings, no ends. Only endless sagging middles.

I put her letter aside and stared into the semidark room as above me on Hope Street a few cars slurred by, and I could hear a number of drunken student voices on the pavement.

The last letter in the packet was from Mrs. Giordano, Billy's mother. She had written a few times before—always lonely and afraid, with her only son in a war zone on the other side of the planet. She offered gossipy news of Billy and my classmates, and I recognized the looping vowels and double-crossed *t*'s on the envelope addressed to "Mister Jay Parini." But somehow I knew at a glance this time—the shaky handwriting worried me—that her letter was not just another of her newsy ramblings.

I read it without breathing, leaping ahead to the phrases I guessed were there. "There isn't a lot of information. The army doesn't know much, which I can't understand. Isn't that their job, to know things? But the sad truth is that Billy was killed by a sniper while on patrol. An ambush, they said. The officers came to our house to tell us. (I felt sorry for those boys, who had to break the news.)" The rest of his platoon had made it back safely, she said. Billy had been taken by a helicopter to a medical station at a base nearby, "but it wasn't possible to save him, given the extent." At the end of the letter, all underlined, she said, "Please write something for us to read at the mass for Billy. I would be very grateful and so would Joe, who sends his hello." It was signed "Anne-Marie Giordano, with affection and sadness."

Sadness, indeed. The restrained dignity, brevity, and clarity of her letter startled me. I sat on my bed as the light dwindled into perfect darkness, not moving, not even thinking I would ever move again. I'd turned to stone inside.

Eventually I made it to the kitchen, my legs under me like ghost sticks. In the cabinet under the sink I found a bottle of whisky. I didn't usually rely on alcohol, but I saw no other option tonight. Was this for real? Had Billy really been jerked away like this, taken from me, from his family? Would I never have a chance to complain to him again in miserable self-involved letters about my thesis, my worries, my unrequited love for Bella? In my head I was already telling him about Borges and our dash through the Highlands in Rocinante, and I planned to write to him at length soon. He would have loved this story.

I poured a tumbler of Scotch to the brim, then took the bottle with me into the dim adjacent room and sat at the table, where I could see the faint outline of myself in a mirror.

It frightened me, that mirror. Had it been here all the while? Had I been too obsessed by my thoughts even to glance at myself and consider what I found there?

I looked older than I imagined, haggard, unkempt, my face unshaven for a couple days. I reeked, and no wonder. My hair needed washing, and I hadn't changed my clothes for days; there was the residue of Loch Ness in my shirt, and a faint whiff of vomit like an invisible cloak. I perspired now, though I hadn't lit a fire and the temperature in the room had fallen. I could feel the sweat on my forehead, under my arms, and cold.

I sipped the whisky steadily. When I finished the glass, I poured a second.

My head swirled with memories of Billy. I had a picture of him on my dresser in the bedroom, a fuzzy Polaroid taken during my senior year, when he was already out of school. The picture showed him with the wavy shoulder-length hair that had so annoyed his parents. He wore his favorite tie-dyed T-shirt and cut-off shorts. When he came to see me, he'd often linger on his motorbike in the driveway, sometimes gunning it. My mother would go out and insist that he should park the bike and come into the house for iced tea and banana bread. She would scold him for driving "that thing" and berate him for his long hair. "You're such a hippie," she would say.

"I don't even know what a hippie is," he would answer.

And this was true. He was more like James Dean than anyone protesting the war or smoking dope in some Berkeley park. He was Dean Moriarty in *On the Road*, though he never read books like that and wouldn't have liked my pretension in bringing it up. "Tone it down, Socrates," he would say. "I don't care about knowing shit. Forgetting is hard enough."

I fell into a drowse, my head in my hands. When a light knocking came at the door, I thought I might be dreaming. I flipped on a light in the hall and went to the entryway.

It was Borges.

"Giuseppe! I am missing you!"

"Borges?"

"I remain Borges. Although I sometimes question the meaning of this appellation. Which is the real Borges? The man who writes or the old man who presents himself in your doorway, who shifts from foot to painful foot and awaits an invitation to enter this dark and terrifying establishment?"

Alastair hovered on the pavement above, under a streetlamp. Why hadn't he accompanied Borges down to my flat? Perhaps his guest had wished for our little story to have a denouement and asked for a moment of privacy. He'd obviously disliked our abrupt separation in Guardbridge, this interrupted narrative, a story without a proper ending.

I turned on the light in the entryway and led Borges to the table where I'd been sitting.

"You missed a good dinner at Pilmour," he said.

"I wasn't hungry."

He looked around with his blank eyes, as if picking out objects. His head filled the room, massive, like a Roman bust. "Your flat is something of a cave," he said, tipping his cane against the table.

"I live here alone."

"This I have never done."

"I sympathize."

"You've been drinking? My nose, as you know, is a delicate instrument."

"I've had some news."

"And what's this?"

"My friend Billy. I told you about him, the friend from school. I've had a letter from his mother. He was killed in Vietnam."

After a long pause, a soft, unhappy gasp followed, with a thin line of anguish in the vibrations. Had I sighed? Or was it Borges? Eerily, I stood beside myself, as if looking on, and I saw and heard that I wept. An eerie stillness widened, pressed at the walls of the room, and pulsed. Was the room spinning?

"Are you all right, Borges?" I asked, though the question made no sense.

"Dear boy, I don't know much about these matters or I'd comfort you with my knowledge. I'm not a priest. My life has been something of a flight to oblivion. We lose everything in the end, as with your friend Billy, who lost his altitude too quickly." He reached for me and touched my eyes, finding them wet with tears, as he suspected. "Spinoza, dear brilliant Spinoza, he said that all things long to persist in their own state. A stone wishes to remain a stone. A tiger wants to be a tiger. I want to be Borges and cannot help myself in being Borges, and there is something admirable in this, something eternal. And you, Giuseppe, you will persist as Giuseppe—even when these body rags, they fall away. We have discussed this perhaps, a little. How we persist in ourselves." After a pause, he asked, "Is there comfort there?"

"A little," I said. "Thank you."

We stood together in the nearly dark hallway for quite

a long time. It was, somehow, no longer necessary to talk. We had done that. And this was different.

"Alastair asked me to invite you for dinner, for tomorrow night," he said, at last. "We must celebrate the end of my Scottish adventure." It would be his last night in St. Andrews, he explained, as he must move on. There was "a man in Edinburgh" he wished to see, and Oxford beckoned. And there was, of course, his inamorata, this "lovely girl, Maria Kodama," his former student, who was several decades younger. He would meet her in Oxford in a few weeks. "I am," he said, "with you on Hope Street, and so wonderful this hope."

"You're running away with a beautiful and much younger woman," I said.

"Don't tease an old man. What you say has the ring of truth, which doesn't mean it's true." He sighed, looking up at the ceiling. "Alastair is outside."

I didn't want to see Alastair just now, as I wasn't fit for conversation or ready to deal with him, a man who so quickly had occupied a huge space in my life, though he had faded in the past week, lost in the bright blasts of light from Borges. I thanked Borges for coming and opened the door for him.

Before he climbed the stairs, he drew close to me, his nose two or three inches from mine. And pulled me close, wrapping both arms around me. Did he kiss my cheek? Even my eyes?

"Giuseppe, listen," he said gravely. "When you come to Pilmour tomorrow night, bring the letters from your army. It's the only thing I ask you. I insist!"

26

WAKING WITH DAWN, I groaned, sitting in bed. It felt as if the throats of two frogs pulsed at my temples. I had slept badly, slipping through shelves of nightmares, walking in terror through big-finned jungles along the DMZ. Jerked from sleep repeatedly, I had longed for the reprieve of morning, but the reality of Billy's death proved even more difficult in full daylight, when I could no longer pretend to myself that it was a dream.

I swallowed a couple of aspirins and made myself a strong cup of tea, but the thought of food sickened me. I couldn't imagine I would eat again for days.

About nine, feeling marginally better, I took a very hot bath, dressed in fresh jeans and a sweater, and made my way to Hamilton Hall, arriving just as the girls were finishing breakfast in the dining room. The big windows blazed with light.

"You're up early!" said Miss Wright, the last person in the world I wanted to see right then. Her bright smile, ringed by ruby lipstick, was too much for me, a sunspot burning into my retinas. I blinked rapidly.

"I've been up for a while," I said.

"Bravo! You're quite the chap, I think. I heard from Professor Falconer last week that you're doing splendid work. Mackenzie Brown? Hurray."

"*Mackay* Brown. There's a long way to go."

She offered a faint, uncertain smile. "It's a long way, yes. Art is long but life is short. And how is Alastair? Have you seen him lately?"

"Oh, he's very well," I said, feeling no inclination to prolong this conversation.

"Ah, well, that's good. Good!"

That she was in her usual hurry relieved me, and it made the superficiality of our exchange less awkward. She blew me a kiss as she departed, wishing me luck with my research. "Onward and upward!" she called. "MacDougal Brown?"

"That's it," I said.

I climbed the broad stairwell to Bella's floor and was on the verge of knocking on her door when I realized that she could be in bed with Angus. She might come to the door breathless, in a cloud of sex-smell; I imagined glimpsing, on the sunlit bed, the bare pale ass of her lover. Had I any right to intrude like this, at this time of day and without prior notice? Even if Angus weren't here, she could be deep in sleep, having studied late into the night for her looming exams. I realized I knew so little about her, her habits or deep desires.

Yet I could hear Borges in my head, urging me to take action. And I thought about stepping without hesitation into Ailith's room at the hotel in Stromness.

I knocked, but there was no answer, though I might have heard a rustling of some kind behind the door.

I waited, then turned away. It was all quite pointless. I hoped to tell her about Billy, or perhaps not tell her. But I knew this visit had something to do with Billy as well as something to do with my feelings for her.

"Yes?"

Bella's sleepy head poked around the door.

"Hi," I said. "It's Jay."

"I see you."

Those three syllables, flat and passionless, made me want to evaporate. What on earth had I been thinking, coming here like this?

"Would you like a coffee?"

"I would, yes," I said. "Thank you." I could feel a tear on my cheek and wiped it away. She mustn't know how fragile I was.

"Come in."

She had, as she told me, "overslept," and wore a white cotton nightdress that stopped just below her knees. Her hair was unkempt but lovely asunder. Her cheeks were puffed a little from sleep, her eyes full of dew. A coverlet on the bed was turned down, and the sheets (I couldn't help but think, letting myself wax poetic) almost sighed with the absence of her body. I wanted to crawl into them, to bury my face in her pillow. The room smelled of her strongly, beautifully—so distinct and appealing.

"You've found me a terrible state," she said.

"Not at all. I'm sorry to bother you."

"Don't apologize. I'm glad to see you. Sit down."

"Really?"

"I liked your letter—letters! And the poem. I have a couple of suggestions. The line breaks worry me. There is . . . slack."

"Slack?"

"Here and there. Don't look so worried!"

There was a hint of scolding in her tone, as if I'd stepped over some invisible line.

"Should I come back later?"

"No. You're here."

It wasn't an enthusiastic welcome, but I sat in the shabby chair she used for reading. A copy of Borges's *Labyrinths* lay on the stand by her bed. Had my letters piqued her interest? She opened the window shades, and light poured in. There was an imposing view of the West Sands from this vantage, and the wide bay gleamed. The air tingled with possibility.

"What a beautiful day," she said.

"Spring does its thing again."

"And without warning."

"It was stormy yesterday. We drove from Loch Lomond, Borges and I. My car broke down, so I walked in the rain from Guardbridge."

"You've had an adventure . . ."

"That's a way to frame it."

"I've been reading his stories. He's like nothing else in the world." She handed me the paperback of *Labyrinths*.

"I've got one," I said.

"It's a magic carpet. Alastair did some of these translations, I noticed," she said. "I like them the best." She put instant coffee into the cups. "So what was he like, up close? Borges? You got to know him. Lucky you."

I wasn't sure what I could say in a short space that would equal the reality. But I made a feeble attempt. "He's a very complicated man, a beautiful man. He's read and remembers everything. His mind, it's a spinning wheel. A spiral? Bad metaphors. I'm at a loss . . ."

"One has to read the pieces slowly, taking time over each story or essay," she said. "He dismantles the genres."

I leafed through the book, turning to the tiny story called "Borges and I," which I'd read on the ferry. Some of the phrases were things he'd just said to me—about Spinoza, and tigers wanting to be tigers—but this didn't disappoint me. If anything, it made me feel a flush of privilege. In our days together, Borges had been offering his sense of the world, putting his way of being forward for consideration. He had personally introduced me to his stories in a sly, roundabout fashion. And that made sense now.

The ending of "Borges and I" struck me with its aptness: "And so my life is a flight, and I lose everything and everything belongs to oblivion, or to Borges."

Bella leaned over my shoulder, handing me a mug. "That little one is good, no?"

I groaned, biting my lip, putting a finger to one of my temples.

"You don't like my coffee?"

Was it fair to unload my problems, to tell her about Billy? I had never liked that moment in *Othello* when the Moor says, "She loved me for the dangers I had passed, / And I loved her that she did pity them." This was no way to attract a woman's sympathy or affection. Pity was not love.

"I've had news about a friend," I said, working to hold myself together. "A letter from his mother. He was killed in Vietnam a few weeks ago."

"Good god!"

My eyes watered as she drew near, knelt close, and folded her arms around me, saying nothing but emanating sympathy. And I knew that we had arrived at a fresh juncture in whatever this was, a "relationship," a "friendship." The appropriate word would come later. But somehow I was prepared for both possibilities, and willing to accept either.

I went back to my flat with a wild new energy, feeling a pressure inside, the urge to write a poem I would call "This Reaping." I wrote it quickly, then typed it. It felt to me like the best thing I'd ever written:

> *They are all going out around us,*
> *popping off like lights—*
> *the professors crumpled over desks,*
> *the doctors with entrails hanging from their ears,*
> *the operators dead at the end of lines.*
>
> *They are all going out, shut off*
> *at the source without warning—*
> *the student tumbled from the bike in traffic,*
> *the child in the cradle, choking,*
> *the nun in the faulty subway.*

And nobody knows the hour,
whether now or later, whether
neatly with a snap in the night
or, less discreetly, dragged
by a bus through busy corners.

What a business, this reaping
in private or public places
with so little sowing:
let us pray that somewhere
on sweaty beds of complete affection
there are lovers
doubling themselves in the lively dark.

I finished a draft to my satisfaction and rushed to attend the noon mass at All Saints, an Anglican church in North Castle Street that I liked. I felt an urgency to do this, a need to pray—for Billy, of course, but also for myself. After a short service (with only three others in the congregation) I sat alone at the back of the chancel, which filled with a gold-and-blue light parceled by the stained glass windows overhead. I felt close to Billy there, maybe even to God—or whatever I meant when using that word. In my heart I felt—I *knew*—that Billy was safe wherever he was, and that death was an opening, a springboard. The persistence of souls was an old Platonic idea I could live with. Of course we all proceed, as Borges put it, "on insufficient knowledge," and I was no different from anyone else in this. My faith was probably no more than a gut-level trust in the power of the universe to lift us when we needed lifting.

In late afternoon I packed the bundle of letters from the draft board into my rucksack, as Borges had insisted, then picked up Bella and took her to Alastair's house. I knew he would welcome her, and she had expressed a wish to see Borges again before he left. I really liked the idea of seeing them together again. In fact I *needed* to see them like this, these two parts of my dream life in a daylight reality.

The light was strong, with blades of sun knifing through gilt-edged clouds above the sea. A wind rose from inside the sea and struggled to get out, pushing at the surface. I could smell the dirt under my feet, still wet from the hard rains of the day before. A fragment of the famous psalm filled my head: "This is the day that the Lord has made. Let us rejoice and be glad in it."

As I pushed open the iron gate at Pilmour, there was a flutter above us in the rookery, a peppery spray of birdlife that blackened the sky.

"Ominous," said Bella.

"An omen isn't always ominous, is it?"

"There are good omens and bad ones, I should think."

"I'll take this as a good one."

Softly I knocked at the cottage, noticing how the paint had peeled from the stone of its façade. It looked much smaller than I remembered it.

"The weary traveler," said Alastair, opening the door.

"Where have you been?" Jasper asked.

"Where have *you* been?"

"In London, with Papa."

"How was it?"

"A boy who is tired of London is tired of life," he said.

Was this the cleverest child on Planet Earth? His helmet of dark hair and beautiful big eyes made him so appealing.

"Borges had a good time in the Highlands," Alastair said. "I think he's left his heart there."

"Really?"

"You had a few mishaps . . ."

"That's a way of putting it."

"And how are you, Miss Law?" asked Borges, who pushed into the hallway wearing a psychedelic tie with yellow crocodiles and red waterfalls against an electric-blue background. He knew what Bella meant to me and looked eager to meet her again, perhaps as if Norah Lange had rushed back from his distant past to greet him. "Tell me how you are, please!"

"Very well, sir," Bella said.

"I'm Sir George now? Well and good. My mother and father, I must remind you, called me Georgie."

"I don't," said Alastair.

"I'm Borges to some, Georgie to others. I make no difference."

There was something persistently odd and inscrutable about the way he spoke. Was it a problem of translation, or had he cultivated this opaqueness? Or was it translucence? Light filtered through the mask of Borges: a pale yellow glow with its own enigmatic brilliance. One felt somehow more intelligent, more learned and witty, in his presence. The universe itself felt more pliable and yielding, and so available.

Jasper led Bella and Borges into the sitting room while I slipped into the kitchen with Alastair, who had asked if

I could help him with the soup. It was a ploy, I knew. He wanted a private word.

"How was your trip?" I asked.

"My great-uncle is okay. A mild heart attack. Not a stroke after all. Almost undetectable." He sighed. "Thank you for taking care of Borges."

"An opportunity you handed to me," I said. "I know that."

"And not a pleasure?"

"I'm not sure *pleasure* is the word."

"Like boating on the Amazon. You're glad to have the story. Being there, well—too many biting flies, alligators, blisters, cannibals."

"We found all of those in the Highlands."

He handed me a glass of wine.

"I'm sorry about your friend."

"Billy."

"Borges told me."

"It's sad. But I somehow expected it."

Alastair held my gaze as if it were a goblet of crystal. "I could feel it coming, too," he said. "I lost a good friend in the Pacific. Bruce Donaldson, 'Donald the Bruce,' I called him. We were at school together in Whithorn, sang in the choir at my father's church—not much of a choir. We played hooky, hitchhiked to Glasgow for a day trip once that turned into a night on the town. My mother was furious. Who cared?" He put a hand on my wrist. "Are you all right?"

"Not really."

"You can come here anytime. Day or night."

"I know that. Thank you."

"Don't withdraw. Don't go silent."

"Sometimes my breath sort of stops. I feel strange, disconnected."

"Anguish is pain multiplied by resistance. So they say, and I believe them. You will have to grieve."

The word itself, *grieve*, puzzled me. I didn't know how this process might unfold but guessed I would come to accept Billy's death in due course. What choice did I have?

Alastair took a tray of his usual brownies from the Aga.

"*Voilà!* The brownies," he said.

He pulled from the fridge a porcelain bowl filled with a dark creamy chocolate icing, which he lathered over the brownies with a spatula.

"The various parts of the mind," said Alastair, "usually fail to communicate. My brownies are what I call a facilitator. A shortcut to bliss. But what's wrong with taking the straight rather than the roundabout way to a destination? In Anglo-Saxon, the 'straight' way was the direct way. 'Wrong' simply meant going roundabout, the crooked way. Sometimes I think the whole world moves roundabout. Speaking of which," he added, "you've made a connection with Bella, so I see."

"I think so, yes."

"Let it go where it goes. Or fails to go."

He finished icing the brownies, swirling it with little peaks of chocolate.

"Borges likes you," he said.

"Really?" It somehow surprised me to hear this stated plainly. And pleased me, too, more than I might've been prepared to acknowledge.

"Very much so," he said. "He's a magician, a sorcerer, a fraud, and a genius."

"And a priest."

"That, too. When you read him, you'll see."

"Mackay Brown gave me a copy of *Labyrinths*."

"Good for George. Everything you need is there." He licked the spatula clean. "The rest is icing, but we all like icing, don't we? Borges—on the page—takes a lifetime to absorb. I don't have so many years left."

"I read the one about Pascal this afternoon."

"A good one. Borges makes these perfect little texts, essays that are stories. It's all poetry, a kind of spell. After reading Borges, if you miss a train, the event will feel drenched in meaning." Alastair had taken flight, his eyes wide, his nostrils almost flaring like a bull's before his charge, and I guessed he'd sampled his brownie mix at some point earlier in the afternoon. "Literature, after Borges, must change."

Borges stepped into the kitchen. "I'm hearing my name, and taken in vain!"

"Borges," said Alastair.

His name hung in the air, more concept than address. And Borges savored this.

"I've been introduced to the Highlands by your friend," he said. "He is Giuseppe, but he is Sancho, too—the great formulator of homely wisdom."

"There *is* something homely, now that you mention it," Alastair said.

Bella came into the kitchen now and looked fondly in my direction. She was followed by Jasper and Jeff.

"Papa made brownies," said Jasper.

"Not for you, Jasp," said Alastair, with a narrow glance.

"How old do you have to be for brownies?" asked Jeff. I hadn't known he was back from his travels. We would have a lot to talk about in the coming weeks, I was quite sure, and he would be his usual genial and wise self, willing to listen and advise. I was so damned lucky, I thought. And in so many ways.

"You have to be old as Homer," said Borges. "Give me a brownie, Alejandro."

Alastair obliged, lifting a fat one into the outstretched palm of the Master. He gave another to Jeff, who greedily accepted the offering.

"Miss Law, you will have a brownie?" Alastair asked. "They're potent, I warn you."

"I love potency!" she said, taking a brownie and biting into it with gusto. With the back of her hand, she wiped a bit of icing from her lips. "They say that chocolate is love," she added.

"And perhaps more reliable in its effects," said Borges. "Dante should have had access to this drug. Beatrice, as you know, lived forever in his mind. But to her, Dante had very little presence. On the other hand, when they meet at the end of the *Purgatorio*, she guides him toward heaven. She cared deeply for his soul, but not for his body."

"Very unfortunate," said Alastair. "Was she Scottish?"

Bella laughed at this, and never looked more beautiful. She wore a diaphanous light yellow shift, with tiny cornflowers in a design that played off her red sneakers—always the red sneakers, with white ankle socks that accented them.

I devoured a large brownie myself, eager to join this gladdening circle.

Music pulsed from the big speakers near the windows. Alastair was especially fond of Bach, and what we were hearing was, I knew, *The Art of the Fugue,* which often played in the background at Pilmour. It was, I think, a kind of weaving together of various elements in the air, a single strand of melody absorbing the disparate parts and making a whole of the room, the occasion, the voices.

Tuning in to the music, with a slight dancing step as he crossed the room, Borges seemed animated, more so than usual, his face burning. He called to me: "Giuseppe! Have you brought the letters?"

"They're in my rucksack."

"Such a charming word, *rucksack.* The world hides in your rucksack."

"I need a rucksack," said Jeff.

Taking the cue, I went into the front hall, where I had dropped this fabled rucksack, and returned holding up the passel of unopened letters, seven of them, bound by a rubber band.

"The letters," I said.

"We must incinerate them," said Borges. "Ashes to ashes, no? This is the only solution. I think from the Book of Genesis. The origin of all stories."

As soon as Borges said this, I felt the wisdom—even the necessity—of his proposal. I must burn the letters as a kind of benediction for Billy, as an elegy for my younger self. It felt as right as anything had felt since my arrival in St. Andrews.

Alastair, as he would, understood that we required a ceremony.

He led us, with that impish glow in his eyes, out of the house and across the grassy links to the West Sands. We were a grateful train, Borges and Bella, me, Alastair and Jeff, and young Jasper: silhouettes against the sky. We passed several bemused golfers in plus-fours, who tipped their caps in our direction. It was still quite bright, with a strange milky pink glow on the sea as we moved through wiry brush and dunes to the broad flat beach.

"I can make a fire," said Jasper.

"You *are* a fire," said Alastair.

Jeff suggested they look for kindling together, and Alastair followed them into the brush.

I stood alone with Bella and Borges on the wide sands. Beyond us, the clouds hung like a massive bronze chandelier over the sea. A gannet moved past the edge of a cloud, and I watched it swoop and pierce the surf, then lift off with a fish for its meal. The beach itself was pale and soft, almost pink, full of bladderwrack that spilled its oily guts and the skeletal display of cuttlefish bones. The remains of crab and dogfish mingled with driftwood, the white bare limbs in tangled patterns, a residue of the falling tide. Everything would in due course be exposed.

Soon Jasper, Jeff, and Alastair brought kindling and erected a small temple in a sand pit, stacking driftwood and sticks in a pyramid above the twigs and dry leaves. With the pyromaniac glee of a child, Jasper lit the fire and blew on it, and before long we heard the low snap-crackle of flames.

"*Voilà!*" said Jasper, a phrase copied from his father.

"*Un pequeño fuego,*" said Alastair.

Borges drew close. He could see the flames, I was sure. He quoted Hopkins: "'And the fire that breaks from thee then, a billion / Times told lovelier, more dangerous!'"

"Your letters," Alastair said to me, as the time had come.

We gathered in a circle around the fire, and I felt strangely, even crazily, high now, elated, trembling. Did I want to go ahead with this? Bella could intuit my hesitation, and she touched me on the elbow, squeezing in reassurance. When I turned to her, her eyes were wide and deep with acceptance. And she smiled.

Everyone watched as I dropped the envelopes into the flames, one by one. Seven of them: the mystical number. They turned orange at first, then curled at the edges, brown and black, blistering, curling into themselves. The flakes rose—ashes to ashes, at last.

"Dust to dust," said Jeff.

"These are blessed transformations," Borges told us. "They go on and on. One cannot stop them, the glorious changes. I was such a young man once, so tender. And now, you see . . ."

"A tender old man," said Jeff.

"And soon only dust. But we come again. You know Whitman? 'I bequeath myself to the dirt to grow from the grass I love.'"

Alastair chimed in: "'If you want me again, look for me under your boot-soles.'"

To my amazement, Bella continued. "'You will hardly know who I am or what I mean / But I shall be good health to you nonetheless.'"

Borges added, completing the stanza: "'And filter and fiber your blood.'"

Was there music in the air? I could hear it distinctly, feel it coursing through me—a strong and palpable sound, with a scent of cinnamon, a tingle in the air. There were drums, too, and perhaps bagpipes as well, and an unseen guitar with a rhythmic stroke that scraped across strings in bold fashion. I saw Borges begin to sway, his eyes closing, his shoulders swiveling, caught in the tune. He gave a little step, a leap, then reached one hand out to the side for Alastair, who grabbed it, while Jeff took the other; and they began to bob, moving in sideways intricate steps as they sang in Spanish. And then Jasper took his father's other hand, and the four of them began to dance around the fire to this strangely wonderful melody.

Bella drifted by herself toward the sea, where she slipped off her red sneakers and socks and stepped barefoot into the surf. She raised her shift so that her long legs glistened in unsurprising beauty. The sea washed around her knees, a foamy mix. The wind picked up slightly, and her dress opened, almost disappeared. The music was like thunder, everywhere on the beach, as the surf rose and crashed.

I took off my own shoes and walked toward her. The light was palpable, soft, succulent. I could taste the pink-orange of the clouds as the sun pulsed and shone in the water. The sea itself was a sprawl of diamonds.

Bella smiled at me, an invitation.

And I walked toward her into the quivering water.

Afterword

THIS NARRATIVE LIVED in memory for fifty years, its contours enhanced or distorted in the usual ways by time and retelling. I've told these stories countless times—my wife recalls one of our first dates, in the late seventies, when I talked at length about Borges, Alastair, Jasper, and Jeff. She seemed especially to like "the night of the pissing," as I referred to our stop in Killiecrankie. It was fun when, shortly thereafter, she met Alastair, who amplified my stories, filling in parts I had missed. (Alastair remained a beloved member of our family until his death in 2014. And it wouldn't be a stretch to say that I miss his company every day of my life.)

I'd written a few segments of this story before, some of them dating to the midseventies. But it wasn't until Ross Clarke, an English filmmaker, suggested that this would make a good movie that I began, at his urging, to write down a complete narrative. *Borges and Me* began as a novel, with Jay called Luke (though his biographical details mirrored my own in most ways). I finished the novel but soon realized it was indeed a story whose truth was confirmed by memory, so I refashioned it, moving toward a kind of novelistic memoir, a "narrative" or Borgesian "fiction." It's a bit of a palimpsest, a text written over another text, with many erasures; the underlying text is barely legible but nonetheless important, its bones poking through the skin. This story was shaped as fiction, or auto fiction, and the residue of that shaping survives in its transformation into this text, "An Encounter."

Needless to say, I was not hiding a tape recorder in my pocket as I sat with Alastair at his kitchen table or drove in my car with Borges or walked through the streets of Orkney with George Mackay Brown. Memory is a stepchild of the imagination, and the conversations in this book are reconstructed, with fidelity to voices that have played in my head over five decades. (I did have a handful of notes, with scraps of conversation, in my journal from this year.) As it were, many of the incidents and scenes depicted here have taken on a mythic resonance for me, as I think they did for Alastair as well. On the day Borges died, Alastair called and said, with his usual whimsy, "He's looking for Mr. Singleton elsewhere."

Borges and Me is in obvious ways a refraction and reconsideration of "Borges y Yo." I only hope it offers a fraction of the pleasure that piece has given to me over the years. The journey with Borges was in fact two trips, which I combined here for narrative efficiency. The characters in the story are real, most of them in possession of their actual names: Alastair, Jasper, Borges, Jeff, Professor Falconer, Anne Wright, and George Mackay Brown. Mr. Singleton is real, though probably buried in New Zealand by now. The girl with the red sneakers draws on several women who were close to me. "Ailith" I never saw again, as we lived in such different worlds. Billy Giordano is a composite of three friends from my high school who fought in Vietnam, one of whom (the one who was closest to me) died in that impossible war during my first year as a graduate student in St. Andrews. His death left me with a feeling of melancholy that took years to erase.

On an incidental note: I switched the topic of my doctoral thesis from George Mackay Brown to Theodore Roethke soon after the period described in this narrative, having discovered a trove of manuscripts by the recently deceased American poet that would make my project more palatable to Professor Falconer. "I'm so glad that he's dead," Falconer said to me when I suggested this.

There is a line in Roethke's "The Far Field" that I think nicely frames the nature of *Borges and Me*: "The pure serene of memory in one man."

Acknowledgments

Various friends read this story and offered suggestions, including Andy Paterson, Ross Clarke, Heather Neilson, Patrick Flanery, Nick Spengler, and Jeff Lerner—the Jeff in the story—and my wife, Devon Jersild. I had wonderfully detailed feedback from my friend Michael Lowenthal. I owe all of these readers my deepest thanks. As ever, Gerald Howard, my longtime editor at Doubleday, has been wonderfully supportive and helpful. I've been lucky to work with him over many years.

BENJAMIN'S CROSSING

It is 1940. For the past decade, Walter Benjamin—the German-Jewish critic and philosopher—has been writing his masterpiece in a library in Paris, a city he loves. Now Nazi tanks have overrun the suburbs, and Benjamin is forced to flee. With a battered briefcase that contains his precious manuscript of a thousand handwritten pages, he sets off for the border and is led by chance to a young anti-Nazi who is taking Jews and other refugees over the Pyrenees into Spain, where they may (with luck) make their way to freedom in Portugal or South America. Part tragedy, part dark comedy, this sharply realized historical novel tells one of the great and most moving peripheral stories of the Holocaust.

Fiction

THE DAMASCUS ROAD

In the years after Christ's crucifixion, Paul of Tarsus, a prosperous tentmaker and Jewish scholar, took it upon himself to persecute the small groups of Christ's followers that sprung up. But on the road to Damascus, he had some sort of blinding vision, a profound conversion experience that transformed Paul into the most effective and influential messenger Christianity has ever had. In *The Damascus Road*, novelist Jay Parini brings this fascinating and ever-controversial figure to full human life, capturing his visionary passions and vast contradictions. In relating Paul's epic journeys, both geographical and spiritual, Parini unfolds a vivid panorama of the ancient world on the verge of epochal change.

Fiction/Historical

EMPIRE OF SELF
A Life of Gore Vidal

The product of thirty years of friendship and conversation, Jay Parini's *Empire of Self* digs behind the glittering surface of Gore Vidal's colorful career to reveal the complex emotional and sexual truths underlying his celebrity-strewn life. But there is plenty of glittering surface as well—a virtual Who's Who of the twentieth century, from Eleanor Roosevelt and Amelia Earhart through the Kennedys, Johnny Carson, Leonard Bernstein, and the crème de la crème of Hollywood along with a generous helping of feuds with the likes of William F. Buckley, Norman Mailer, Truman Capote, and *The New York Times*, among other adversaries. The life of Gore Vidal teemed with notable incidents, famous people, and lasting achievements that call out for careful evocation and examination. Jay Parini crafts Vidal's life into an accessible, entertaining story that puts the experience of one of the great American figures of the postwar era into context.

Biography

ALSO AVAILABLE

The Last Station
The Passages of H. M.
Promised Land

ANCHOR BOOKS
Available wherever books are sold.
www.anchorbooks.com

P.O. 0005309666 20230324